THE FUTURE OF TRAUMA THEORY

This collection analyses the future of 'trauma theory', a major theoretical discourse in contemporary criticism and theory. The chapters advance the current state of the field by exploring new areas, asking new questions and making new connections.

Part I, *History and Culture*, begins by developing trauma theory in its more familiar post-deconstructive mode and explores how these insights might still be productive. It goes on, via a critique of existing positions, to relocate trauma theory in a postcolonial and globalized world—theoretically, aesthetically and materially—and focuses on non-Western accounts and understandings of trauma, memory and suffering. Part II, *Politics and Subjectivity*, turns explicitly to politics and subjectivity, focusing on the state and the various forms of subjection to which it gives rise, and on human rights, biopolitics and community.

Each chapter, in different ways, advocates a movement beyond the sorts of texts and concepts that are the usual focus for trauma criticism and moves this dynamic network of ideas forward.

With contributions from an international selection of leading critics and thinkers from the US and Europe, this volume will be a key critical intervention in one of the most important areas in contemporary literary criticism and theory.

Gert Buelens is Professor of English at Ghent University, Belgium, and a founder member of LITRA, the Centre for Literature and Trauma.

Sam Durrant is Senior Lecturer in Postcolonial Literature at the University of Leeds, UK.

Robert Eaglestone is Professor of Contemporary Literature and Thought and Deputy Director of the Holocaust Research Centre at Royal Holloway, University of London, UK.

THE FUTURE OF TRAUMA THEORY

Contemporary literary and cultural criticism

*Edited by Gert Buelens,
Sam Durrant and Robert Eaglestone*

LONDON AND NEW YORK

First published 2014
by Routledge
2 Park Square, Milton Park, Abingdon, Oxon OX14 4RN

Simultaneously published in the USA and Canada
by Routledge
711 Third Avenue, New York, NY 10017

Routledge is an imprint of the Taylor & Francis Group, an informa business

© 2014 Gert Buelens, Sam Durrant and Robert Eaglestone for selection and editorial matter; individual contributions the contributors

The right of Gert Buelens, Sam Durrant and Robert Eaglestone to be identified as the authors of the editorial material, and of the authors for their individual chapters, has been asserted in accordance with sections 77 and 78 of the Copyright, Designs and Patents Act 1988.

All rights reserved. No part of this book may be reprinted or reproduced or utilised in any form or by any electronic, mechanical, or other means, now known or hereafter invented, including photocopying and recording, or in any information storage or retrieval system, without permission in writing from the publishers.

Trademark notice: Product or corporate names may be trademarks or registered trademarks, and are used only for identification and explanation without intent to infringe.

British Library Cataloguing in Publication Data
A catalogue record for this book is available from the British Library

Library of Congress Cataloging in Publication Data
A catalog record for this title has been requested

ISBN: 978-0-415-69458-2 (hbk)
ISBN: 978-0-415-69459-9 (pbk)
ISBN: 978-0-203-49310-6 (ebk)

Typeset in Bembo
by Saxon Graphics Ltd, Derby

CONTENTS

Contributors   *vii*
Acknowledgements   *x*

Preface: beyond Tancred and Clorinda—trauma studies for
implicated subjects   xi
Michael Rothberg

Introduction   1
Gert Buelens, Sam Durrant and Robert Eaglestone

PART I
History and culture   9

1   Knowledge, 'afterwardsness' and the future of trauma theory   11
    Robert Eaglestone

2   Fascism and the sacred: sites of inquiry after (or along with)
    trauma   23
    Dominick LaCapra

3   Beyond Eurocentrism: trauma theory in the global age   45
    Stef Craps

4   Affect, body, place: trauma theory in the world   63
    Ananya Jahanara Kabir

5 Trauma ties: chiasmus and community in Lebanese
   civil war literature   77
   Nouri Gana

6 Undoing sovereignty: towards a theory of critical mourning   91
   Sam Durrant

PART II
Politics and subjectivity   **111**

7 'That which you are denying us': refugees, rights and
   writing in Arendt   113
   Lyndsey Stonebridge

8 Time, personhood, politics   127
   Jenny Edkins

9 The biopolitics of trauma   141
   Pieter Vermeulen

10 Future shock: science fiction and the trauma paradigm   157
   Roger Luckhurst

Index   *169*

NOTES ON CONTRIBUTORS

Gert Buelens is Professor of English at Ghent University, where he directs a long-term research project on the concept of authorship, and chairs the Department of Literary Studies. He edits the e-journal *Authorship*, is the author of some 60 essays in collections and journals, and has, most recently, co-edited *The Catastrophic Imperative: Subjectivity, Time and Memory in Contemporary Thought* (with Dominiek Hoens and Sigi Jöttkandt). He is currently working on two volumes for the CUP edition of Henry James's fiction.

Stef Craps teaches English at Ghent University, Belgium, where he also directs the Centre for Literature and Trauma. He is the author of *Postcolonial Witnessing: Trauma Out of Bounds* (Palgrave Macmillan, 2013) and *Trauma and Ethics in the Novels of Graham Swift: No Short-Cuts to Salvation* (Sussex Academic Press, 2005), and has guest-edited special issues of *Criticism: A Quarterly for Literature and the Arts* (2011; with Michael Rothberg) and *Studies in the Novel* (2008; with Gert Buelens) on the topics of, respectively, transcultural negotiations of Holocaust memory and postcolonial trauma novels. His next book project is an introductory guide to the concept of trauma for Routledge's New Critical Idiom series.

Sam Durrant is Associate Professor of Postcolonial Literature at Leeds University. His first monograph *Postcolonial Narrative and the Work of Mourning: J. M. Coetzee, Wilson Harris and Toni Morrison* was published by State University of New York Press in 2004. He co-edited *Essays in Migratory Aesthetics* with Catherine Lord (Rodopi, 2007) and has published numerous articles on postcolonial literature and aspects of critical theory. His current monograph, due from Routledge in 2014, is entitled *Mourning and Postapartheid Literature: Reconciliation and its Discontents*.

Robert Eaglestone is Professor of Contemporary Literature and Thought at Royal Holloway, University of London. He works on contemporary literature and literary theory, contemporary philosophy and on Holocaust and Genocide studies. He is the author of five books, including *The Holocaust and the Postmodern* (2004) and *Contemporary Fiction* (2013), and the editor or co-editor of six more. His work has been translated into five languages.

Jenny Edkins is Professor of International Politics at Aberystwyth University; her most recent books are *Missing: Persons and Politics* (Cornell, 2011) and *Trauma and the Memory of Politics* (Cambridge, 2003). She is editor with Maja Zehfuss of the textbook *Global Politics: A New Introduction*, and series editor with Nick Vaughan-Williams of the Routledge Interventions book series.

Nouri Gana is Associate Professor of Comparative Literature and Near Eastern Languages and Cultures at the University of California, Los Angeles. He has published numerous articles and chapters on the literatures and cultures of the Arab world and its diasporas in such scholarly venues as *Comparative Literature Studies*, *PMLA*, *Public Culture* and *Social Text*. He has also contributed op-eds to such magazines and international newspapers as *The Guardian*, *El Pais*, *The Electronic Intifada*, *Jadaliyya* and *CounterPunch*. Author of *Signifying Loss: Towards a Poetics of Narrative Mourning* (Bucknell UP, 2011), he is currently completing a book manuscript on the politics of melancholia in the Arab world and another on the cultural politics of the Tunisia revolution. In addition, he is the editor of *The Tunisian Revolution: Contexts, Architects, Prospects* and of *The Edinburgh Companion to the Arab Novel in English* (Edinburgh UP, 2013).

Ananya Jahanara Kabir is Professor of English Literature at King's College London. She is the author of *Territory of Desire: Representing Kashmir* (2009) and *Partition's Post-Amnesias: 1947, 1971 and Modern South Asia* (2013). From 2013 to 2018 she will lead a project funded by a European Research Council Advanced Grant, titled Modern Moves: Kinetic Transnationalism and Afro-Diasporic Rhythm Cultures.

Dominick LaCapra is Emeritus Professor of History and Comparative Literature and Bryce and Edith M. Bowmar Professor of Humanistic Studies at Cornell University. He is the editor of two books and the author of fourteen, including *Writing History, Writing Trauma*, *History in Transit: Experience, Identity, Critical Theory*, *History and Its Limits: Human, Animal, Violence*, and *History, Literature, Critical Theory*.

Roger Luckhurst is Professor of Modern Literature at Birkbeck College, University of London. He published *The Mummy's Curse: The True History of a Dark Fantasy* (Oxford) in 2012 and *The Shining* for the BFI Classics series in 2013.

Michael Rothberg is Professor of English and Conrad Humanities Scholar at the University of Illinois at Urbana-Champaign, where he is also Director of the Holocaust, Genocide, and Memory Studies Initiative. Affiliated with the Unit for

Criticism and Interpretive Theory, the Department of Germanic Languages and Literatures, and the Programs in Comparative Literature and Jewish Culture and Society, Rothberg works in the fields of critical theory and cultural studies, Holocaust studies, postcolonial studies and contemporary literatures. His latest book is *Multidirectional Memory: Remembering the Holocaust in the Age of Decolonization* (2009), published by Stanford University Press in its Cultural Memory in the Present series. He is also the author of *Traumatic Realism: The Demands of Holocaust Representation* (2000) and co-editor with Neil Levi of *The Holocaust: Theoretical Readings* (2003).

Lyndsey Stonebridge is Professor of Literature and Critical Theory at the University of East Anglia. She is the author, most recently, of *The Judicial Imagination: Writing After Nuremberg* (2011). Other publications include: *The Writing of Anxiety* (2007), *The Destructive Element: British Psychoanalysis and Modernism* (1998), *British Fiction after Modernism: The Novel at Mid-Century*, edited with Marina MacKay (2007), and *Reading Melanie Klein*, edited with John Phillips (1998). She is currently working on a new project, *Refugee Writing: States, Statelessness and Modern Literature*.

Pieter Vermeulen is Assistant Professor of English Literature at Stockholm University. He works in the fields of critical theory, the contemporary novel, and memory studies. His writing has appeared or will appear in journals such as *Arcadia, Criticism, Critique, Journal of Modern Literature, Memory Studies, Modern Fiction Studies, Mosaic, Studies in the Novel*, and *Textual Practice*. His book *Romanticism after the Holocaust* was republished in paperback by Continuum/Bloomsbury in 2012. He is currently at work on a book-length study of the paradoxical productivity of early-twenty-first century discourses of the end of the novel.

ACKNOWLEDGEMENTS

We would like to thank the Centre for Literature and Trauma at the University of Ghent (LITRA), and in particular Stef Craps, for organizing an international research cluster in this field. We would also like to thank the Flemish Academic Centre for Science and the Arts (VLAC) for funding the research team whose work forms the kernel of this book: the VLAC Fellows were Gert Buelens, Stef Craps, Ortwin de Graef, Sam Durrant, Robert Eaglestone, Dominick LaCapra, Roger Luckhurst and Michael Rothberg. Kristiaan Versluys was extremely supportive of this initiative, for which we are grateful. We'd also like to acknowledge the informative and inspiring discussions we have had on these matters with many colleagues from five continents over several years. The editors would also like to thank all those at Taylor and Francis, including Elizabeth Levine, Polly Dodson and Ruth Moody, for their guidance, help and support.

PREFACE

Beyond Tancred and Clorinda—trauma studies for implicated subjects

Michael Rothberg

What do we talk about when we talk about trauma? Any assessment of the future of trauma studies must start with that question. The answer—even, or especially, in a book that asks us to reflect on the future—will necessarily be historical: we need to start from the assumption that answers will vary across time and across cultural context. Trauma today is probably not the trauma of twenty years ago and certainly not the trauma of the early twentieth century. Yet the way we talk about trauma today and tomorrow will certainly bear the traces of those earlier layers of historical accretion. Trauma is perhaps best thought of not as any kind of singular object, but rather—in the helpful conceptualization Roger Luckhurst adapts from Bruno Latour—as one of those 'knots' or 'hybrid assemblages' that 'tangle up questions of science, law, technology, capitalism, politics, medicine and risk' (Luckhurst 14–15). Luckhurst's capacious genealogy of the trauma knot helps us avoid familiar, reductive accounts that simply link the rise of trauma studies to the expansion of Holocaust consciousness or the context of post-Vietnam America (although these are surely crucial). Instead, he reveals how, over the course of more than a century, the problem of individual psychic suffering became 'tangled up' with an array of the larger problems of modernity, including industrialization, bureaucracy, and war.

Thinking genealogically about trauma is one essential means of opening it towards possible, alternative futures. Genealogical thinking loosens up the reified common sense that tends to cluster around concepts that achieve a rapid rise in popularity, as trauma clearly has in the humanities since the publication of Cathy Caruth's landmark edited volume *Trauma: Explorations in Memory* (1995). If the explosion of interest in trauma seemed to come out of nowhere, Luckhurst demonstrates how it actually emerged from a whole host of somewheres. With a focus more on what is to come than on what has been, the chapters in *The Future of Trauma Theory* nevertheless derive from a similar critical engagement with the current state of the field. While recognizing their debt to the intellectual genealogy that culminated in the poststructuralist theorization of trauma in the 1990s, the contributors are not bound to or by it. Both individually and, most powerfully, taken together, they make an irrefutable argument that in the future—and, really, already in the present—trauma studies will need to travel further and add a whole new series of destinations to its agenda.

Some of those new destinations are geographical or geo-cultural, and inhabiting them will require recalibrating inherited concepts. As Stef Craps makes clear in his chapter, we cannot assume that a category crafted in Europe and North America can travel smoothly to all other cultural locations: 'the PTSD construct reflects a Eurocentric, monocultural orientation'. Several of the other contributors to *The Future of Trauma Theory* help us begin envisioning what an alternate orientation might look like. Without by any means abandoning all the insights crafted in Europe, Ananya Kabir leads us through the dispersed 'affect-worlds' of the black Atlantic, Cambodian Buddhism and the Sufi-inflected Islamicate; Nouri Gana asks us to consider what it would mean to dwell in the post-catastrophic context of civil war Lebanon; and Lyndsey Stonebridge moves us from a refugee camp in Australia to the uncanny imaginary landscapes of Kafka, while gesturing at the all-too-real urgencies of contemporary Palestine.

But even those who remain focused on Europe and North America argue for the need to rethink the central categories of trauma studies. History, after all, moves on, even if we stay in place. Thus, Jenny Edkins continues her reflections on how, in the post-9/11 moment, the state has colonized a previously disruptive traumatic temporality and integrated it into its sovereign chronologies; Dominick LaCapra invites us to rethink fascism and Nazism from a lens inflected by 'post-secular' concerns; Pieter Vermeulen alerts us to the changing biopolitical horizon in which trauma is both produced and policed; and Luckhurst himself evokes science fiction in order to turn us toward potential futures in which the technological transformation of subjectivity will (if it doesn't already) necessitate a transformed notion of trauma (for more on 'trauma future-tense', see Kaplan).

In their different ways, then, the essays collected here call on us to nuance our notions of trauma by revealing their cultural and historical specificity. But if we are to redirect the field of trauma studies, the simple call for specificity must lead to a second moment of theoretical re-elaboration. For, however we conceive it, trauma is also a category that ought to trouble the historicist gesture of much contemporary criticism as well as its concomitant notions of history and culture. Theorists such as Cathy Caruth have famously claimed that trauma dislocates history and makes it difficult, if not impossible, to think in terms of singular historical or cultural contexts (Caruth, *Trauma*; *Unclaimed Experience*). Critics of Caruth—including several here—have pointed to the limits of classical trauma theory's dislocation of its own context of emergence (i.e. its failure to transcend a Eurocentric frame), but that does not necessarily negate Caruth's point. Indeed, it is difficult for me to imagine trauma as not involving dislocation of subjects, histories, and cultures. These dislocations are everywhere in the non-European archives evoked here: in the alienating work of the Lebanese novelist Elias Khoury discussed by Gana, in the kinetic *kuduro* dance moves of post-civil war Angola vividly described by Kabir, and in the activist and aesthetic resistance of the Woomera inmates in Stonebridge's reflections. Even if we must conceive of multiple forms of dislocation—those that result from events, from systemic violence, and, in LaCapra's terms, from transhistorical, structural trauma (LaCapra, 'Trauma, Absence, Loss')—we can only maintain trauma as a theoretical category by recognizing overlaps and similarities across the historical and cultural contexts we track. As Edkins argues in similar terms, event-like 'ontic' trauma reveals structural, 'ontological' lack. This is the work of theory: in Kabir's words, 'theory's drive is to generate connections and paradigms that must work in, and despite, different contexts.'

Here, I think, the 'new' trauma theory is still in the process of developing paradigms to match those of its classical, psychoanalysis-inspired predecessors. That is, classical trauma theory provided us with a powerful hermeneutic for linking events of extreme violence, structures of subjective and collective experience, and discursive and aesthetic forms. Once we have revealed the specificities hiding under the apparently neutral and universal face of this understanding of trauma—its attention to events and not systems; its assumption of privileged, secure subject positions; its investment in fragmented modernist aesthetics—it is incumbent on us to provide the counter-forms that would maintain trauma as an object of inquiry. Pluralization alone is not enough. In various ways, this cutting-edge collection makes moves towards a new paradigm that might link up apparently divergent sites and moments. One of the most promising may be the biopolitical framework developed in several of the essays. Via the approach inspired by Foucault and developed by Agamben and Esposito, among others, questions of power and life itself have begun to enter more fully into the field of trauma studies, as the essays of Edkins and Vermeulen, especially, demonstrate.

Even as we seek to maintain trauma as a theoretical category, we should not, of course, attempt to subsume all forms of violence, dislocation, and psychic pain under its categorical singularity. The project of building a non-Eurocentric, fully historicized trauma theory should not be an imperial one. I agree with LaCapra that it can be productive to talk about trauma without explicitly naming it, but I would add that we might also want to think about the relationship between trauma (named or not) and *other* disruptive social forces. We should be suspicious of overgeneralizing the trauma concept because, as Vermeulen points out, its circulation 'risk[s] strengthening "immunitary" tendencies that perpetuate rather than minimize trauma … especially in an age of globalization.' That is, when power operates biopolitically as the management of life, trauma talk in the centers of political sovereignty may activate concerns about security and contagion that lead to asymmetrical forms of violence rather than egalitarian, global solidarity. The post-9/11 United States is the most obvious example of such a phenomenon.

In the face of the paradoxical need to pluralize trauma while recognizing the limits of its applicability, I would like to suggest that we think of the trauma category as *necessary but not sufficient* for diagnosing the problems that concern us as scholars and human beings. To explore what it might mean to declare the category of trauma necessary but not sufficient, I want very briefly to add two examples of contemporary and future urgency to the important areas of concern discussed elsewhere in this volume: the status of labor under globalization and the impact of climate change. These examples both confirm the necessity of de-provincializing trauma and suggest in turn how such a move necessitates that trauma studies join with other fields and methodologies of inquiry that, like the critique of biopolitics, address the mutations of power and the conditions of life.

In the fall of 2012, two factory fires in South Asia killed hundreds of garment workers who were making clothes for subcontractors of European and American companies such as H&M, Wal-Mart, and Gap. In September, a fire killed at least 262 workers in a factory in Karachi, Pakistan, while 112 died in November during a fire in Dhaka, Bangladesh (see Bajaj; Walsh and Greenhouse). These events are not exceptions—more than 500 Bangladeshi workers had already died in fires in the last six years before the recent catastrophe—and they are obviously not limited to South Asia. Surely there is plenty of evidence of trauma here, but conceptual clarity is crucial if we want to move beyond a confirmation of what we already know and a simple denunciation of global capitalism (as worthy as such denunciation is!). To start with the obvious: trauma is not a category that encompasses death directly, but rather draws our attention to the *survival* of subjects in and beyond sites of violence and *in proximity* to death. The dead workers are not the victims of trauma, and thus trauma theory can only partially reckon with their death. But if trauma theory cannot fully encompass the event, that does not imply that a renovated trauma studies is of no use. What kinds of violence are at stake here and how does trauma fit into this scenario?

We clearly have an intersection of two forms of violence that concern the contributors to this volume. We have a sudden event of extreme violence that could very well have traumatized survivors of the fires and families and loved ones of the workers who perished, even if we cannot predict precisely what their experience will have been or the form their response to it will take. But, in addition, that event takes place on the site of—and thoroughly embedded within—a system of violence that is neither sudden nor accidental: exploitation in an age of globalized neo-liberal capitalism. To be sure, exploitation can be both physically and psychically traumatic, and yet, as with the problem of death, the category of trauma cannot subsume it without an important loss of analytical clarity—in this case, the sort of clarity that a Marxist critique of political economy can provide. Despite their non-coincidence, however, this example does succinctly illustrate how tightly exploitation and trauma are interwoven. The mechanisms of neoliberal accumulation not only seem to require the everyday regimen of sweatshop exploitation under inhuman circumstances, but also enable the 'extraordinary' (if still predictable) event of the factory fire. As the *New York Times* reported, it is precisely the neo-liberal structure of voluntary, 'industry-backed "social-auditing"' of workplace conditions that makes possible, even likely, such devastating fires (Walsh and Greenhouse). Here we see how an event-focused trauma theory needs to understand the conditions of structural violence. At the same time, we can speculate that sociological accounts of structural violence could benefit from event-based models in order to understand the psychic effects of systemic exploitation, effects that would have implications for organizing resistance to such structures.

But another step is necessary to encourage us to move beyond an isolated conception of trauma studies: the structures of globalization undergirding this (all too ordinary) example necessitate a turn back on the producer of theory in a way that classical trauma theory has not always demanded. That is, 'we' producers of theory in the Euro-American academy—as all the contributors to this volume are—are part of this picture: our seemingly insatiable consumption of clothes and gadgets and our habituation to the benefits of globalization (in many realms, if not in all) drive the regime of accumulation in factories like these as much as do the corporate drive for profits and the devious system of factory inspection. Trauma theory has helped us to think about the relation between perpetrators and victims—even if it has, in the (in)famous example of Tancred and Clorinda, sometimes confused them (Caruth, *Unclaimed Experience*; Leys; Novak; Rothberg, *Multidirectional Memory*; Craps, in this volume). But these categories alone are not sufficient to understand 'our' positioning in this globalized scenario of exploitation and trauma. Nor is the third term usually brought in at this point sufficient: the bystander. We are more than bystanders and something other than direct perpetrators in the violence of global capital. Rather, in the terms I have been developing in other contexts, we are *implicated subjects*, beneficiaries of a system that generates dispersed and uneven experiences of trauma and wellbeing simultaneously (see Rothberg, 'Multidirectional Memory' and 'Progress, Progression, Procession').

The notion of the implicated subject—neither simply perpetrator nor victim, though potentially either or both at other moments—also proves useful for thinking about the second context of violence and trauma I want to explore: climate change. Taking account of the devastation wrought by human-induced climate change and environmental degradation similarly requires a move beyond event-centered accounts of violence, as Rob Nixon suggests with his concept of 'slow violence.' In order to understand the impact of ecological disaster on the environments of the world's poor—in other words, the same people most directly and harshly affected by the neo-liberal regime of accumulation—Nixon argues that we need to comprehend 'a violence that is neither spectacular nor instantaneous, but rather incremental and accretive, its calamitous repercussions playing out across a range of temporal scales' (Nixon 2). This 'violence of delayed destruction,' this 'attritional violence that is typically not viewed as violence at all' (2), also results, I would add, in more familiar and 'visible' forms of trauma, such as wars and punctual ('natural') disasters. As with the case of exploitation and factory fires, climate change is a site of knotted and mutually dependent forms of violence; and, as in the previous case, the impact of both slow and punctual forms of violence can surely be traumatic. But is trauma theory—even one that is non-Eurocentric and open to systemic, non-spectacular violence—the only or best lens for exploring the environment's 'long dyings', to which Nixon wants to draw our attention? At most, it seems to me, trauma studies could play a subsidiary role in addressing a problem that demands multi-faceted, interdisciplinary approaches.

The slow violence of climate change does not only require a shift in temporal perception away from the shattering event of classically conceived trauma; it also requires a recalibrated understanding of humanist history and subjectivity that displaces (without entirely eliminating) the positions of victim and perpetrator. Although distributed unevenly, and disproportionately impacting the poor and the global south, as Nixon reminds us powerfully, climate catastrophe ultimately implicates us all. (Hurricane Sandy's flooding of the Wall Street area of New York City in October 2012 might serve as an allegory of that fact.) According to Dipesh Chakrabarty, the evidence of climate change thus requires a new, post-humanist philosophy of history that would trouble not only key presuppositions of classical trauma theory but also those of Marxist and postcolonial theory. Drawing on scientists' proposal of a new geological era—the Anthropocene—in which, for the first time, 'humans act as a main determinant of the environment of the planet' due to the large-scale use of fossil fuel, Chakrabarty argues provocatively that '[h]umans now wield a geological force' (Chakrabarty 209, 206). What he calls humanity's 'geological agency' in the Anthropocene—a period chemist Paul Crutzen dates to the late eighteenth century (Chakrabarty 209)—entails the collapse of the distance between '[g]eological time and the chronology of human histories' (208).

In Nixon's account, slow violence already challenges our usual historical chronologies as well as the categories of perpetration and victimhood, but his account stays relatively close to Marxist and postcolonial understandings of history in highlighting the unevenness of the effects of climate change across rich and poor regions. Chakrabarty's adoption of the Anthropocene to describe our contemporaneity and his linked notion of 'geological agency' lead him to supplement Marxist and postcolonial visions with a more encompassing notion of our implication as a species in a common and novel problematic. Such a shift to a more universal implication, Chakrabarty clarifies, 'is not to deny the historical role that the richer and mainly Western nations have played in emitting greenhouse gases … [b]ut scientists' discovery of the fact that human beings have in the process [of capitalist modernization] become a geological agent points to a shared catastrophe that we have all fallen into' (218). Chakrabarty's analysis suggests a paradox in the impact of geological agency, which he sees as an 'unintended consequence of human actions' (221): geological agency 'scale[s] up our imagination of the human' (206) by recognizing our planetary impact, but it simultaneously installs limits in the potentials of human freedom and in the possibilities for control over our environment. One may quarrel with Chakrabarty's relative emphasis of commonality over unevenness—his universalization of what I've called implication under the heading of the 'species' (21–2). Yet his formulation of a paradoxical human agency of unintended consequences helps us to grasp what he calls in his title 'the climate of history' as a problem of violence involving vastly different scales of temporality and modes of subjectivity than we in trauma studies have yet ventured to address.

The linked examples of globalized industrial production and human-induced climate change suggest a number of consequences for the future of trauma studies that are also evoked in different terms by the essays in this volume. First, they confirm the necessity, evinced by all the contributors here, of broadening and differentiating our understanding of what trauma is, along with our account of the conditions under which it is produced. As these examples and several of the essays demonstrate, the site of theoretical production of trauma theory—the Euro-American academy—has remained distant from many of the sites of trauma's impact. Thus, second, we must continue to trouble the West/non-West binary that is at the root of Eurocentric thinking (and some forms of resistance to it): the distinctions between event-based, systemic, and structural trauma do not map onto any simple, geo-cultural map, but cut across all borders (even if their distribution is markedly uneven). In addition, the different sites of trauma—as well as the different sites of trauma theory—are linked in networks of causality, feedback, and mediation that require a more sophisticated tracing of knots and assemblages of violence than early work on trauma provided. Furthermore, not all violence and suffering are best described by trauma—even if something we can recognize as trauma often accompanies those other forms of violence and suffering. Exploitation and ecological devastation can be traumatic—and can certainly lead indirectly to trauma of various sorts—but their essence (also) lies elsewhere. We need better ways of understanding how different forms of suffering and violence may inhabit the same social spaces and we need to understand what such overlap entails for the possibilities of resistance, healing, and social change. Finally, both examples discussed here suggest that developing a *necessary-but-not-sufficient* trauma theory entails reflection on *implicated subject positions* beyond those of perpetrator and victim, such as the beneficiaries of neo-liberal capitalism and the inhabitants of the Anthropocene. As we contemplate the future of trauma studies and the changing nature of violence and power, this volume inspires us to construct new parables beyond Tancred and Clorinda.

Works cited

Bajaj, Vikas. 'Factory Fire Kills More Than 100 People in Bangladesh.' *New York Times* 25 November 2012. Available online at www.nytimes.com/2012/11/26/world/asia/bangladesh-fire-kills-more-than-100-and-injures-many.html.

Caruth, Cathy, ed. *Trauma: Explorations in Memory*. Baltimore: Johns Hopkins UP, 1995.

Caruth, Cathy. *Unclaimed Experience: Trauma, Narrative, and History*. Baltimore: Johns Hopkins UP, 1996.

Chakrabarty, Dipesh. 'The Climate of History: Four Theses.' *Critical Inquiry* 35.2 (2009): 197–222.

Kaplan, E. Ann. 'Trauma Future-Tense (with reference to Alfonso Cuarón's *Children of Men* 2006).' In Julia Koehne, ed. *Trauma and Cinema*. Berlin: Kadmos P, 2012. 364–380.

LaCapra, Dominick. 'Trauma, Absence, Loss,' *Writing History, Writing Trauma*. Baltimore: Johns Hopkins UP, 2000. 43–85.

Leys, Ruth. *Trauma: A Genealogy*. Chicago: U of Chicago P, 2000.

Luckhurst, Roger. *The Trauma Question*. London: Routledge, 2008.

Nixon, Rob. *Slow Violence and the Environmentalism of the Poor*. Cambridge: Harvard UP, 2009.

Novak, Amy. 'Who Speaks? Who Listens? The Problem of Address in Two Nigerian Trauma Novels.' In Stef Craps and Gert Buelens, eds. *Postcolonial Trauma Novels*. Spec. issue of *Studies in the Novel* 40.1–2 (2008): 31–51.

Rothberg, Michael. *Multidirectional Memory: Remembering the Holocaust in the Age of Decolonization*. Stanford: Stanford UP, 2009.

Rothberg, Michael. 'Progress, Progression, Procession: William Kentridge and the Narratology of Transitional Justice.' *Narrative* 20.1 (2012): 1–24.

Rothberg, Michael. 'Multidirectional Memory and the Implicated Subject: On Sebald and Kentridge.' In Liedeke Plate and Anneke Smelik, eds. *Performing Memory in the Arts and Popular Culture*. New York: Routledge, 2013. 39–58.

Walsh, Declan and Steven Greenhouse. 'Certified Safe, a Factory in Karachi Still Quickly Burned.' *New York Times* 7 December 2012. Available online at www.nytimes.com/2012/12/08/world/asia/pakistan-factory-fire-shows-flaws-in-monitoring.html.

INTRODUCTION

Gert Buelens, Sam Durrant and Robert Eaglestone

Like waves breaking on the shore, every discipline, every field and sub-field, every theoretical movement tells and retells the story of its genesis, until a pattern is written on the sand, awkward points are eroded and the beach seems stable and calm: a seemingly inevitable result of natural processes. The shoreline then becomes a place from which to view the horizon, to survey the future in serenity or with wild surmise. However, in a collection that concerns the messy complexities of trauma, this paradoxically stabilizing flow seems to be a problem. It is clear that the names 'trauma' or 'trauma theory' mark a rising tide in the humanities and beyond, and that the concepts and approaches that make up this surge come from many currents and flow from many sources. These often run into each other, contradict, agitate, creating not a smooth, gently shelving beach but shifting, unpredictable sands and turbulent waters. Charting the future of trauma studies is not meant to channel these waters in one, reassuringly navigable direction, which would, after all, be a disavowal of the unexpected nature of trauma itself. Rather, this collection seeks to trace the contradictions within the field that might continue to render its turbulence productive.

As the work of Roger Luckhurst and others has shown, the modern concept of trauma developed, in the West, through the interlocking areas of 'law, psychiatry and industrialized warfare' (Luckhurst 19). From around the time of the Second World War to the present, the concept has been increasingly medicalized but also and importantly linked into wider political frames: survivor narratives, responses to persecution and prejudice, and to the Holocaust and other acts of mass atrocity and genocide. In all of these discourses, as Luckhurst argues, the concept of trauma is neither fully material or somatic, nor simply psychic, nor fully cultural or easily located in its appropriative or disruptive relation to the symbolic order, nor simply historic or structural, but a point at which all these currents meet. It is precisely because it is a point of intersection, of turbulence, that 'trauma' is such a powerful force.

It is certainly true that 'trauma theory' is a response to the developing and changing impact of the Holocaust, at least in the West. Equally, there is something in Aimé Césaire's declaration that before the Nazis' 'supreme barbarism', many in Europe

> absolved it, shut their eyes to it, legitimized it, because, until then, it had been applied only to non-European peoples; that they are responsible for it, and that before engulfing the whole of Western, Christian civilisations in its reddening waters, it oozes, seeps and trickles from every crack.
> *(Césaire 14)*

Recognition of this, the world history of barbarity, also underlies 'trauma'. It is also true that there has been an increased medical attention to trauma, from the declaration by the American Psychiatric Association that post-traumatic stress disorder was a disease. However, these wider shifts are, in some way, beyond the remit of this book, which is concerned with the future of trauma theory in contemporary cultural and literary criticism and theory.

In terms of its growth within literary studies and cognate disciplines, trauma theory again comes from a range of sources. There was, in history, a turn to 'memory', in part stimulated by the work of Pierre Nora in the 1980s and Yosef Yerushalmi's influential book *Zakhor: Jewish History and Jewish Memory* (1982) (see Klein). Michel Foucault, too, invoked a politics of memory and, tracing this out, Ian Hacking explored what he named 'memoro-politics' (Hacking, 1994). This turn to memory often involved a rediscovery and translation of Maurice Halbwachs's work on collective memory from the 1920s (Halbwachs was murdered at Buchenwald in 1945). This shift in historical discourse not only seemed to align much in that field with similar questions about representation, politics and ethics and historical understanding in literary and cultural studies but also seemed to beg questions about trauma. Ian Hacking (1994), for example, wrote that 'there are interconnections between group memory and personal memory. One obvious link is trauma' (211).

But a strand in literary and cultural theory in general in the 1980s and 1990s seemed to turn towards trauma for other reasons. Research in the nascent medical humanities, sometimes inspired by Judith Lewis Herman's *Trauma and Recovery* (1992) or Arthur Frank's *The Wounded Storyteller* (1995) focused on traumatic events and the ways that individuals might come to terms with them. The work of theorists inspired by Lacan, or by Slavoj Žižek's Hegelian–Lacanian politicized psychoanalysis (or perhaps psychoanalytic politics) often use trauma as a core concept. The work of Judith Butler, too, turned to issues of trauma, grief and mourning in books like *Precarious Life* (2004) and *Frames of War* (2009). However, perhaps the most powerful stream came from the work of Cathy Caruth and Shoshana Felman in work developed from the impact of Derrida, Paul de Man and deconstruction.

Many have argued that there is something profoundly traumatic in the impulse that underlies deconstruction and Derrida's work, and that this work both enacts and responds to trauma (see Critchley; Eaglestone; Ofrat). The recent Derrida biography suggests some traumatic political events from his life (see Peters).

However, it is also the case that in the late 1980s and early 1990s, Derrida and those inspired by his work were being widely criticized from the right and from the left because many found the work overly textual and far away from the 'real world', unable to address political or ethical issues. (This was aggravated by the Paul de Man scandal, in which the influential Belgian-born critic was discovered to have published a handful of literary articles in a collaborationist newspaper in occupied Belgium during the War). Much of Derrida's work in the 1990s and afterwards, and much scholarship on his work, aimed to correct this impression. It is in this context that Caruth's and Felman's work developed.

Caruth's edited collection, *Trauma: Explorations in Memory* (1995), drew on a wide interdisciplinary range of critics and theorists, film-makers and medical experts and practitioners. Her introduction to the volume serves almost as a 'mission statement' for this form of 'trauma theory' and is, perhaps, the most widely cited piece in this field. It is here that the claim is made that trauma consists 'in the structure of its experience or reception: the event is not assimilated fully at the time, but only belatedly, in its repeated possession of the one who experiences it.' (Caruth 1995: 4–5). While this statement has been explored and problematized— indeed, many of the chapters in this volume cite it and use it as the basis of their critique—it remains a crucial insight. But her 1996 book, too, *Unclaimed Experience: Trauma, Narrative and History* made important interventions in the field, especially in relation to the relationship between experience and representation. Similarly, Shoshana Felman and Dori Laub's *Testimony* (1992) had a huge impact. *Testimony* has an explicit debt to psychoanalysis and to deconstruction and has at its core a sense of oddness and peculiarity which is connected to trauma: texts 'that testify do not simply report facts but, in a different way, encounter—and make us encounter— strangeness' (Felman and Laub 7). Felman and Laub argue that the strangeness of trauma cannot be easily domesticated. While some of the claims of the book have been questioned, its impact remains powerful (see Trezise, and Laub's response), not least in the academy itself, where so may have followed Felman's lead in organizing their modules around questions of trauma, testimony and witnessing.

The work of the intellectual historian Dominick LaCapra, too, draws on these discussions of memory, historiography and trauma to make significant interventions in this growing field. These publications, and the others that made up the sources of this field, led to a huge burst of intellectual and critical creativity consisting of new readings of texts, critical disputes and revisions.

Despite the importance of Caruth and Felman, 'trauma theory' is perhaps less a field or a methodology than a coming together of concerns and disciplines. The work done in it is usually profoundly interdisciplinary, drawing on literary and cultural studies, history, politics, sociology, psychology and philosophy. Some of the promise of Caruth's collection – of an engagement with more strictly medical knowledge – has not yet been fulfilled, but emergent fields such as 'neuro-criticism' may well have much to offer.

It is against this background, then, that this collection offers not a reflection on the past of trauma theory, but a consideration of its future. The chapters point to areas of change in the field, especially in relation to issues of globalization and postcolonialism. They also respond to the very nature of 'becoming a field' itself: it is very easy for a series of complex ideas to become a concrete 'method', and so to lose both the capability of self-reflection and the original questioning, investigative (and in this case, ethical) impulse. Part of the point of this book is to prevent this from happening.

As we have suggested, issues of trauma theory are characterized by a 'knot' tying together representation, the past, the self, the political and suffering. Reflecting this, each of these chapters is woven with these complex threads. However, we have divided them into two parts: the first part tends to deal more with the role of *history and culture*, the second more with the importance of *politics and subjectivity*. Each chapter explores how 'trauma theory' might move beyond its current phase. Various strands bind them together. They all, in different ways, stress the importance of politics, yet none offer simplistic resolutions. Each, again in different ways, advocates a movement beyond the sort of modernist or postmodern narrative texts that are the usual focus of trauma criticism. Many are concerned with the body as a site of meaning and trauma. And each is, within the remit of the humanities, profoundly interdisciplinary, responding to the interweaving that trauma itself gestures towards.

The first part of the book, 'History and Culture', begins with more traditional accounts of trauma theory in its post-deconstructive mode. Robert Eaglestone and Dominick LaCapra discuss the ways in which trauma theory engages with representations of the Holocaust and how this might still be productive for reflection and analysis. Following numerous critiques of the centrality of the Holocaust to the development of trauma studies, however, contributions from Stef Craps, Ananya Jahanara Kabir, Nouri Gana and Sam Durrant relocate trauma theory in a postcolonial and globalized world, theoretically and materially.

In his chapter 'Knowledge, "afterwardsness" and the future of trauma theory', Robert Eaglestone turns to *Landscapes of the Metropolis of Death*, the memoir of Otto Dov Kulka, which is a sort of modernist precipitate of a historical work, something strange and powerful formed from, but separate to, the solution of history. Eaglestone argues that in this memoir it is possible to see how trauma opens up a wider range of disciplines and texts, how trauma destabilizes our wider senses of temporality, and how trauma theory, in its classic Eurocentric and post-deconstructive mode, connects with a range of wider intellectual and existential currents of thought related to the 'structure of experience'. He suggests that the experience of trauma has shifted some profound part of western discourse.

Similarly, Dominick LaCapra's 'Fascism and the sacred: sites of inquiry after (or along with) trauma', uses the advances made through the study of trauma to explore how issues of religion underlie fascism. A discussion of Derrida's essay 'Faith and Knowledge: The Two Sources of "Religion" at the limits of Reason Alone' introduces the themes of holiness and the sacred which in turn LaCapra uses to illuminate fascism. He suggests that much about the Holocaust and its traumatic effects is transformed by seeing it through this religious or 'postsecular' prism.

In a productive counterpoint to these two chapters, Stef Craps, in 'Beyond Eurocentrism: trauma theory in the global age', argues that many of the founding texts in the field seemed to promise a wider cultural engagement precisely through trauma – Caruth wrote that that 'trauma itself may provide the very link between cultures' (1996: 11) – than has in fact taken place. Often, texts on trauma theory marginalise the traumatic experience of non-western cultures, assume the definitions of trauma and recovery that the West has developed are universal and often favour a distinctively modernist form in order to 'bear witness' to trauma. Craps suggests that Caruth's reading of *Hiroshima mon amour* – essentially a Western story in which the Japanese setting and character are foils for the French woman's trauma – is an example of this. In order to open up trauma theory to become more inclusive and less Western-focused, Craps critiques the implicit Western construction of PTSD. He also reads Aminatta Forna's novel, *The Memory of Love* (2010), set in Sierre Leone just after the civil war, in a way that both highlights the Westernized approach to trauma and its failings in a country where the 'Western standards of normality … are actually the exception rather than the rule'. The future of trauma studies must work with and through these critiques.

Along similar lines, Ananya Jahanara Kabir's chapter 'Affect, body, place: trauma theory in the world' begins with two lines from an anthology of poetry from the Taliban and suggests that there are limitations and blind spots in trauma theory which stem from the contexts from within which it has arisen. The chapter then seeks to explore these blind spots within a broader, more global framework. Her own work on the partition of India revealed that the 'Holocaust-centric' forms of trauma theory, while useful, were not capacious enough, especially to deal with a global range of literary, musical and cinematic forms, the multiple, often contradictory messages therein and the complex role of affect. Kabir traces similar sites of complication and challenge to the (European) model of trauma in Phnom Penh, in Angola and in Iraq. While Kabir acknowledges Rothberg's model of 'multi-directional memory', she suggests that this model is still rooted in a Freudian vocabulary that occludes vernacular (and in particular non-narrative) modes of response to trauma and their origins in complexly differentiated 'affect-worlds'.

Nouri Gana, in 'Trauma ties: chiasmus and community in Lebanese civil war literature', argues that devastation and war are so much part of today's world that they threaten to institutionalize 'ungrievability, disposability and post-traumatic stress disorders as ineluctable contradictions of human existence'. Structural accounts of trauma need to be carefully distinguished from the historical, often colonial origins of suffering in regions such as Iraq, Palestine and Lebanon, not least because such structural accounts threaten to obscure the possibility of justice, redress and forgiveness. 'Counter-narratives' are needed that aim to make sense of war and engage with and process its traumatic effects. However, this process of making sense demands an intricate attention to the formal complexity of representing traumatic experience. Accordingly Gana turns to one of contemporary Arabic literature's most experimental novels, Elias Khoury's *City Gates* (2007;

Abwāb al-madina, 1981). Gana identifies in the novel a 'poetics of occlosure' in which opposing stresses exist in a chiasmus: between the excess of the traumatic event and its unrepresentability; between closure and a resistance to closure; between event and its repetition; between wholeness and fragmentation. Chiasmus emerges as 'the figure of traumatic survival and vulnerability' that binds the stranger to the 'community of the traumatized'.

Sam Durrant's chapter, 'Undoing sovereignty: towards a theory of critical mourning', serves as a hinge between the two parts of the collection, concerned as it is with how postcolonial attempts to memorialize the traumatic histories of colonialism structurally reproduce state processes of subjection. Following Judith Butler's lead, Durrant explores how trauma's capacity to breach what Freud posited as the subject's protective shield might be put to political use in producing a shared consciousness of corporeal vulnerability. Transposing her argument into the realm of aesthetics, he explores how the artwork can only give rise to such a consciousness by undoing its own protective shield, namely the self-legitimating ideology of its own form. He turns to a poetry cycle by Ingrid de Kok in order to show how the artwork maintains a mimetic solidarity with corporeal suffering by suspending not only the cathartic logic of South Africa's Truth and Reconciliation Commission, but also the transcendent logic of its own lyric form.

The second part of the book focuses even more clearly on issues of politics and subjectivity, on the state and the various states of subjection to which it gives rise. Stonebridge considers rights and refugees, Edkins the relation between personhood and the political, and Vermeulen, using similar intellectual resources, considers biopolitics and community. Finally Luckhurst speculates on trauma after subjectivity through a reflection on science fiction.

If, Lyndsey Stonebridge argues in '"That which you are denying us": refugees, rights and writing in Arendt', trauma theory began with a contemplation of the Holocaust, the detention centres of the twenty-first century are where a part of that legacy endures and so the future of trauma theory must be tied up with the fate of today's refugees. Identifying a 'critical lyricism' in refugee writing, and drawing on Hannah Arendt, herself 'stateless' for 17 years, Stonebridge argues that, for a refugee, 'to claim rights is first of all to criticize the linguistic and political mystifications on which they rest'. At the core of lyrical texts is the idea of the human, and (as de Man argued) a mourning for the human. Again, after Arendt, Stonebridge identifies the development of a 'new kind of human beings' in Kafka and in other writers as a response to and broadening of trauma.

In her book *Trauma and the Memory of Politics*, Jenny Edkins developed the concept of 'trauma time', a temporality that challenges sovereign power through the latter's reliance on linear time. Her chapter in this book, 'Time, personhood, politics', argues that, by producing a permanent state of exception, the state has attempted to take control of this trauma time. Following Agamben's contrast between 'chronological time' (in which we become 'spectators continually missing themselves') and 'messianic time' (the time we, in fact, are) she explores how time and personhood are related in the political. The 'missing person', in a range of senses, is the focus of this analysis and forms, in the end, a locus from which a resistance to the state in the figure of the 'neighbour' can be analysed.

Pieter Vermeulen's 'The biopolitics of trauma' analyses a concern that trauma studies, in its focusing on suffering and woundedness, may add to a politics of recrimination and vengeance. Drawing on the work of Judith Butler, Giorgio Agamben and others, he measures a shift in the analysis of power from the 'domain of culture to the problematic of life' and to the policing of life: to, in short, biopolitics. In his chapter, he shows how trauma and discourses of trauma are resituated in the context of biopolitics. While biopolitics disguises itself as 'mere management or bureaucracy' with the aim of 'preserving' life, in fact it generates a constant 'insidious trauma' (Vermeulen cites Laura Brown). These daily traumata shape and affect us, and – turning to Foucault and Esposito – Vermeulen argues that trauma theory can be seen as an 'immunitary technology' involved with life and the care of life. Where Durrant transposes Butler's politics of vulnerability into a critical aesthetics, Vermeulen reminds us that 'unprotected exposure to contagion and contamination is not a livable option', repositioning trauma studies as working towards a condition of 'sustainable exposure'.

Both Edkins and Vermeulen imagine a roughly contemporary form of subjectivity; in the final chapter of the collection, 'Future shock: science fiction and the trauma paradigm', Roger Luckhurst uses 'hard science fiction' to challenge this. In 1970, Alvin Toffler published a book called *Future Shock*. Luckhurst argues that many of the terms the book introduced (such as 'adaptational breakdown') have now been replaced with a discourse of trauma. While trauma theory has, to date, largely turned to elitist modernist texts, it has been suspicious of popular genres such as science fiction; yet science fiction may well be, Luckhurst suggests, the best place to examine the future, the future here now, and the future of trauma. 'The most challenging contemporary science fiction', he writes, leads us to rethink trauma itself. Ballard and Vonnegut, for example, are both seen to have transmuted wartime traumatic experiences into demanding science fiction. But Luckhurst suggests that in 'hard SF', drawing on advances in hard sciences such as neurology, even more of a challenge is offered, as the imagining of 'post-human futures' questions what a 'post-human' trauma might be. John Brunner's *The Shockwave Rider* (1975) and William Gibson's *Pattern Recognition* (2003) both challenge models of subjectivity, and so of the trauma that subjectivity might endure. Other, even 'harder' works of science fiction work to question and reform trauma even further. Yet, as Luckhurst points out, they function as a correlate to the new, scientific understandings of trauma that are arising in the contemporary moment.

Trauma theory is perhaps, at root, an attempt to trace the inexhaustible shapes both of human suffering and of our responses to that suffering. By gathering these scholars together, and allowing a range of views and approaches to develop, we hope that we are contributing productively to the continuing debates around these most serious and painful of matters.

Works cited

Caruth, Cathy, ed. *Trauma: Explorations in Memory*. London: Johns Hopkins University Press, 1995.
Caruth, Cathy. *Unclaimed Experience: Trauma, Narrative and History*. London: John Hopkins University Press, 1996.
Césaire, Aimé. *Discourse on Colonialism*.1955. Trans. Joan Pinkham. New York: Monthly Review Press, 1972.
Critchley, Simon. *Ethics–Politics–Subjectivity*. London: Verso, 1999.
Eaglestone, Robert. *The Holocaust and the Postmodern*. Oxford: Oxford University Press, 2004.
Edkins, Jenny. *Trauma and the Memory of Politics*. Cambridge: Cambridge University Press, 2003.
Felman, Shoshana and Dori Laub. *Testimony: Crises of Witnessing in Literature, Psychoanalysis, and History*. London: Routledge, 1992.
Hacking, Ian. 'Memoro-Politics, Trauma and the Soul.' *History of the Human Sciences* 7.2 (1994).
Hacking, Ian. *Rewriting the Soul: Multiple Personality and the Sciences of Memory*. Princeton: Princeton University Press, 1995.
Klein, Kerwin Lee. 'On the Emergence of Memory in Historical Discourse.' *Representations* 69 (2000): 127–150.
Laub, Dori. 'On Holocaust Testimony and Its "Reception" within Its Own Frame, as a Process in Its Own Right: A Response to "Between History and Psychoanalysis" by Thomas Trezise.' *History & Memory* 21.1 (2009): 127–150.
Luckhurst, Roger. *The Trauma Question*. London: Routledge, 2008.
Ofrat, Gideon. *The Jewish Derrida*. Trans. Peretz Kidron. Syracuse: Syracuse University Press, 2001.
Peters, Benoît. *Derrida*. Trans. Andrew Brown. London: Polity, 2013.
Trezise, Thomas. 'Between History and Psychoanalysis: A Case Study in the Reception of Holocaust Survivor Testimony.' *History & Memory* 20.1 (2008): 7–47.

PART I
History and culture

1
KNOWLEDGE, 'AFTERWARDSNESS' AND THE FUTURE OF TRAUMA THEORY

Robert Eaglestone

'We are singing like little angels, our voices providing an accompaniment to the processions of the people in black who are slowly swallowed up into the crematoria' (Kulka 27). When he was a boy of eleven, Otto Dov Kulka, now a very eminent Holocaust historian, a survivor of Auschwitz and the son of a survivor from Auschwitz, sang the 'Ode to Joy' in a children's choir at Birkenau. All through his life since then, he has asked himself what drove the conductor to choose that famous declaration of human dignity: was it a protest, 'as long as man breathes he breathes freedom, something like that' (27)? Or was it 'an act of extreme sarcasm … of self amusement, of a person in control of naïve beings and implanting in them naïve values, sublime and wonderful values, all the while knowing that there is no point or purpose and no meaning to those values' (27)? Kulka can find no answer to this profound, historical and existential question. He chooses first one possibility and then the other. The first, somehow more hopeful, shapes what he is 'occupied with and believes in' (28) during his working life. However, when he considers the rise of the Nazis, the second haunts him and seems, 'I will not say realistic – but more authentic' (28). Each choice, like any truly existential choice, 'is in fact the whole unfolding of my existence or of my confrontation both with the past and with the present from then until today' (29). There are enough Holocaust survivor testimonies by historians to make a fascinating little canon (see Popkin). *When Memory Comes* by Saul Friedlander is a classic of this small genre and Kulka's *Landscapes of the Metropolis of Death* deserves a place on a par with that volume.

I begin with this moment in Kulka's astonishing testimony because, in our attempts to understand it, it draws attention to a number of crucial points about trauma. These seem central to me for the future of trauma theory, for the thinking about what questions and insights might be generated by this responsive and responsible conceptual apparatus – if it is anything so organized as an 'apparatus' and not, rather, conceptual threads turned into a pattern by observers keen to convert critical thought into a programme or a doctrine. I am going to focus on three interrelated aspects, each drawn from Kulka's work. The first is the sense that trauma is both the origin and disruption not only of memorial work or fiction but of discipline-specific knowledge in other fields too: the impact of trauma and the theory that studies it respects no academic boundaries and shapes not only affective 'feelings' but also more formally recognized knowledge. Second, and again central to the form of Kulka's testimony, I am going to draw attention to the way that trauma has an impact on our experience of time, our temporality, and its structure as 'afterwardsness'. Freud's idea of '*Nachträglichkeit*' is theoretically complex but – oddly – experientially easy, as each of us lives it, often unnoticed, each day. It is not in itself traumatic but roughly corresponds to Kirkegaard's observation, so often misquoted that it is now an old saw, that while life is lived forwards, it 'can only be understood backwards'. Third, stemming from this moment in Kulka's work and from the understanding of 'afterwardsness', is the idea that the questions posed by trauma (and investigated by trauma theory) are existential questions which are to do with the time of a whole life and so with its relation to ethics. In this way, much that underlies trauma theory is tied into not only post-deconstructive thought but wider currents of contemporary intellectual life.

Yet trauma theory does have its origins in post-deconstructive work. The story of the origins of trauma theory is fairly well-established: developing from the Yale school of deconstruction and part of the 'ethical turn' in literary theory and European philosophy, it grew – centrally through the work of Cathy Caruth and Shoshana Felman – to become a critical-theoretical way of attending to and addressing the representation of human suffering and 'wounding', both literal and metaphorical, both personal and communal. Of course, there are other strands of 'trauma theory', too, woven into this tapestry: some stem from the work of Judith Herman, for example, or come out of memory studies and critical historiography. The concept of 'trauma' itself has a much longer life as, for example, Roger Luckhurst has shown, but it is this recognizably post-deconstructive strand that I take to be central in trauma theory. Indeed, this strand of critical thought represents one answer to the question – asked repeatedly in the 1990s – about the 'ethics of deconstruction'. And, in its many sinuous appearances, trauma theory attempts to unite what we might call (perhaps too quickly) a formalist concern for text and problems of interpretation (what Paul de Man called the 'internal laws' of literature) with a historicist concern for application and response to the world (the 'external relations' of literature).

Any current in the seas of scholarship can sometimes flow too fast and, on a quick tide, in the fast surge of novelty, barks are launched when their hulls have not been checked carefully enough for ill-fitting planks and outright holes. Many scholars, such as Michael Rothberg, Jane Kilby and Susannah Radstone, have pointed to flaws, omissions and areas in which trauma theory needs to develop and expand. Stef Craps correctly points out that trauma theory has tended to focus too much on the Holocaust as the paradigm of individual and communal trauma, and so has marginalized other atrocious events. He suggests that it has been too

Eurocentric in its development and risks appropriating other, non-Western events into a Western model of traumatic suffering: his work and the work of others seeks to address this. Some, such as Wulf Kansteiner in a series of articles (see Kansteiner 2004; 2008), have found the whole project (if it is a project) misbegotten, an 'interdisciplinary research trajectory that has gone astray' (Kansteiner 2004: 195). In a parallel to Craps, but with less sympathy, Kansteiner finds it obliterates 'historical precision and moral specificity' (194) (I am uncertain what 'moral specificity' is, but lacking it is clearly a bad thing). 'Trauma theory', he argues, conflates the traumatic and non-traumatic (194) and provides instead an 'aestheticised, morally and politically imprecise concept of cultural trauma, which provides little insight into the social and cultural repercussions of historical traumata' (194).

His substantive issue – from which all the others stem – is what he sees as the 'misleading symbolic equivalency' (194) between the 'allegedly traumatic component of all human conversation' (194) and the 'concrete suffering of victims of physical and mental trauma' (194). Kansteiner suggests that the core reason that this happens is because Cathy Caruth

> focuses on the question of trauma because the phenomenon appears to her as a perfect, particularly vivid illustration of her understanding of the workings of language, which she adopts from Paul de Man.
>
> *(203)*

That is, Kansteiner argues that Caruth, and those who come after her, are less interested in the particular histories of a traumatic event, and more interested in using that event to demonstrate their view of language itself. Kansteiner fails to offer his view of 'the workings of language' but it seems fairly clear that he thinks of language in an unproblematic, positivistic kind of way, as a vehicle to carry (presumably extra-linguistic) concepts between people. One does not have to be an eighties-style deconstructor to find this 'folk psychology' concept of language limited: indeed, the whole 'linguistic turn' across the humanities in the twentieth century throws this concept of language into doubt. Moreover, Kansteiner also implicitly begs a question: if Caruth gets her understanding from de Man, what are his ideas about the working of language and where does he get them from? This question is too large to answer here, so I will focus on one aspect. De Man's thought was influenced by Derrida's work, and while Derrida does not, I think, offer a theory of how language works, he offers approaches to understanding why, at least, Kansteiner's version doesn't. (There is also a strong argument – too extensive to be made here – to say that Derrida's work itself is an ethical response to trauma; see Eaglestone.) Kansteiner's view of language fails to work because any moment of language works only in differentiation to a huge backdrop of language that is not there, is absent: absent in space and also absent in time. Kansteiner, very decently, says that moral 'honesty and conceptual and historical precision demand that trauma be first and foremost read from the perspective of the victim' (214): however, these same scholarly virtues point out that this 'reading' is just not possible in a straightforward way. It is not that Caruth (or de Man or Derrida) does not appreciate pain, suffering and so on, but their concern is with the understanding, and the limits of understanding, of these things. Trauma is not the chance example that exposes, from a deconstructive position, how language and reference works: instead, a deconstructive approach to language and reference is that which allows us better to understand trauma. This is obviously not to say, *pace* the critique of Kilby, Craps and others, that this approach is a final and complete form of understanding, but it is to say that the bland positivism of other approaches is not able to engage with the profound questions that a serious consideration of trauma asks. The future of trauma theory is most usefully to be found by exploring it through its deconstructive past.

The reason that these post-deconstructive insights are most effect is because, as Caruth argued, the pathology of trauma is not the event itself, or the distortion of the event in memory, but 'consists, rather, solely, in the structure of its experience or reception: the event is not assimilated or experienced fully at the time, but only belatedly, in its repeated possession of the one who experiences it' (Caruth 4). While other scholars rightly broaden out and reflect on the nature of trauma in the wider, non-western world, this chapter aims to explore the future of trauma by thinking through these deconstructive terms, to explore what impact the idea of the 'structure of experience' can offer for the future of trauma theory. As I have suggested, I want to suggest that it is still illuminating in three areas: in the range of applicability across a number of forms of representation (including, for example, the writing of history); in terms of the idea of 'afterwardsness' and in relation to the widest and most demanding existential questions. And I want to suggest that all these consequences are shown in a most striking form in Kulka's extraordinary work.

Trauma as history

Raul Hilberg, reflecting on Adorno's famous remark, wonders if footnotes 'after the Holocaust' are 'less barbaric?' (138). Similarly, Shoshana Felman and Dori Laub ask if 'contemporary narrative' can bear witness to how the 'impact of *history as Holocaust* has modified, affected, shifted the very modes of relationship between narrative and history?'(94–5). This is a more detailed version of the question asked, occasionally too dramatically perhaps, about 'how can we live after the Holocaust?' If we do think that the Holocaust has had a profound impact on what it is to be a human being, how has it shifted the very frames by which narrative and language work? In disagreement with thinkers like Pascal Bruckner, who find the West too laden with guilt, I am more tempted to broaden this out to consider the huge array of atrocity and genocide of which we are now more excruciatingly and often shamefully aware, of that Europe 'where they are never done talking of Man, yet murder men everywhere they find them … in all corners of the globe' (Fanon 251). Even these questions – and to them we can add the arguments about hearing the voices of the victims that helped motivate the style of Saul Friedlander's monumental final historical work – begin to show how historians, for example, are aware of the impact of the nature of trauma not simply as a 'wound' to individuals but to disciplines of thought (see also Ball).

Landscapes of the Metropolis of Death shows this 'from the inside'. It is hard to know what to call Kulka's book – perhaps it is a work of 'traumatic meta-history'. It is a sort of modernist precipitate of a historical work, something strange and powerful formed from, but separate to, the solution of history. It is not 'against' history but 'beyond' or 'below' history, striving to illuminate what Kulka calls the 'tremendous "meta-dimensional" baggage and tensions' (82), philosophical and personal, which underlie his historical work. It is an account, in fractured, modernist prose, mixed with photographs and clearly influenced by the work of W. G. Sebald, of his thoughts, dreams, diaries, visits, moments of epiphany and memory, of his unconscious and rarely spoken 'mythology' of the 'Metropolis of Death', of Auschwitz. He names the 'Great Death' (the gas chambers) but also the 'Small Death' (the electrified fence) and the 'Life beyond Death', recalling the occasion where he was electrified on the fence, hanging a moment 'after death' – 'I am dead, and the world as I see it has not changed! Is this what the world looks like after death?' (34) – he was saved by being pushed off by a pole, 'or maybe it was a shovel' (35), held by a Soviet POW. Most of all, perhaps, it is about his attempts to face his own history. There is a narrative, a map, but it is told not as a chronicle but as a series of moments, flashes, impressions, ideas, illuminations, poems, even dreams and recalled daydreams. The style is terse, often simply descriptive.

Crucially of interest here is Kulka's relationship to himself as a historian. Kulka describes how he went out of his way to separate himself from his research. So successful was he in this that, for example, in 1978, on hearing he planned to visit Auschwitz, a well-meaning colleague suggested that he ignore the main camp and 'go to Birkenau – that is the real Auschwitz' (3). He writes of his 'paradoxical duality' (82) in which he was both historian of that period and at the same time managed totally to avoid 'integrating any detail of biographical involvement' (82). This is discussed in the book and then illustrated by an appended meta-text, his scholarly article 'Ghetto in an Annihilation Camp: Jewish Social History in the Holocaust Period and its Ultimate Limits'. As a historian, he both poses and answers the question of why the inmates of the 'family camp' – the sub-camp in Auschwitz in which he was held – were treated so differently. The 'family camp' was planned as a 'show camp' for the Red Cross and was suddenly 'liquidated' when the Nazis found it was no longer necessary. Identifying himself as a survivor, in the book but not the article, he discusses his intense memories and associations. This doubleness and the use of meta-texts are, of course, recognized tropes of texts that deal with trauma.

Kulka writes that he hoped that his highly regarded historical research would be 'infused' with a consciousness of the intensity of those events he witnessed, or that the 'scientific historical research' (82) would somehow help him break into the 'metropolis of death'. However, he finds that

> the truth, as it seems to me now, is that I only tried to bypass here the barrier of that gate, to enter it with the whole force of my being, in the guise of, or

in the metamorphosis of, perhaps, a Trojan horse, intended, finally, to smash the gate and shatter the invisible wall of the city forbidden to me, outside whose domain I had decreed that I would remain.

(82)

Disguised or hidden as a historian he sought to come to terms with, to work *at*, if not 'work through' perhaps, the childhood experiences from which he had, in some profound way, exiled himself. But quite the opposite happened: the 'safe and well-paved way of scientific discipline' (82) led him to skirt precisely the violence, the murder and torture he had seen, 'as perhaps I skirted the piles of skeletons in Auschwitz on my way to the youth hut' (83). The 'safe passage' (83) of the discipline of history led him, he thinks, both not to be able to convey 'the message' (83) that was 'burned into' (83) his being but at the same time to cope with precisely that inability to tell it. And yet, in these passages over these few pages, he writes that the message that he could not tell, indeed, that made him 'cower at the vague awareness that I had no way, and would never attempt, to embark on the path of an attempt to disclose' (83–4) is that 'the world, with the Metropolis and the immutable law of the Great Death having been, can no longer, and will never again be able to free itself of their being part of its existence' (84).

Kulka's work shows up something crucial for trauma theory. E. H. Carr famously wrote, in his jolly English way, that one should study 'the historian before you begin to study the facts. This is, after all, not very abstruse … When you read a work of history, always listen out for the buzzing. If you can detect none, either you are tone deaf or your historian is a dull dog' (18). Listening for the 'buzzing' is not to depreciate the work, clearly, but to better understand it. Among historians of the Holocaust and of other atrocities, there is of course a great deal of 'buzzing': much of this is, quite rightly, 'metahistorical' in the Hayden White sense. But some 'buzzing' is more personal and harder to quantify or qualify: Browning's work, for example, as he admits, is in part shaped by his early response to Vietnam, and Saul Friedlander's 'turn' from a more traditional, empiricist historian to later work can be seen to occur around the time of his self-exposing memoir. However, in relation to historical work and in relation, perhaps, to other work in the human and social sciences (see Simon), trauma theory alerts us to more than just buzzing. It alerts us vividly to the other forces – fears, hopes, experiences – at play in a historical work, other forces which are quite as revealing in bearing witness to the Holocaust, or to any traumata, as 'the facts'.

'Afterwardsness'

A recurring trope in Kulka's work is the coming together of two different times, as the past reappears in the present. He has, for example, a sudden and absolute feeling, on his first visit to the Temple Mount (in the 1960s), that he had been there before, because the desolation there, and at a 'ruined' Auschwitz in 1946 (he was there to give evidence at a trial), was so 'charged with historic meaning' (74).

He discusses the blueness of the sky over Israel, and, with a child's eye, he describes how he admired the beauty of the blue skies of summer over Auschwitz while imprisoned there, and how he was almost immune to the frightful disorientation of the camps, a disorientation which itself killed adults, since he knew no other order. Indeed, both these examples invoke three different times: the past at Auschwitz, the represented present (at the Temple Mount, for example) and the present of the narration (the time of writing of the book). It is not just the disciplinary limits that shape *Landscapes of the Metropolis of Death* but also those of time and the representation of time, centrally that of 'afterwardsness'. Trauma is not only a disruption of how we experience time, but of how we represent it, too.

Trauma theory asks questions about the 'structure of experience', and so, inevitably, about the complexities of 'afterwardsness'. As I have suggested, 'afterwardsness' – often thought of in terms of Freud's idea of '*Nachträglichkeit*' – is very close to us: indeed, it is part of our daily experience (everyone is first a historian of themselves, after all). However, the common forms of narrative and representation, especially those of the human sciences and even more especially those which use narrative most and assume a 'god's-eye view point', run counter to and confuse our sense of 'afterwardsness'. In 1989, David Wood suggested that the 'century-long linguistic turn' would be followed by a 'spiralling return to time as the focus and horizon of all our thought and experience' (xi). He continued: for 'this to happen time has to be freed from the shackles of its traditional moral and metaphysical understanding' (xi). One place where this change has been more obvious has been in contemporary fiction and in contemporary film which both show a heightened interest in 'playing' with the representation of time (see Currie). One might go further, and (as I'll suggest below) trauma theory picks up on a shift of interest in trauma which goes hand in hand with this shifting sense of how time is, and how it is represented. How this 'afterwardsness' is to be understood is both complex and huge: indeed, if it represents a shift as huge as that of the 'linguistic turn' as Wood suggests, then its impact is almost too huge to easily comprehend. But, *contra* Kansteiner, I want to suggest that the explicit study of 'afterwardsness' in trauma studies can be re-imported into the wider humanities. If the expansion of the thinking through of this concept is encouraged, rather than delimited, it may illuminate a number of complex matters. For example, it may be that the same structure inhabits a whole range of non-traumatic discourses that seem to have some similar characteristics to those analyzed in trauma studies. People often say, to those with young children, that 'the time flies by' and that the quotidian events of childrearing must be savoured. The implication is that the event of early child parenting is, as Caruth suggests of traumatic events, not 'assimilated or experienced fully at the time, but only belatedly' (Caruth 4). Similarly, experiences of great joy are not experienced fully at the time ('the day went like a flash' people say, 'it was all over too quickly'). Yet these are in no way historically or structurally traumatic events. In *Anna Karenina*, for example, we see Anna and Vronsky flirting, in anticipatory love, and then falling from love, into dejection and despair. But we never see – indeed, the narrative purposely jumps over – a moment of happiness.

Here, the representation of their happiness – clearly not traumatic – has some of the hallmarks of trauma. One of the futures of trauma theory, then, is perhaps to look closely and more carefully not simply at the trauma, but at the structure of experience within which trauma is made manifest.

Ethics, 'afterwardsness' and trauma

This rethinking of 'afterwardsness' and the structure of experience and time is inextricably tied to language not only through the sinews of tense, but also through the deeper existential questions that it asks. In his memoir, Kulka writes that he avoids artistic and memorial representations of the Holocaust because 'I cannot find in them what they seek to convey' (80). However, he turns to Kafka's 'Before the Law' as a way of coming to understand how he can arrive at the 'gate' of comprehension but not, as it were, pass through it. Kulka suggests that his mythology exists, perhaps, only for himself, and no other 'gate' will open for him. However, he recalls that, in Kafka's story, the man sees, faintly, a light glowing from behind the gate of the law. The questions posed by 'afterwardsness' are also, and immediately, ethical questions. This is because questions of ethics are woven inescapably into questions of narrative and of time.

In the Aristotelian tradition, the 'good life' of the virtues can only be seen rightly in relation to our death and finitude. Aristotle writes that the man who has achieved happiness is

> 'one who realises in action a goodness that is complete and that is adequately furnished with external goods, and that not for some limited period but throughout a well-rounded life spent in that way'. And perhaps we must add to our definition 'one who shall live in this way and whose death shall be consistent with his life'. For the future is dark to us, and happiness we maintain to be an 'end' and in every way final and complete. If this be so, then those who have or shall have the blessings we have enumerated shall be pronounced by us entirely happy in terms of human happiness.
>
> *(48)*

This thought – glossed as 'call no man happy until he is dead' – reveals that there is a profound link between the stories we tell and our sense, however vague, of the ethical. And nonetheless we are aware, as Kulka shows, that the relationship between ethics and trauma makes this complicated.

When we tell the stories of others, we are keen to make them unified and give their lives a theme (and it may be that some people have lives to which this fits). It is this unification that so often plays a role in our ethical thinking. However, reading Kulka through the eyes of trauma theory reveals that this 'unification' is clearly externally imposed: his own life feels, to him, disjointed, fragmented, doubled, disunified. One crucial symptom of this is the way in which Kulka explores how he both feels he has a 'message' (83), one to do in some way with ethics, with how we live, and is also aware that the trauma, from which this message comes and about which it is concerned, is almost impossible to express. If we are to respond to traumatic events, it must be to analyse not only the ways that these atrocities outrage the principles and virtues by which we live, but also the ways that they disrupt even how these principles and virtues come to be understood. Thus, it seems to me that the insights of trauma theory need to spread more widely across the humanities, not simply to awaken guilt but to assist in the rethinking of how we tell and think about ourselves.

Conclusion: hyperbolic suggestion

But – and here I offer only a hyperbolic suggestion – perhaps this is happening already. My suggestion throughout this chapter has been that 'trauma theory' is not really a new disciplinary paradigm, but that it forms a network of ideas that offers a new way of paying attention to forms of texts. Then again, forms of interpretive responsiveness stem from the texts and the world to which they are called to respond. That is to say that the wave of books with titles like *Trauma*, *Trauma Culture*, *Culture Trauma*, *Texts of Trauma*, *Traumatic Texts*, *Traumatic Realism*, *Worlds of Hurt*, *Post-traumatic Culture* and the misery memoirs, verbatim theatre of terrible atrocities, narratives of suffering and so on are both a symptom of, and a response to, some wider change. Perhaps – and this is just hyperbole – there has been some shift in the language (at least) of the West, perhaps the world. A shift in what the later Foucault would call the 'discourse' in relation to 'afterwardsness', ethics and trauma. And this change would be, and be visible, first, and most, in and by language.

We know, of course, that language meaning changes over time: we can see this easily within our own lifetimes. We also know that what we might call 'language sensibility' changes over time. For example, think of how in the UK, after the First World War, the Edwardian discourse of 'Play up, play up and play the game' was undercut with such terrible irony by its speakers that it could not be used again: or of the change, in the West, from a formal public discourse to a much more informal one during and after the 1960s. These things are charted in the writings before and after these changes and are easily observed by all. The hyperbolic suggestion, then, is that the change in language and acts of culture is itself a response to trauma and that what's called 'trauma theory' is the place where this change has been responded to most clearly. This is not a unique idea. Something similar is at the core of Foucault's argument in *The Order of Things*. To simplify the argument of that complex book, Foucault suggests that there was, in the early modern period, an 'immense reorganisation of culture' (43) around the nature of the sign and its relation to (what we now call) its referent. Prior to this, Foucault argues, the 'value of language lay in the fact it was the sign of things' (33) and that there was

> no difference between the visible marks that God stamped upon the surface of the earth, so that we may know its inner secrets, and the legible word of the Scriptures, or the sages of Antiquity … in both cases there are signs to be discovered.
>
> *(33)*

To choose a crude example, in medieval medicine, plants that echo the shape of the head or liver were taken to be beneficial to illnesses of the head or liver and were read as such in 'the book of nature'. Similarly, written words were assumed to be 'coeval with the institution of God' (34). (The shadow of this idea remains in the present world in various guises, some serious, some not. For example, one less serious, but illuminating example is the representation of magic in stories: in the Harry Potter series of children's books, uttering a pseudo-Latin noun or verb for something in a spell gives one power over an object or person: the archaism of the word points to the old idea, preserved as an 'idea fossil', that a word has power directly over a thing because a word is intertwined, not simply arbitrarily associated, with that thing.) The change that occurred with the early modern period happened at the level of reference: that is, how language itself worked changed. Language, 'instead of existing as the material writing of things, was to find its area of being restricted to the general organisation of representative signs' (42). 'Discourse', Foucault writes, was 'still to have the task of speaking that which is, but it was no longer to be anything more than what it said' (43). My hyperbolic thought-experiment suggests that such a change has occurred now. The impact of the Holocaust, of our increasing knowledge of the world-wide impacts of global genocides and atrocity, of our general ability to cause immense suffering to each other, of what Judith Butler calls 'precarious life' has changed how language works. It is the post-deconstructive understanding of language that, perhaps clumsily, gestures towards this most clearly.

Perhaps even this hyperbolic idea is too totalizing and hegemonic. Wittgenstein's famous metaphor of language like an ancient city, with streets, new quarters and old districts, suburbs and so on, is useful here. He means to suggest that the 'shape' of language varies in each suburb: different levels of, say, accuracy and meaning, or of quality of reference. The language of chemistry or the notations of calculus are quite different from, say, the language of art criticism, the discourse of love or, here, accounts of suffering and testimony. If the claim that the whole of language has been altered by atrocity is too hyperbolic after all, then, perhaps, one could argue that one suburb is growing rapidly and in this suburb, different rules apply: we have to feel our way around, find out the shape of things. In this way, the future of trauma theory is to continue to reflect on and to attempt to understand the damages that we do to each other, and in so doing draw our attention to both our terrible strength and our utter weakness.

Works cited

Aristotle. *Ethics*. Trans J. A. K. Thomson. London: Penguin Books, 1953.
Ball, Karyn. *Disciplining the Holocaust*. Albany: SUNY Press, 2008.
Browning, Christopher. *Ordinary Men: Reserve Police Battalion 101 and the Final Solution*. 2nd edn. London: HarperCollins, 1998.
Bruckner, Pascal. *The Tyranny of Guilt*. Princeton: Princeton University Press, 2010.
Butler, Judith. *Precarious Life*. London: Verso, 2004.
Carr, E. H. *What is History?* Basingstoke: Palgrave, 1986.

Caruth, Cathy, ed. *Trauma: Explorations in Memory*. London: Johns Hopkins University Press, 1995.
Craps, Stef. *Postcolonial Witnessing: Trauma Out of Bounds*. London: Palgrave Macmillan, 2013.
Currie, Mark. *About Time: Narrative, Fiction and the Philosophy of time*. Edinburgh: Edinburgh University Press, 2007.
Eaglestone, Robert. *The Holocaust and the Postmodern*. Oxford: Oxford University Press, 2004.
Fanon, Frantz. *The Wretched of the Earth*. Trans. Constance Farrington. London: Penguin, 1990.
Felman, Shoshona and Dori Laub. *Testimony: Crises of Witnessing in Literature, Psychoanalysis and History*. London: Routledge, 1992.
Foucault, Michel. *The Order of Things*. London: Tavistock, 1970.
Friedländer, Saul. *When Memory Comes*. Trans. Helen R. Lane. New York: Discus Books, 1980.
Hilberg, Raul. *The Politics of Memory*. Chicago: Ivan R. Dee, 1996.
Kansteiner, Wulf. 'Genealogy of a Category Mistake: A Critical Intellectual History of the Cultural Trauma Metaphor.' *Rethinking History* 8 (2004): 193–221.
Kansteiner, Wulf (with Harald Weilnböck). 'Against the Concept of Cultural Trauma or How I Learned to Love the Suffering of Others without the Help of Psychotherapy.' In Astrid Erll, Ansgar Nünning, eds. *Cultural Memory Studies: An International and Interdisciplinary Handbook*. New York: de Gruyter, 2008. 229–240.
Kilby, Jane. *Violence and the Cultural Politics of Trauma*. Edinburgh: Edinburgh University Press, 2007.
Kulka, Otto Dov. *Landscapes of the Metropolis of Death*. London: Penguin, 2013.
Popkin, Jeremy D. 'Holocaust Memories, Historians' Memoirs: First-Person Narrative and the Memory of the Holocaust.' *History & Memory* 15:1 (2003): 49–84.
Radstone, Susannah. *The Sexual Politics of Time: Confession, Nostalgia, Memory*. London: Routledge, 2007.
Radstone, Susannah and B. Schwarz, eds. *Memory: Histories, Theories, Debates*. New York: Fordham University Press, 2007.
Rothberg, Michael. *Multidirectional Memory: Remembering the Holocaust in the Age of Decolonization*. Stanford: Stanford University Press, 2009.
Simon, David. 'To and through the UK: Holocaust Refugee Ethnographies of Escape, Education, Internment and Careers in Development.' *Contemporary Social Science* (2012): 21–38.
Wood, David. *The Deconstruction of Time*. Atlantic Highlands, NJ: Humanities Press International, 1989.

2
FASCISM AND THE SACRED

Sites of inquiry after (or along with) trauma

Dominick LaCapra

Where does one go after the recent surge in trauma studies? I think that the study of trauma is not a passing fad or trend. The problems posed by trauma, both individual and collective, are real problems, and the study of trauma has begun to take differentiated and self-critical forms. Such study has provided newer ways of seeing both older and recent problems. But instead of rehearsing what has already been extensively discussed with respect to trauma and the debates surrounding it, or applying trauma studies to another text (although there may still be much to accomplish in the latter respect), we may have reached a point where problems can be addressed without always ringing the trauma bell. Instead one may choose to indicate the role of trauma when suitable, but often leave its pertinence implicit, especially when that pertinence would seem obvious. In my recent book, *History and Its Limits: Human, Animal, Violence*, I have extensively discussed the relevance of trauma in a variety of areas, including the study of the Nazi genocide or 'final solution'. Here I would like to pursue that inquiry, touching especially on the way the potentially shattering experience of trauma may either be averted or transfigured through a form of sacralization or sublimation (in the sense of rendering sublime), specifically in the case of certain perpetrators.

I would, however, note that I am not an expert in comparative fascism. And, despite a few allusions, I shall not discuss all versions of fascism or fascist tendencies. As will be evident in the approach I shall take, the focus of some of my own work has been representations of the Holocaust, memory, trauma, and the understanding of Nazism. I would also note that my approach is exploratory and that my title is almost an equation with two unknowns. I shall come to fascism and the problem of its relationship to Nazism,[1] but it is important to keep in mind throughout my discussion that the sacred and religion are contested concepts, including their relation to presumably secular phenomena, such as politics, aesthetics, ideology, and trauma.

One dimension of the 'final solution', and perhaps of certain forms of anti-Semitism and racial prejudice more generally, is an acting-out in practice of ideologically reinforced, anxiety-producing, indeed potentially traumatizing phantasms about the radically other, prominently including the Jew as phobic, quasi-ritual threat, source of pollution or contamination, world-historical power, and abject victim or pest. Such phantasms might be all the more disconcerting to the extent one sensed their self-contradictoriness or absurdity, yet tried nonetheless, through a self-fulfilling performativity, to reduce the other to the state of degradation and threat they impute to that other. Moreover, anti-Semitism, while having distinctive features, is best seen in a larger framework of racism and victimization that may also have ritual or quasi-sacrificial aspects (notably a desire for purification and regeneration through violence) that may apply to other groups, such as Slavs, 'Gypsies', people of colour, and those judged to be unacceptable or unintegratable components of the community (for example, the mentally ill, the disabled, or 'asocials') who may be swept up into a dynamic of violence and victimization.

I would like to explore this complex set of contentions or hypotheses in relation to a much-debated question: whether fascism (or at least Nazism) can, at least in certain ways, be seen as a civil or secular religion, in one formulation, a political religion, and in another, a postsecular phenomenon – to invoke a term with some currency in recent thought. This issue is typically addressed on the basis of the very questionable assumption that we understand and know what we mean by religion and secularity along with other concepts often invoked in discussions of them (such as the aesthetic or even the literary, for example, the 'aestheticization of violence' or 'literary politics'). Despite the dubiousness of any clear-cut definitions of these concepts, I would nonetheless like to inquire into the role of the religious or the sacred in fascism, and especially Nazism, without pretending to offer definitive answers or an inclusive and exhaustive account of the complex phenomena in question. I am addressing only one complex strand or network of factors in a more complicated process.

Of interest here is a late essay by Jacques Derrida, a typically intricate, difficult, questioning, and self-questioning essay entitled 'Faith and Knowledge: the Two Sources of "Religion" at the Limits of Reason Alone' (in Derrida and Vattimo 1998: 1–78). I shall say a few words about this essay and perforce simplify and make a selective use of Derrida's analysis without dwelling on aspects of it with which I would take issue.[2]

What I find pertinent for my purposes is how Derrida worries, works, and unsettles the concepts of religion and secularity, along with related concepts, to indicate how little we can say we know or understand with any degree of confidence, much less certainty (a not unfamiliar strategy in Derrida). He does not simply introduce a necessary degree of hesitancy and self-critical doubt that may be missing, or at least not taken beyond a certain point, in the work of some if not many historians and social scientists. He also tries to sketch out the meanings given to religion and more or less related phenomena that deserve serious critical attention. The title of his essay involves a dual reference to works of Kant and Bergson – initiators of two discursive practices or traditions that have interacted in complex ways in French and, more generally, modern thought. And in discussing the problem of religion Derrida stresses the importance of the pragmatic question of recent uses and abuses of the term, including how it is invoked in the confused idea of the return of religion (did it ever go away?). He also raises doubts about a presumably disenchanted or secular modernity as well as the way religion is sometimes linked ideologically to fascism, as in the ideologically charged, dubious concept of Islamo-fascism.

Derrida also emphasizes the duality – what unsurprisingly emerges in the course of the essay as the multiplicity – of the meanings attributed to religion. Still, he elaborates the idea of two senses or 'sources' of religion. One is the sense that relates it to faith – 'the *fiduciary* (trustworthiness, fidelity, credit, belief or faith, "good faith" implied in the worst "bad faith")' (Derrida 1998: 63). He also treats the relation of faith to the 'totally other' (63). Thus in his first sense or somewhat heterogeneous set of senses of religion, Derrida stresses faith as well as the totally other.

The second set of senses relates religion to the sacred and the holy, between which there are also divergences and tensions. (The German '*heilig*' is translated as either 'holy' or 'sacred', whereas the French has two terms: '*saint*' – as in *le Saint Esprit* – and '*sacré*'.) I would note that the definition or conception of religion in terms of the sacred, rather than, say, a belief in immortality or in God (as well as the totally other), has been very important in a French tradition of thought to which Derrida is to some degree indebted or by which he is himself hailed or interpellated – the Durkheimian tradition, including such important figures as Marcel Mauss, Georges Bataille, Roger Caillois, René Girard, Julia Kristeva in certain ways (at least via Mary Douglas), and many others, including to some extent Henri Bergson. Derrida also indicates the importance of the holy and the problem of the relation between the sacred and the holy. I would simply suggest in passing that the holy is often related to notions of the radical transcendence of divinity (as is the totally other and perhaps even faith or at least the 'leap of faith'). The sacred relates to more immanent, this-worldly, at times carnivalesque forces such as ritual, including (but not reducible to) sacrifice, which Derrida discusses in many places, including his *Gift of Death*. (Yet it is interesting that one refers to the 'holy' rather than the 'sacred' fool – as well as the indwelling of the Holy Spirit – but to the 'sacred' monster – *le monstre sacré* – such as Derrida himself.) The holy as the *heilig* is very important in German thought, including Heidegger's thought, in a sense privileged for Derrida for an interesting reason, because of 'its extreme character and of what it tells us, in these times, about a certain "extremity"' (59), from which Derrida himself is not immune. One may also mention Rudolf Otto, whom Derrida does not discuss.

Derrida sees the holy or *heilig* as related to hailing and the way one is hailed by an address to which one must respond. One thinks, say, of Abraham or Moses as well as the hailing of Mary. Derrida refers to a possible division

> in the alternative between sacredness without belief (index of this algebra: 'Heidegger') and faith in a holiness without sacredness, in a desacralizing truth, even making of a certain disenchantment the condition of authentic holiness (index: 'Levinas' – notably the author of *From the Sacred to the Holy*).
> *(64)*

With respect to the reference to Levinas and disenchanted holiness, one might add Karl Barth or Rudolf Bultmann – indicating a meeting of a certain Judaism and a certain Protestantism, both of which tend to desacralize or 'disenchant' the world through a notion of the radical transcendence of a totally other, hidden God who may be both the ultimate object of desire and the most extreme, dangerously traumatizing force – arguably similar in certain ways to the 'real' in Lacan. Derrida does not mention what is pertinent to problems I shall discuss shortly: the role of address or hailing in the fascist salute and forms of address such as *Heil Hitler* or *Sieg Heil*. He nonetheless emphasizes how the *heilig* conveys notions of the unscathed, the pure, the undefiled, the uncontaminated, the immune that is safe and sound, in one sense the avoidance or voiding of the traumatizing or anxiety-producing, and, in Nazi Germany, the quest to be *Judenfrei*.

This notion of the unscathed, pure, and uncontaminated has been a crucial object of critical inquiry throughout Derrida's thought. It is related to his deconstruction of pure binary oppositions through which one attains purity in a concept or a phenomenon by concentrating and projecting onto the other all internal alterity, or difference from oneself, to arrive at the pure, integral, unscathed, presumably self-identical entity or concept. This procedure is crucial both to a logic of pure identity and difference and to a sacrificial scapegoat mechanism. For Derrida such a logic undermines itself by repressing or disavowing internal alterity (the female in the male, the animal in the human, the heteronomous in the autonomous, or the Jew in the German, say, as well as the sacred in the holy). This process of generating what radically questions pure identity and pure difference is what he designates by various terms over time: perhaps most famously, *différance*, related to the intertwined processes of temporalization and spacing. And the issue of more or less flexible limits and of the problematic but necessary role of non-absolute distinctions in the wake of the deconstruction of binary oppositions is crucial in the bearing of deconstruction on historical, ethical, and political analysis.

I have intimated that Derrida has joined others in referring, perhaps at times in an extreme, questionable fashion, to auto-immunity in the sense of the way a system generates its own antibodies that unsettle its pure identity and, at a certain threshold, its very being or life. I would also note that the process of *différance*, which takes a particular swerve in auto-immunity and which I would relate to internal dialogization, self-questioning, and self-contestation, also helps one to understand Derrida's oft-repeated and rather bewilderingly paradoxical assertion that a condition of possibility is a condition of impossibility. I would gloss this assertion as meaning that something's condition of possibility is the very condition of its impossibility 'as such' – as a pure, undivided, integral, autonomous, 'uncontaminated' entity or essence – hence implying the impossibility of the 'as such' as such. (Conversely, something's condition of impossibility as such is its very condition of possibility as what it is with its internal alterity, marking, trace-structure, or difference from itself, in a sense, its originary hybridity that threatens any simple opposition between a pure, integral inside and an outside.) In his essay on 'Faith and Knowledge', Derrida also makes observations indicating that the waters of the two sources of religion are themselves typically mingled in a veiled and even muddied, impure, or secret manner.

Towards the end of the essay, he asserts that 'the experience of witnessing situates a convergence of *these* two sources: the unscathed and the fiduciary' (65) – a thought that resonates with the widespread turn to experience, trauma, witnessing, and testimony in the recent past. Perhaps surprisingly for some readers, Derrida also argues that an elementary testimonial trust precedes all questioning, indeed that the slightest testimony 'must still appeal to faith as would a miracle'. And he makes the provocative, in certain ways problematic, assertions that the experience of disenchantment itself 'is only one modality of this "miraculous" experience' (64), that disenchantment is 'the *very resource of the religious*,' and that 'the possibility of *radical evil* both destroys and institutes the religious' (65) – views that I think apply more to the 'faith' side of the 'sources' of religion. In the present context I cannot inquire further into these assertions. I would simply observe that attempts to separate and oppose the 'two sources' or their analogues are contestable and may be conjoined with conflict and even with wars, as in the wars of religion and the Reformation.

Derrida also discusses two putative etymological sources of the term religion that in a sense cut across, or form tributaries to, his two main sources. One is *relegere*, important in the Ciceronian tradition and meaning harvest or gather. The other and perhaps more prevalent is *religare*, to bind, link, obligate – related to having scruples that hold one back from doing or thinking possibly transgressive things. I have intimated that I think that the more prominent concepts, at least in Christian theology, that are related to the two main sources specified by Derrida – to simplify, the sacred-holy-pure and faith-radical alterity – are immanence and transcendence. The relation or nonrelation between transcendence and immanence has, I think, a claim to being the paradigmatic aporia or paradox of Christianity (notably with respect to what, for Kierkegaard, was the 'scandal' of the incarnation – a 'scandal' that messianism tries to defer – the 'scandal' of the transcendent becoming immanent or God, man). The transcendence/immanence aporia or paradox (or its displacements and allegories) may even have this paradigmatic status in the so-called Western tradition more generally – something intimated in what was for some time, at least in the English-speaking world, Derrida's signature essay, 'Structure, Sign, and Play in the Discourse of the Human Sciences' (in Derrida 1978: chapter 10), specifically his analysis of the problem of the centre as both inside and outside (immanent and transcendent to) the circle it determines. One may also refer to dimensions of Derrida's early and later thought that are not explicitly brought together and thematized as a problem – the famous assertions that there is no 'outside-the-text' (a notion more on the side of immanence) and that every other is totally other (*tout autre est tout autre*), a generalization of radical transcendence. The transcendence/immanence aporia or paradox is also operative in a displaced manner in theories of meaning as immanent to its vehicles or signs or, on the contrary, arbitrary and, in a sense, transcendent with respect to them. One might even ask whether 'meaning' has become a 'god-term' in studies of history, culture, and society that see their goal as the determination or recovery of meaning.

The immanent sacred is related to a multiplicity of phenomena – notably sacraments and rituals, including sacrifice but not reducible to it. The transcendent sacred (possibly construed as the holy) may be figured as the unrepresentable, the ineffable, the totally other, the hidden God. It may serve as a bar to mediations, including sacraments and rituals, including sacrifice. I would note in passing, and later return to the point, that to the extent fascism and especially Nazism arguably have a significant relation to the religious and the sacred, it is, I think, more to a specific form of the immanent sacred, especially when the latter is absolutized and bound up with a quest for total purity that may generate anxiety about contamination and prompt a turn to rituals, including purifying and sacrificial rituals that get rid of phobic, anxiety-producing, typically scapegoated others. From a transcendent perspective, Nazism may be seen as a diabolical, immanent, political religion, as it was by Eric Voegelin and others (see Ustorf; Vondung).

Allow me to mention another distinction, at times taken to binary, oppositional, or separatist extremes: that between faith and works or actions. Faith (like certain transhistorical, universalizing approaches to theory) is more on the side of the radically transcendent, and works are more on the side of the immanent, this-worldly, and mediated. (Yet a this-worldly figure such as Hitler may be the object of a certain kind of faith.) The problem of faith and works was, of course, an issue in the Reformation. I would suggest that there are analogous concepts and concerns in historiography and social science, especially with respect to the relation between ideology or belief, even theory, and practice. Recently in history there have been attempts to stress the importance of practice, often correlated with Bourdieu's notion of habitus as what is embedded, goes without saying or is simply assumed. I would refer you, for example, to a recent book, *Practicing History: New Directions in the Writing of History after the Linguistic Turn*, edited by Gabrielle Spiegel. Bourdieu was himself within the Durkheimian tradition, and for Durkheim sacred practices, including rituals, constituted, at least in traditional societies, a habitus.

Most historians would see fascism and Nazism as somehow combining practice and ideology. Of course much depends on what one means by ideology, whose senses are also multiple, which is not to say that the concepts of practice and habitus are transparent. (Spiegel acknowledges that conceptions of practice along with practice theory are, for example, far from clear and, to the best of my knowledge, fascism and Nazism have not been explicit topics in practice theory.) I shall simply touch on the two extremes or at least two sources or currents of ideology that are often opposed or separated from one another. One is the systematically articulated networks of concepts or beliefs. You find at least an approximation of this in highly self-conscious intellectuals, say, Kant, Hegel, or Marx. Whether any modern movement or regime has an ideology in this sense is very problematic. A regime may have a doctrinal or dogmatic basis, but it may be a stretch to compare this with an articulated system. Very few historians would see Nazism as having a systematic ideology, although many would see it as having a doctrinal or dogmatic basis in racism, especially racially oriented anti-Semitism and the desire for a racially pure, unscathed, *Judenfrei*, utopian *Volksgemeinschaft* – a racial utopia.

The second, and I think more historically pertinent, notion of ideology is formulated by Althusser and taken up by many others. It has curious resonances with aspects of 'religion'. This is ideology that addresses, hails, or interpellates one and calls for a response. In more secular terms, it says 'hey you'. In more 'religious', or at least affectively charged and even visceral terms, it may say 'Hail Adolf' or even '*Heil Hitler*'. It is related to subject formation, and it need not appeal to systematic thought. Indeed a systematic ideology that is explicit and well-articulated opens itself to scrutiny and may invite criticism. An ideology that hails or interpellates can be more vague, even confused, and linked more compellingly, more bindingly, and more unreflectively to practices, even rituals and more or less structured forms, of acting out phantasms.

I shall also invoke another concept that has become prominent recently – the postsecular (for example, in the work of Eric Santner and Jane Bennett, among others). The postsecular is neither the secular nor the religious or sacred but somehow both – or betwixt and between. It comes into its own in the attempt to re-enchant the world, even to evoke a sense of the uncanny, the epiphanous, the extraordinariness of the ordinary, indeed the miraculous or the endowed with grace, charisma, the gift of grace. And the postsecular has very labile, often rather confused relations to the aesthetic, including notably the performative, the uncanny, and the sublime. My own appeal to the concept of the postsecular involves both use and mention, indicating a desire to leave open certain questions I raise.

I would note what deserves more inquiry: the possible relations of the sacred and the sublime as seemingly religious and secular, or perhaps postsecular, correlates – the sublime as a displacement or at least analogue of the transcendent sacred (or perhaps the holy), indeed what is out of this world – in a phrase often used with reference to works of art. (Beauty is more immanent and mediated – less excessive or extreme. The uncanny disorients beauty but, insofar as it may be seen as a returning repressed, it is closer to the immanent (for Freud, ultimately the mother's genitals or womb), with the return of the sacred in the secular, including the sublime, as a somewhat paradoxical, particularly disorienting mode of the uncanny.) One may also mention what I term 'traumatropisms' – different attempts to transfigure trauma into the sublime or the sacred, for example, in the sacralization or sublimation of founding traumas such as the Crucifixion, the French Revolution, the Holocaust, and possibly the First World War for Hitler and others (for example, Ernst Jünger with respect to the *Fronterlebnis*). For Hitler the devastating disappointment of loss of the war was exacerbated by the evangelical promise of its outbreak. (In Germany, this sense of devastation was further aggravated by developments in the interwar period, including runaway inflation followed by the great depression.) As Hitler put it in *Mein Kampf*:

> For me, as for every other German, the most memorable period of my life now began. Face to face with that mighty struggle all the past fell away into oblivion. For me these hours came as a deliverance from the distress that had weighed upon me during the days of my youth. I am not ashamed to

> acknowledge today that I was carried away by the enthusiasm of the moment and that I sank down upon my knees and thanked Heaven out of the fullness of my heart for the favour of having been permitted to live in such a time.
>
> *(50)*

The general question of the labile, often confused relations between the sacred or the religious and the aesthetic are, I think, very important in certain currents in modernity, including but in no sense restricted to fascism. I would recall in passing T. E. Hulme's definition of Romanticism as spilt religion – something quoted by M. H. Abrams in *Natural Supernaturalism* in the course of tracing the complex relations of Romanticism to religion, its structures, and motifs – a problem, of course, discussed by many others, including Northrop Frye and Hans Blumenberg. And the religion of art or the role of art as a surrogate or competitor with respect to religion has played an important role in 'modern times', including Freud's role-reversing reference in *Civilization and Its Discontents* to those who may need religion because they do not have art or *Kultur*. Of course this is not the only thing of interest in Freud concerning the complex relations between religion and seemingly secular formations, including psychoanalysis (for example, as involving attempts at exorcism of haunting, possessive forces).

Allowing for the very problematic meaning or meanings of religion, the sacred, and the aesthetic, let us cautiously move on to fascism and especially Nazism and ask whether they can be seen in any significant way – not entirely or even essentially – but in any significant way as related to the religious and the sacred, including their contested and often confused relations to the aesthetic. I will not go into the more delimited and more readily researchable question of the actual, empirical relations between fascist regimes and religious institutions such as the Catholic Church or the related question of clerico-fascism (see Finchelstein). These relations are intricate and run from compromise to active collaboration; Christian Wiese argues that 'Christian theology and the policy of the Churches, as well as a widespread social mentality determined by demonizing stereotypes of the "alien", dangerous Jew actively and often consciously prepared the ground for the National Socialist policy of disenfranchisement and – a few exceptions apart – contributed to the fate of the Jewish minority through consistent desolidarization and quiet surrender' (Wiese 166).

I have mentioned the conception of ideology that has displaced religious aspects, notably in its role in forming subjects through hailing or (in Althusser's term) interpellation – subjects who may well engage in practices bound up with ideological phantasms, beliefs, or convictions. What is, I think, of general significance during the interwar period is the widespread appeal of fascism, including its appeal for intellectuals, and the extreme lability of ideologies in terms of shifts in position of individuals across the spectrum and of 'borrowings' from ideology to ideology, even when they were militantly opposed to one another – including a tendency to valorize violence in intrinsic or regenerative, even sacrificial, and not limited strategic terms. In the sacrificially oriented Georges Bataille, this led for a while to a defence of what was termed *surfascisme* or taking from fascism its methods presumably in order to oppose fascism – a kind of homeopathic strategy that could well lead to overdosing on the antidote, especially when that antidote involved the typically escalating appeal to violence.

I have been using the problematic term 'fascism'. Allow me to give a list of what have often been taken as its prominent characteristics – what might perhaps be taken as a fascist constellation, if not a fascist minimum.

1. An affirmation of violence often seen not simply instrumentally as a means but as an intrinsic, valorized aspect of action, practice, or policy, at times bringing a so-called cult of violence involving traumatizing terrorism and even sublime elation.
2. A vision or figuration of violence both as originary or generative and as a heroic, typically masculine or virile vehicle of regeneration and purification in a world condemned as degenerate, fallen, mediocre, feminized, bourgeois – a despicable world that had to be radically uprooted and transformed with an apocalyptic sense of urgency.
3. A charismatic notion of leadership – an exciting leader who was chosen to lift up and lead the people out of mediocrity, degeneration, or even bondage. This is something even Bataille stressed in his essay on fascism and saw as a source of its appeal (see Bataille).
4. An enthusiastic, even elated, re-enchanted, mass public that followed the leader. The mass was also to be infused with charisma (not inert or passive). Here one may think of the ecstatic faces in the crowd greeting Hitler at Nuremberg, as seen in Leni Riefenstahl's film *Triumph of the Will*.
5. Extreme nationalism, militarism, and ethnocentrism that might, however, be combined with an idea of fascism as a transnational movement. There was also an idea of a new Europe, even a new world order that might include special affinities among given peoples or nations. Mussolini saw a privileged link between Italy and Argentina with its large percentage of Italian immigrants. Nazis looked to Nordic and 'Aryan' groups.
6. A long series of 'antis' – anti-Marxist, anti-parliamentary, anti-Enlightenment, anti-liberal, anti-bourgeois, anti-intellectual, and with some variation anti-Semitic.
7. A more positive notion of fascism as a third way, neither right nor left, neither capitalistic nor Marxist.
8. A notion of fascism as more spiritual than competing modern ideologies such as Marxism or capitalistic liberalism – more spiritual but also involving thinking with the blood, experientially, even viscerally, not intellectually, critically, or analytically.
9. The importance of movement and the movement (in German *Bewegung*), which is related to the importance of the will and direct action. This was perhaps most prominent in the Nazis. In Italy, where fascists did affirm direct action and will, there was also a pronounced valorization of the state and a top-down corporatist organization of the economy.

One may perhaps add other characteristics (for example, the breakdown of at least a 'liberal' sense of the rule of law), and not all those labelled or self-identifying as fascist accepted all of the above. One problem, however, is the relation of fascism and

Nazism. This question involves the broader issue of totalitarianism, which has been used, with certain qualifications, to include fascism, Nazism, and Soviet communism. The concept, of course, had a pronounced ideological role in the Cold War, almost analogous to that of terrorism and the war on terror today. (One might almost say, paraphrasing Freud, where ideologically totalitarianism once was, there terrorism has come to be.) This ideological role jeopardized the more analytic uses of the concept of totalitarianism. And the question with respect to the latter is whether the concept, even as a model or ideal type that one acknowledges was never fully realized in empirical reality, obscures too many differences. Mussolini and certain of his ideologues did affirm a totalitarian state as a goal. And the concept of totality was prevalent. Stanley Payne and others see political religion (PR) in partial contrast to civil religion (CR) as centred on the state and totalitarian in incentive (see Payne; Sternhell; Paxton; Gentile; Griffin 1993, 2008). But whether totalitarianism is a way to highlight the similarities between Nazism and fascism or fascisms is questionable. Arendt herself, with whom Payne agrees in his book of 1995 (206), argued that the concept of totalitarianism did not apply to Italian fascism and perhaps not even to Nazism, although it might have, had the Nazis won the war. So that leaves the Soviet Union and the problem of the Cold War.

Even without invoking the problematic concept of totalitarianism, one may note that there were obvious overlaps and actual alliances between Nazis and fascists. Interestingly, both claimed to be spiritual – more spiritual than materialistic Marxism and materialistic capitalism. Both appealed to violence in furthering supposedly spiritual ends and valorized violence itself in ways that might even be seen as aestheticizing *and* sacralizing, notably as regenerative if not redemptive, elevating, exhilarating, and perhaps even sublime. And both were expansionist, with the Nazis seeking *Lebensraum* and colonies in Eastern Europe. It has even been argued that the Nazi quest for *Lebensraum* had a causal role or at least was a very significant factor in the Holocaust. Once they invaded the east, the Nazis had to deal with an enormous number of Jews – notably in Russia, Poland, and Hungary. And they had to clear space for ethnic Germans. So the Holocaust could be seen as caused, or at least strongly influenced, by problems in population control. This view fits in with the major tendency in the historiographical literature – that stressing bureaucratic processes and the machinery of destruction, more recently, at least in certain quarters, biopower. I think this approach points to one important set of factors. But I don't think it is sufficient. And it is noteworthy that killing actions began before Nazis controlled large land masses and peoples, and genocidal practices were part and parcel of the conquest of those areas. Dan Michman has even argued that the development of ghettos was not instrumentally rational in motivation but stemmed from deeply internalized fear and repulsion in encountering 'radically other' *Ostjuden* (see Michman 2009, especially 75n; Michman 2008). Some historians have insistently argued that what differentiated Nazism from other fascisms was as important, if not more important, than what they shared, especially the Nazi role in the 'final solution' or the genocidal treatment of Jews as well as the widespread, violent abuse of other victims and victim groups. Genocide has generally not been seen as a necessary dimension of fascism. Saul Friedländer tries to make this argument. But Friedländer, like other historians, recognizes that other nationalities and countries were active collaborators in the genocide, at times even outdoing Nazis or going beyond what was required or even requested of them. It is well known, after Robert Paxton's research, that Vichy France deported children to the camps when this was not required by the Nazis. And Jan T. Gross has told the story of how Poles abused and massacred Jewish neighbours and took over their property without being coerced by Nazis, during the pogrom of July 10, 1941 at Jedwabne (Gross 2002). The book, touching on sensitive issues, provoked a heated controversy (see Polonsky and Michlic; Forum) He has also recounted how, even after ninety per cent of Poland's three-and-a-half million Jews had been eliminated during the Nazi occupation, the deadliest pogrom of twentieth-century Europe took place in the Polish town of Kielce on July 4, 1946, a year after the war ended, as Poles once again killed Jews, this time because they feared Jews would reclaim expropriated property, a fear that may have been reinforced by a sense of guilt or unease about what they themselves had earlier done to Jews and might do again (Gross 2007). For Gross the long-standing accusation of Jewish involvement in ritual murder remained prevalent in Polish society or at least was invoked on numerous occasions. And Polish Gentiles, recognized at Yad Vashem, were afraid to reveal that, at the risk of their own lives, they had helped Jews during the war, because of the expected hostile reaction of their own anti-Semitic neighbours (see, for example, Gross 2002: 82–4).

Another important point that has recently become more prominent is that the Holocaust seems less unique if not seen in a purely Eurocentric context but related to practices and policies with respect to people of colour in the colonies. The French in Africa, the Belgians in the Congo, and the white South Africans were at times quite extreme in their violence against enemies. There has been debate about the occurrence of genocide against native peoples in the Western hemisphere. The practices of Australia with respect to aborigines were assimilative and often quite violent, including killings in the colonial period and, in the twentieth century, the forcible removal of some 20,000 to 50,000 children of mixed parentage from aboriginal families and their placement in institutions or in white foster homes (Levi). All of these important cases and controversies would require extensive discussion sensitive to issues of time, place, and context, for example, with respect to comparisons or analogies with the Holocaust or Nazi genocide, including the treatment of animals in factory farming and experimentation, as in Charles Patterson's *Eternal Treblinka* (the title comes from a phrase of Isaac Bashevis Singer, who was deeply affected by the genocide in which his mother and younger brother were killed) or, in a more qualified way, in Boria Sax's *Animals in the Third Reich*.

It is important to recall what is at times obscured, especially in the insistence on the machinery of destruction. There were two, partially overlapping phases of the Nazi genocide. The first involved the *Einsatzgruppen* (special task forces) and auxiliary groups that accompanied the army in the invasion of the east, the so-called

Operation Barbarossa. This was the phase of hands-on killing – not simply desk murder or arranging train schedules. Here the killers were at first often inexperienced and were spattered with blood and brain as they shot victims in the back of the head. This phase involved the killing of some million and a half Jews and other victims – not an insignificant number. For the most part, Nazis and their affiliates, especially those in the elite SS, did not begin as hardened criminals, and a problem in Nazi ideology and practice was how to become hard and also how to find alternatives to the hands-on killing that might shatter or traumatize the insufficiently hardened. It is well known that a primary reason for the turn to gas was not from concern for the victims but the demoralization of German troops in direct killing actions that included the murder of women and children.

The second, partially overlapping phase was that of the concentration and death camps. The death camps, where the goal was killing and not work or extraction of surplus value, included Auschwitz-Birkenau, Chelmno, Sobibor, Belzec, and Treblinka, with Majdanek also involving much killing. Yet conditions in other camps were also dire and often led to death due to overwork, abuse, and rampant disease.

I intimated that probably the most prevalent explanation of the Holocaust is in terms of the machinery of destruction, the role of bureaucratic mechanisms, and largely 'modernizing' practices that more or less rolled along under their own quasi-mechanistic momentum, without clear attribution of responsibility and in conjunction with modern technologies of war and the stress of battle conditions as well as peer pressure. This view is often correlated with the notion of the banality of evil. One finds problematic resonances of this view in novels such as Bernhard Schlink's *Der Vorleser* (*The Reader*) and Jonathan Littell's much more ambitious *Les Bienveillantes* (*The Kindly Ones*), where, despite Littell's narrator's explicit distance-taking with respect to the notion of the banality of evil, there is *inter alia* a stress on the force of circumstance and at best diminished agency. Hanna, in *The Reader*, is described as 'falling' into her job as a guard with the SS, similar to the way she and her young paramour, the narrator, fall into one another's arms as a towel falls to the ground (the thirty-six-year-old Hanna initially embraces and fondles the fifteen-year-old Michael Berg from behind) (Schlink 1998: 25, 133), and Aue, the narrating officer in *The Kindly Ones*, is, as a putative result of an incestuous relation with his sister, a 'passive' homosexual who, like his fellow SS officers, is swept along by the course of events and ground up by the machinery of destruction as he finds himself involved in an incredible number of atrocities and 'perversities' in an amazing variety of places. Both novels are pervaded by a rather indiscriminately empathic, 'it-could-happen-to-anyone' (or '*mon-semblable-mon-frère*') feel to events.

Without making misleading amalgamations or suggesting a simplistic solution to the complex relation between process or practice and agency, I think one also finds variations of Raul Hilberg's 'machinery-of-destruction' view in Hannah Arendt, Omer Bartov, Christopher Browning, the sociologist Zygmunt Bauman, the deconstructive theorist Philippe Lacoue-Labarthe (in Heideggerian terms pointing to the supposed modern culmination of the Western technological *Gestell* or framework), Giorgio Agamben (in terms of biopower and the modern reduction of life to mere life in a state of exception), and many others. Different inflections among these analysts, as well as curious connections in lines of argument in their texts, are worth extensive analysis, some of which I have attempted elsewhere (LaCapra 1994, 1998, 2001, 2004, 2009; the last two books contain extensive critical analyses of Agamben).

The extreme, indeed visceral reaction to the Hilberg orientation is that of Daniel Jonah Goldhagen in *Hitler's Willing Executioners*, a book that has been criticized by historians but has also found a large popular following, both in the United States and abroad, notably in Germany. Goldhagen also, bizarrely enough, insists on an embedded habitus or culture on the level of what goes without saying, but he applies it to a putative generations-long eliminationist anti-Semitism in Germany that, with the Nazis, metastasized (in his term) into exterminationist anti-Semitism or genocide. This habitus rather mysteriously disappeared because of institutional changes after the war in a way that seems to credit denazification with rather amazing powers of success. Goldhagen also feels free to feel his way into, read, and render the subjective experience of perpetrators, actually, I think, the experience of perpetrators as fantasized by someone identifying with victims – most questionably perpetrators as they proceeded to escort and kill Jewish girls around the age of puberty. What I would like to argue in conclusion is different from Goldhagen's perspective.

What I would like to argue, or at least suggest, is that what is ignored in both the machinery-of-destruction and the generations-old eliminationist-habitus approaches is the way the Nazi genocide may have involved 'religious', purifying, apocalyptic, regenerative, even redemptive dimensions – one might conceivably call them postsecular – that were in some confused and confusing way at times bound up with numerous other factors, including aesthetic concerns, perhaps even an accentuatedly negative yet possibly exhilarating aesthetic of the sublime (with a role for the beautiful as well, which the 'ugly', anti-aesthetic Jews impaired or destroyed). I think these dimensions are especially applicable to the actions and motivations of certain elite Nazis and perhaps some others as well, including such figures as Hitler and Himmler, who were bound together by a strongly cathected nexus, with Hitler becoming for Himmler a kind of anxiety-inducing, indeed traumatizing, godlike figure who issued sacred orders. Obedience to Hitler's sacred orders, based on a faith, a fidelity, and a trust, uncontested by criticism and allowing for no critical distance in relation to their objects, was proclaimed as a Nazi, and especially an SS, cardinal virtue. In the words of Hermann Göring, 'there is something mystical, unsayable, almost incomprehensible about this man … we love Adolf Hitler, because we believe, with a faith that is deep and unshakable, that he was sent to us by God to save Germany'. In the analysis of Joachim Remak: 'For reason, [National Socialism] substituted faith – faith in "the movement", faith, to an even greater extent, in Hitler' (Remak 41; the affirmation from Göring's *Aufbau einer Nation* is quoted on 69). The object of faith was more the movement (*die Bewegung*) and, of course, Hitler, than the party or the state, although there might be a metaphoric identification between Hitler, the party, and the nation or the *Volk* (as in Rudolf Hess's speech filmed in Riefenstahl's *Triumph of the Will*).

The broader suggestion I would make is that, to the extent they were operative, Nazism's postsecular dimensions do not represent some regression to barbarism, much less 'brutishness', but instead make up an intricate dimension of 'modernity' – what might in its most perplexing form be termed a constitutive outside: what is inside modernity as its uncanny repressed or disavowed other. This 'extimate' other (to use Lacan's term) may emerge, possibly with a virulence related to its repressed or disavowed status, but at times it also comes to be articulated in a more or less explicit way. One place this articulation arguably occurs is, I think, in Himmler's Posen speech (or speeches) of October 1943, which I have discussed in other places and to which I shall allude later. One might even speculate that the seemingly uncanny return of ritual murder charges against Jews in late nineteenth- and early twentieth-century Europe itself resulted from a projection of phobic, ritualistic attitudes towards them (Spector). What I am pointing to in particular is a symbolically, even quasi-ritually 'purifying' and not simply hygienic response to Jews and possibly other victims who were projective objects of anxiety, allowing Nazis – and not only Nazis – to deny sources of disquiet in themselves by construing alienated others as causes of pollution or contamination, as well as ugliness, in the *Volksgemeinschaft*. These phobic, toxic, contaminating presences had to be gotten rid of – *entfernen* – in order for the sacred community to achieve quasi-ritual purity, integrity, and regeneration – a new beauty and even sublimity, indeed redemption or salvation in a racial utopia – *Endlösung* as *Auslösung* and *Erlösung* – 'final solution' as release and redemption or salvation. The sense of regeneration, or being born again and possibly redeemed, was fuelled in ecstatic collective rituals, celebrations, rallies, parades, and related events that were not simply aesthetic or dramatic performances, although they were that as well.

The dominant historiographical stress on the 'machinery of destruction' and bureaucracy, even when combined with a view of Hitler as a charismatic leader, may obscure the role of a postsecular dimension in the Nazi genocide related to scapegoating, the elimination of polluting presences, and the attendant quest for purification, regeneration, and even redemption that would 'restore' the intact, putatively lost *Volksgemeinschaft*. There may even have been a quasi-sacrificialism that did not conform to a pristine model of sacrifice that at best might conceivably be found or at least approximated in a stabilized, formalized institution. Nazi quasi-sacrificialism, if such it may be termed, was unbalanced, extreme, even deranged. Yet it is significant that Jews, with respect to the Shoah, were in a crucial sense innocent of the 'crimes' Nazis projected onto them, something certain Nazis and certainly other Germans may well have sensed. The metaphor of 'sheep to slaughter' was often invoked both during and after the Holocaust, at times by Nazis, at times by demoralized and devastated Jews in the ghettos, and at times by Jewish resisters (such as Abba Kovner) who wanted to foster a sense of resistance by urging Jews not to be led like sheep to the slaughter. And, while they were perceived as abject by Nazis and anti-Semites, Jews were not simply taken to be abject pests or outlaws, for they were also figured as powerful, indeed hidden or secret manipulators of a world-wide conspiracy, even a Bolshevik revolutionary force, that threatened the

Nazi regime with destruction. Moreover, the entire discourse of martyrdom that is often used with respect to Holocaust victims (as well as other victims of disasters, such as the bombing of Hiroshima and Nagasaki) lends itself to a sacrificial frame of reference. In German, the dual meaning of the word *Opfer* as both victim and sacrifice almost invites a sacrificial understanding of victimization.

In any case, Jews were, at times along with other victim groups, localized and targeted as racially impure, threatening recipients of projective animosity and violence. Hence they could be ambivalent objects of phobic, quasi-ritualistic animus – not simply mere life or homo sacer (*pace* Agamben and Žižek). Jews were, in some non-trivial sense, neither one thing nor another – or, in however contradictory a fashion, both one thing and the other – both abject and powerful threats, both repulsive and compelling if not desired – betwixt and between, hence not fitting into a well-ordered yet ecstatic community of the people. It is, of course, also possible that, in one dimension of a complex Nazi reaction, a cynical reason of disavowal was at play which granted that Jews were not 'worthy' objects of sacrifice but would be sacrificed nonetheless because, for whatever reason, this was the sacred order of the *Führer* and the destined path to renewed glory and salvation. Extremely important as well, and not incompatible with more 'religious' conviction, is the sense that a sacred duty was being fulfilled in eliminating Jews, which had to be undertaken with something like purity of intention. As Himmler puts it at Posen:

> A number of SS men have offended against this order [to take nothing of goods confiscated from Jews for oneself]. There are not many, and they will be dead men – WITHOUT MERCY [GNADENLOS – the one time Himmler emphatically raises his voice during the speech]. We have the moral right, we had the duty to our people to do it, to kill this people who want to kill us. But we do not have the right to enrich ourselves with even one fur, one Mark, with one cigarette, with one watch, with anything … We have carried out this most difficult task for the love of our people. And we have taken on no defect [or damage] within us, in our soul, in our character [*keinen Schaden in unserem Innern, in unserer Seele, in unserem Charakter daran genommen*].
> (Dawidowicz 44–45; translation modified)

Moreover, the nature of the elation in extremely transgressive violence is problematic. Summarizing some of the scenes depicted in the documents collected in the book *'The Good Old Days': The Holocaust as Seen by its Perpetrators and Bystanders*, Hugh Trevor-Roper writes:

> The most horrible photographs, and some of the most horrible narratives, in this book record the earlier stages in this [genocidal] process, for the first massacres, especially those in the Baltic states, were carried out in public. In Kaunas, Lithuania, where Einsatzkommando 3 operated, the Jews were clubbed to death with crowbars, before cheering crowds, mothers holding

up their children to see the fun, and German soldiers clustered round like spectators at a football match. At the end, while the streets ran with blood, the chief murderer stood on the pile of corpses as a triumphant hero and played the Lithuanian national anthem on an accordion.

(Klee, Dressen and Riess xii)

What were the source and the nature of the elation or excitement that seems evident in such scenes? Was it uncanny, sublime, carnivalesque, sadistic, vengeful, an accompaniment to fanatical self-righteousness or to 'brutality' (an anthropocentric misnomer that explains nothing), or some confused amalgam of tangled emotions and resentments? And how does one parse Himmler's words to high-ranking SS insiders at Posen, with his references to the shudder caused by the Night of the Long Knives (*es hat jeden geschauert*), the experience shared by those who have been through it (*durchgestanden*) and know what it means to see 'a hundred corpses lie side by side, or five hundred, or a thousand'? How does one understand his formula for becoming hard and avoiding traumatic breakdown by enduring the aporia or combining in oneself the antinomies of decency or uprightness (*anständig geblieben zu sein*) and sticking out scenes of mass murder? Why do such events constitute, for Himmler, 'an unwritten, never-to-be-written page of glory' in German history? And why does the speech end with apocalyptic apprehensions and then a prayer-like invocation that enjoins his listeners to 'direct [their] thoughts to the Führer, our Führer, Adolf Hitler, who will create the Germanic Reich and will lead us into the Germanic future'? And then a dedication: 'To our Führer Adolf Hitler: *Sieg Heil! Sieg Heil! Sieg Heil!*' Can an acceptable response to these questions be reduced to the contention that Nazis were simply hardened criminals, ignoring the process by which they became hard, and baldly asserting that any notion of a role for the negative sublime in their orientation or outlook is simply beside the point? Can Kant (or a certain selective, idealized version of Kant) – even in the dubious ideological aspect of his understanding of the sublime as attesting invidiously to the moral superiority and dignity of the 'upright' human being, in contrast to the rest of nature, including other animals (apparently you cannot be dignified if you go on all fours) – be held up as fully authoritative and even kept unscathed as the good German whose sublime must in all ways be opposed to anything operative in the Nazis? Can Bataille's sacred, despite its equivocations with respect to sacrificial violence, useless expenditure, mutilating torture, death, and ecstatic elation, be sharply separated from certain abyssal practices, even if it cannot simply be conflated with them? Without pretending that definitive answers are available, I raise these questions because I think the propensity to reduce the Nazis to hardened criminals, take Kant as incontestably authoritative, and dismiss any notion of a negative sublime as operative in Nazis and, in particular, in Himmler's Posen speech, as well as to adopt an insufficiently nuanced and critical approach to Bataille, is at play in certain recent analyses (see Kligerman; Richman and Surya both offer ameliorative, participatory approaches; at the other extreme, Bataille is simply a 'left fascist' in Wolin; see also my discussion of Bataille in LaCapra 2009).

Before concluding, I would like to be as explicit as possible about the nature of my argument. I am not trying to present a 'concept of the Nazi perpetrator', even an ideal-typical one. I am even further from the idea of offering an overall account of motivation of the vast majority of Germans under the Nazi regime, even those who devotedly followed the leader. I am trying to explore what I think are aspects of the perpetration of genocide and perhaps extreme collective action in general that have not been adequately researched or conceptualized. The task for empirical research would be to see whether, and to what extent, archival sources substantiate or run counter to the notion of a quasi-ritual animus related to feelings of contamination or pollution by the other, notably the Jew, whose elimination was deemed necessary for liberation or even a kind of redemption of the *Volksgemeinschaft*. I think such an animus is rather clear in Hitler and in dimensions of others, including Himmler, at least in terms of his bond with, or even adulation of, Hitler. I also think it is there in certain elated participants in killing actions, perhaps less so in the more routinized activities in the camps. And while the Jews had a specific salience for certain key Nazis, including Hitler, Himmler, Goebbels, and Eichmann, the 'redemptive' dynamic, involving purification and regeneration through violence and victimization, might possibly apply to other groups as well, thus placing the concept of 'redemptive anti-Semitism' in a somewhat larger context and opening it to careful, critical comparative study.

The question with respect to any individual perpetrator or even collaborator and bystander would be what role, if any, there was for a quasi-ritual, purifying, at times negatively 'sublime', even more or less sacrificial impetus or motivation – in any case, for an intricate constellation of forces that cannot be reduced to deceptive catch-all terms such as 'brutality'. It is altogether possible and perhaps likely, that in certain cases or circumstances such a constellation was not in evidence. Here one has both a question of types of perpetrators and of dimensions of individual perpetrators that could be interrelated in complex and perhaps even contradictory fashion. My own argument tries to bring into greater prominence an aspect of the problem that I think has been underplayed, perhaps because it is difficult to substantiate convincingly in empirical terms. This difficulty is less pronounced with respect to the 'machinery of destruction', including tactical and technocratic dimensions, which were indeed important and are more readily substantiated empirically, although the exact nature of their variable articulation with more 'ritualistic' or quasi-religious concerns is a difficult problem that is often not even formulated as an explicit problem. Yet the combination of types of perpetration and of forces within the same individuals is a crucial issue for historical understanding.

Formulated in somewhat different terms, I have been trying to investigate the nature of the claim that might be made for 'redemptive anti-Semitism', set in a larger framework of racism, victimization, and quasi-sacrificial purification and regeneration through violence, thereby exploring in certain ways the term that is central to Saul Friedländer's *Nazi Germany and the Jews* but remains, I think, insufficiently elaborated on a conceptual or theoretical level in that very important work (Friedländer 1997, 2007; the term is most discussed in 1997, chapter 3). Here a crucial problem is to investigate the relations between 'ritual' or quasi-religious considerations and other forces or factors active in the Nazi genocide by pointing out and critically analyzing, while resisting the tendency to elide or even repeat, the equivocations and confusions of Nazi discourse and practice themselves.

Acknowledging complications in any specific empirical analysis, I would nonetheless like to conclude with the question of the extent to which 'postsecular', sacralizing forces are quite important in history, even in what we term 'modernity', especially in the form of scapegoating and purifying, victimizing practices, along with their relation to 'aesthetic' factors such as circumscribed, exclusionary conceptions of beauty and a desire for sublime exaltation as well as carnivalesque glee, notably through scenes of intrinsically valorized, regenerative violence. I would repeat that, with reference to the Nazi genocide, I am not presenting these forces as total explanations. But I think they are often not explicitly articulated as concerns, and their relations to other factors or forces may also remain unformulated as a problem or elided in an insufficiently examined manner. They may even be neglected or disavowed. Yet they are significant, especially on the level of motivation and lived ideology, which in its quasi-ritual or 'religious' dimensions might best be understood not as a vestige of an old sacrificial order, as reversals, kinks, or feedback loops in a 'dialectic of enlightenment', or as a regression to barbarism if not brutality, but as an often repressed or disavowed yet constitutive outside or extimate other of 'modernity'. I think they had this significance at least for a committed group of more or less elite Nazis and some others as well. And these forces may have been, in part, active recently with respect to the empire of evil, the enemy other, the haters of freedom, the elusive, omnipresent spectre of terror, and the ill-defined terrorist, which often seem to be very 'spiritual' and mystified categories.

In any event, with respect to what I have been arguing, a crucial issue is how to assess the role and to elaborate a critical account of a victimizing, purifying frame of reference in ways that further at least two things:

1. An informed, critical, nonsacrificial understanding of problems on the levels of foreign policy, economic exploitation, and social structure, including gaps in wealth and income, both across and within societies.
2. An attempt to critically disengage scapegoating and victimization, as well as any notion of originary, regenerative, or divine violence, from the sacred and to raise the question of what in the sacred or the postsecular is defensible or of value, or at least what might be of value in a significantly transformed institutional context. (Here I would make special mention of oblation or gift-giving insofar as it may be disentangled from victimization, and rituals for transitional points in social and personal life, including non-invidious carnivalesque practices.)

Notes

1 After finishing what I thought was the final version of this essay, I came across a volume of essays addressing questions in a way pertinent to my discussion: Roger Griffin, Robert

Mallett and John Tortorice's *The Sacred in Twentieth-Century Politics: Essays in Honour of Professor Stanley G. Payne*. The pertinent essays largely support the argument I make.

2   For example, I do not agree with the notion of an originary *coup de force* or performative decision that precedes and founds all law, institution, or constitution (17–18), a theme familiar from Derrida's 'Force of Law: The "Mystical" Foundation of Authority' (esp. 941–43). See also my commentary on this essay as it was presented at a conference at Cardozo Law School, where it did not include the footnotes and 'post-scriptum' on Nazism and the 'final solution' (973–74 and 1040–45). My response is entitled 'Violence, Justice, and the Force of Law'. See as well my discussion in *History and Its Limits: Human, Animal, Violence*, 98–102. I would also question what seems at times to be a biomechanistic fatalism that construes in absolute and transcendental, rather than explicitly speculative and analogical, terms a notion of the auto-immune that not only must be self-defeating but also go to the extreme in the direction of excess, violence, and sacrifice – what Derrida at one point refers to as 'the terrifying but fatal logic of the *auto-immunity of the unscathed*' (Derrida 1998: 44) and what might perhaps be seen as a variant of the death drive. But I would see as more suggestive the idea that anything seemingly immune or unscathed runs 'a risk of auto-immunity' that 'haunts the community and its system of immunitary survival like the hyperbole of its own possibility' (47).

Works cited

Abrams, M. H. *Natural Supernaturalism: Tradition and Revolution in Romantic Literature*. New York: W. W. Norton, 1971.

Bataille, Georges. 'The Psychological Structure of Fascism.' In Allan Stoekl, ed. *Visions of Excess: Selected Writings 1927–1939*. Trans. Allan Stoekl with Carl R. Lovitt and Donald M. Leslie, Jr. Minneapolis: University of Minnesota Press, 1985. 137–60.

Dawidowicz, Lucy, ed. and trans. *A Holocaust Reader*. West Orange, N. J. : Behrman House, 1976.

Derrida, Jacques. *Writing and Difference*. Originally 1967. Trans. Alan Bass. Chicago: University of Chicago Press, 1978. Chap. 10.

Derrida, Jacques. 'Force of Law: The "Mystical" Foundation of Authority.' *Cardozo Law Review* 11 (1990): 920–1045.

Derrida, Jacques. *Gift of Death*. Trans. David Wells. Chicago: University of Chicago Press, 1995.

Derrida, Jacques and Gianni Vattimo, eds. *Religion*. Stanford: Stanford University Press, 1998.

Finchelstein, Federico. *Transatlantic Fascism: Ideology, Violence, and the Sacred in Argentina and Italy 1919–1945*. Durham, NC: Duke University Press, 2010.

Forum. *The Slavic Review* 61:3 (Autumn 2002): 453–89.

Freud, Sigmund. *Civilization and Its Discontents*. Trans. and ed. James Strachey. London: Hogarth Press, 1961. 57–145.

Friedländer, Saul. *Nazi Germany and the Jews: The Years of Persecution, 1933–1939*, vol. 1. New York: HarperCollins, 1997.

Friedländer, Saul. *Nazi Germany and the Jews: The Years of Extermination, 1939–1945*, vol. 2. New York: HarperCollins, 2007.

Gentile, Emilio. *The Origins of Fascist Ideology 1918–1925*. New York: Enigma, 2005.

Goldhagen, Daniel. *Hitler's Willing Executioners: Ordinary Germans and the Holocaust*. New York: Alfred A. Knopf, 1996.

Griffin, Roger. *The Nature of Fascism*. London: Routledge, 1993.

Griffin, Roger. *A History of Fascism 1914–1945*. Madison: University of Wisconsin Press, 1995.

Griffin, Roger. *A Fascist Century*. London: Palgrave, 2008.

Griffin, Roger, Robert Mallett and John Tortorice, eds. *The Sacred in Twentieth-Century Politics: Essays in Honour of Professor Stanley G. Payne*. New York: Palgrave Macmillan, 2008.

Gross, Jan T. *Neighbors: The Destruction of the Jewish Community in Jedwabne, Poland*. With a new Afterword. New York: Penguin Books, 2002.

Gross, Jan T. *Fear: Anti-Semitism in Poland after Auschwitz, An Essay in Historical Interpretation.* New York: Random House, 2007.
Hitler, Adolf. *Mein Kampf.* Originally 1925. Trans. Ralph Manheim. Boston: Houghton Mifflin, 1971.
Klee, Ernst, Willi Dressen and Volker Riess, eds. *'The Good Old Days': The Holocaust as Seen by its Perpetrators and Bystanders.* Foreword Hugh Trevor-Roper. New York: The Free Press, 1991.
Kligerman, Eric. *Sites of the Uncanny: Paul Celan, Specularity and the Visual Arts.* New York: Walter de Gruyter, 2007.
LaCapra, Dominick. 'Violence, Justice, and the Force of Law.' *Cardozo Law Review* 11 (1990): 1065–78.
LaCapra, Dominick. *Representing the Holocaust: History, Theory, Trauma.* Ithaca: Cornell University Press, 1994.
LaCapra, Dominick. *History and Memory after Auschwitz.* Ithaca: Cornell University Press, 1998.
LaCapra, Dominick. *Writing History, Writing Trauma.* Baltimore: Johns Hopkins University Press, 2001.
LaCapra, Dominick. *History in Transit: Experience, Identity, Critical Theory.* Ithaca: Cornell University Press, 2004.
LaCapra, Dominick. *History and Its Limits: Human, Animal, Violence.* Ithaca: Cornell University Press, 2009.
LaCapra, Dominick. *History, Literature, Critical Theory.* Ithaca: Cornell University Press, 2013.
Levi, Neil. 'No Sensible Comparison? The Place of the Holocaust in Australia's History Wars.' *History & Memory* 19 (2007): 124–56.
Littel, Jonathan. *Les Bienveillantes.* Paris: Gallimard, 2006.
Littel, Jonathan. *The Kindly Ones.* Trans. Charlotte Mandel. New York: Harper, 2009.
Mann, Michael. *Fascists.* Cambridge: Cambridge University Press, 2004.
Michman, Dan. *The Jewish Ghettos During the Shoah: How and Why Did They Emerge? Search and Research* series 11, Jerusalem, 2008.
Michman, Dan. 'Introducing More "Cultural History" into the Study of the Holocaust: A Response to Dan Stone.' *Dapim: Studies on the Shoah* 23 (2009): 69–75.
Patterson, Charles. *Eternal Treblinka: Our Treatment of Animals and the Holocaust.* New York: Lantern Books, 2002.
Paxton, Robert. *The Anatomy of Fascism.* New York: Knopf, 2004.
Payne, Stanley. *A History of Fascism, 1924–1945.* Madison: University of Wisconsin Press, 1995.
Polonsky, Anthony and Joanna B. Michlic, eds. *The Neighbors Respond: The Controversy over the Jedwabne Massacre in Poland.* Princeton: Princeton University Press, 2004.
Remak, Joachim, ed. *The Nazi Years: A Documentary History.* Englewood Cliffs, N. J. : Prentice-Hall, 1969.
Richman, Michèle. *Sacred Revolutions: Durkheim and the Collège de Sociologie.* Minneapolis: University of Minnesota Press, 2002.
Sax, Boria. *Animals in the Third Reich: Pets, Scapegoats and the Holocaust.* Foreword Klaus P. Fischer. New York: Continuum, 2000.
Schlink, Bernhard. *Der Vorleser.* Zurich: Diogenes Taschenbuch Verlag, 1997.
Schlink, Bernhard. *The Reader.* Trans. Carol Brown Janeway. New York: Vintage, 1998.
Spector, Scott. *Violent Sensations: Sexuality, Crime, and Utopia in Vienna and Berlin, 1860–1914.* Forthcoming.
Spiegel, Gabrielle, ed. *Practicing History: New Directions in the Writing of History after the Linguistic Turn.* New York: Routledge, 2005.
Sternhell, Zeev. *The Birth of Fascist Ideology.* Princeton: Princeton University Press, 1994.
Surya, Michel. *Georges Bataille: An Intellectual Biography.* 1992. Trans. Krzysztof Fijalkowski and Michael Richardson. London: Verso, 2002.
Ustorf, Werner. 'The Missiological Roots of the Concept of "Political Religion".' In Roger Griffin, Robert Mallett and John Tortorice, eds. *The Sacred in Twentieth-Century Politics: Essays in Honour of Professor Stanley G. Payne.* New York: Palgrave Macmillan, 2008. 36–50.

Vondung, Klaus. 'What Insights Do We Gain from Interpreting National Socialism as a Political Religion?' In Roger Griffin, Robert Mallett and John Tortorice, eds. *The Sacred in Twentieth-Century Politics: Essays in Honour of Professor Stanley G. Payne*. New York: Palgrave Macmillan, 2008. 107–18.

Wiese, Christian. 'An "Indelible Stigma": The Churches between Silence, Ideological Involvement, and Political Complicity.' In Christian Wiese and Paul Betts, eds. *Years of Persecution, Years of Extermination: Saul Friedländer and the Future of Holocaust Studies*. London and New York: Continuum, 2010. 157–92.

Wolin, Richard. *The Seduction of Unreason: The Intellectual Romance with Fascism from Nietzsche to Postmodernism*. Princeton: Princeton University Press, 2004.

3
BEYOND EUROCENTRISM
Trauma theory in the global age

Stef Craps

Trauma theory is an area of cultural investigation that emerged in the early 1990s as a product of the so-called ethical turn affecting the humanities. It promised to infuse the study of literary and cultural texts with new relevance. Amid accusations that literary scholarship, particularly in its deconstructive, poststructuralist, or textualist guise, had become indifferent or oblivious to 'what goes on in the real world' (the world outside the text: history, politics, ethics), trauma theory confidently announced itself as an essential apparatus for understanding 'the real world' and even as a potential means for changing it for the better.

This epistemological and ethical programme is clearly laid out in the highly influential work of Cathy Caruth, one of the founding figures of trauma theory (along with Shoshana Felman, Dori Laub, Geoffrey Hartman, and Dominick LaCapra). In *Unclaimed Experience: Trauma, Narrative, and History* (1996), Caruth argues that a textualist approach—one which insists that all reference is indirect—need not lead us away from history and into 'political and ethical paralysis' (10). Quite the contrary, she claims, it can afford us unique access to history: 'Through the notion of trauma ... we can understand that a rethinking of reference is aimed not at eliminating history but at resituating it in our understanding, that is, at precisely permitting *history* to arise where *immediate understanding* may not' (11). Caruth conceives history as being inherently traumatic, and trauma as an overwhelming experience that resists integration and expression. According to Caruth, conjoining a psychoanalytic view of trauma with a deconstructive vigilance regarding the indeterminacies of representation in the analysis of texts that bear witness to traumatic histories can grant us a paradoxical mode of access to extreme events and experiences that defy understanding and representation. In this account, textual 'undecidability' or 'unreadability' comes to reflect the inaccessibility of trauma.

Moreover, this reading practice comes invested with ethical significance. Caruth claims that the 'new mode of reading and of listening' (9) that trauma demands can help break the isolation imposed on both individuals and cultures by traumatic experience: 'history, like trauma, is never simply one's own, ... history is precisely the way we are implicated in each other's traumas' (24). In a catastrophic age such as ours, Caruth writes elsewhere, 'trauma itself may provide the very link between cultures' (Caruth 1995: 11). With trauma forming a bridge between disparate historical experiences, so the argument goes, listening to the trauma of another can contribute to cross-cultural solidarity and to the creation of new forms of community.

Remarkably, however, the founding texts of the field (including Caruth's own work) largely fail to live up to this promise of cross-cultural ethical engagement. They fail on at least three counts: they marginalize or ignore traumatic experiences of non-Western or minority cultures; they tend to take for granted the universal validity of definitions of trauma and recovery that have developed out of the history of Western modernity; and they often favour or even prescribe a modernist aesthetic of fragmentation and aporia as uniquely suited to the task of bearing witness to trauma. As a result of all of this, rather than promoting cross-cultural solidarity, trauma theory risks assisting in the perpetuation of the very beliefs, practices, and structures that maintain existing injustices and inequalities.

The urgency of overcoming trauma theory's Eurocentric biases has been underlined by Jane Kilby, who states that while the future of trauma theory is to a large extent unpredictable, 'for certain the question of globalization will dominate' (181). In arguing the need for trauma theory to be globalized more thoroughly and more responsibly, this chapter aims to help make this prognosis a reality. In what follows, I will first try to back up the criticisms that I have just levelled and propose possible solutions. I will address each of the three aforementioned points in turn: first, the marginalization of non-Western and minority traumas, then the supposed universal validity of Western definitions of trauma, and next the problem of normative trauma aesthetics.[1] Finally, I will analyse a literary text—Aminatta Forna's novel *The Memory of Love* (2010)—against this theoretical background.

The trauma of empire

Most attention within trauma theory has been devoted to events that took place in Europe or the United States, most prominently the Holocaust and, more recently, 9/11. The impetus for much of the current theorization about trauma and witnessing was provided by the Nazi genocide of the European Jews. As is apparent from the work of Caruth, Felman and Laub, Hartman, and LaCapra, trauma theory as a field of cultural scholarship developed out of an engagement with Holocaust testimony, literature, and history. However, if trauma theory is to redeem its promise of cross-cultural ethical engagement, the sufferings of those belonging to non-Western or minority cultures must be given due recognition.

In an article on the limitations and exclusions of trauma theory, Susannah Radstone observes that 'it is the sufferings of those, categorized in the West as "other", that tend *not* to be addressed via trauma theory—which becomes in this regard, a theory that supports politicized constructions of those with whom identifications via traumatic sufferings can be forged and those from whom such identifications are withheld' (25). Judith Butler spells out the far-reaching consequences of such constructions in her book *Frames of War: When Is Life Grievable?* (2009), where she argues that the differential distribution of grievability across populations is 'at once a material and a perceptual issue': 'those whose lives are not "regarded" as potentially grievable, and hence valuable, are made to bear the burden of starvation, underemployment, legal disenfranchisement, and differential exposure to violence and death' (25). A one-sided focus on traumas suffered by members of Western cultural traditions could thus have pernicious effects at odds with trauma theory's self-proclaimed ethical mission.

This is not to say, though, that any and all attempts by trauma theory to reach out to the non-Western other are necessarily a step forward. After all, such efforts can turn out to reflect a Eurocentric bias just as well. This is true, for example, of the few descriptions of cross-cultural encounters that we are offered in Caruth's work: her reading of the story of Tancred and Clorinda, her analysis of Freud's *Moses and Monotheism*, and her interpretation of the film *Hiroshima mon amour*. These three cases are central to her formulation of trauma theory, yet they all strike me as highly problematic instances of witnessing across cultural boundaries.

I will limit myself here to a brief discussion of Caruth's treatment of *Hiroshima mon amour*, a film by Alain Resnais and Marguerite Duras, which tells the story of a love affair between a Japanese architect and a French actress who is visiting Hiroshima to make a film about peace. The affair triggers a chain of memories, as the woman relates the traumatic experiences she suffered at the end of the Second World War in the French city of Nevers. The young German soldier she had fallen in love with was shot and killed on the last day of fighting, just before they were to leave the city together. She was subsequently subjected to public disgrace, followed by a period of imprisonment and near-madness in her parents' home. Having recovered, she left home permanently, arriving in Paris on the day the war ended, after the bombing of Hiroshima and Nagasaki. It is her presence in Hiroshima, another site of wartime trauma, and the facilitating role of the Japanese man, who lost his family in the bombing, that enables the woman to recount her story for the first time. According to Caruth, the film demonstrates her thesis that trauma can act as a bridge between cultures: it allegedly opens up 'a new mode of seeing and of listening' to the spectators, 'a seeing and a listening *from the site of trauma*,' which it offers as 'the very possibility, in a catastrophic era, of a link between cultures' (Caruth 1996: 56).

This interpretation seems to me to gloss over the lop-sided quality of the cross-cultural dialogue established in *Hiroshima mon amour*. After all, we only ever get to hear the French woman's story; the traumatic history of Hiroshima in general, or of the Japanese man in particular, remains largely untold. Hiroshima is reduced to a stage on which the drama of a European woman's struggle to come to terms with her personal trauma can be played out; the Japanese man is of interest primarily as a catalyst and facilitator of this process. Caruth notes in passing that the film 'does not tell the story of Hiroshima in 1945 but rather uses the rebuilt Hiroshima as the setting for the telling of another story, the French woman's story of Nevers'

(Caruth 1996: 27), but the asymmetry of the exchange and the appropriation and instrumentalization of Japanese suffering in the service of articulating a European trauma do not stop her from holding up the interaction between the French woman and the Japanese man as an exemplary model of cross-cultural witnessing. Her analysis of *Hiroshima mon amour* thus illustrates how difficult it is for trauma theory to recognize the experience of the racial or cultural other.[2]

Similar arguments can be made in relation to Caruth's interpretations of the story of Tancred and Clorinda and *Moses and Monotheism* (Craps 14–17). The conclusion I think we can draw is that, rather than being evidence of a postcolonial sensibility, Caruth's descriptions of cross-cultural encounters actually reinforce Eurocentrism. Breaking with Eurocentrism requires a commitment, then, not only to broadening the usual focus of trauma theory, but also to acknowledging the traumas of non-Western or minority populations for their own sake. In the next section, I will argue that these traumas must, moreover, be acknowledged on their own terms. This, it seems to me, is another area where trauma theory has tended to fall short.

The empire of trauma

Today the concept of trauma is widely used to describe responses to extreme events across space and time, as well as to guide their treatment. However, as Allan Young reminds us in *The Harmony of Illusions: Inventing Post-Traumatic Stress Disorder* (1995), it is actually a Western artefact, 'invented' in the late nineteenth century. Its origins can be located in a variety of medical and psychological discourses dealing with European and American experiences of industrialization, gender relations, and modern warfare (Micale and Lerner; Saunders; Saunders and Aghaie). This historical and geographical situatedness means that there is nothing self-evident about the notion that Western definitions of trauma can be unproblematically exported to other contexts.

It can even be argued that the uncritical cross-cultural application of psychological concepts developed in the West amounts to a form of cultural imperialism. This claim has been made most forcefully by Derek Summerfield, a psychiatrist who sharply criticizes humanitarian interventions to provide psychological assistance in international conflict situations. 'Psychiatric universalism', he writes, 'risks being imperialistic, reminding us of the colonial era when what was presented to indigenous peoples was that there were different types of knowledge, and theirs was second-rate' (Summerfield 2004: 238). In the assumption that Western-style trauma programmes are necessary to avoid a postwar crop of psychiatric disorders, which is used as a basis for interventions in the lives of war-torn populations around the world, Summerfield hears 'a modern echo of the age of Empire, when Christian missionaries set sail to cool the savagery of primitive peoples and gather their souls, which would otherwise be "lost"' (Summerfield 1999: 1457).

These and similar accusations are reiterated by Ethan Watters in his book *Crazy like Us: The Globalization of the American Psyche* (2010). Watters critiques what he calls 'the grand project of Americanizing the world's understanding of the human mind' (1). Over the past three decades, he writes, Americans have exported their ideas about mental health and illness around the world without regard for cultural differences, imposing their definitions and treatments as the international standards: 'Indigenous forms of mental illness and healing are being bulldozed by disease categories and treatments made in the USA' (3). One of the four case studies Watters examines is post-traumatic stress disorder or PTSD (the others are anorexia, schizophrenia, and depression). He reports on the Western trauma counsellors who arrived in Sri Lanka following the 2004 tsunami and who, in their rush to help the victims, inadvertently trampled local expressions of grief, suffering, and healing, thereby actually causing the community more distress. Both Summerfield and Watters reject the widely held belief that PTSD constitutes a timeless, acultural, psychobiological phenomenon, arguing instead that the PTSD construct reflects a Eurocentric, monocultural orientation.

Much criticism has in fact been levelled at the dominant formulation of PTSD, in the American Psychiatric Association's authoritative diagnostic manual (DSM), for its perceived failures of inclusiveness. Particularly contentious is the definition of what constitutes a traumatic stressor. This is typically thought of as a sudden, unexpected, catastrophic event—indeed, since the beginning of its discussion, trauma has been associated with an image of a single devastating blow or an acute stab that breaks the protective shield of the psyche. Many feminist and multicultural clinicians and researchers have argued that this criterion is too narrow because it makes some important sources of trauma invisible and unknowable. In particular, it tends to ignore 'the normative, quotidian aspects of trauma in the lives of many oppressed and disempowered persons, leading psychotherapists to an inability to grasp how a particular presentation of client distress is in fact posttraumatic' (Brown 18). The narrow range of possible traumas in people's lives implied by the traumatic stressor criterion in its current formulation needs to be expanded, it is argued, as there are many other experiences than those involving 'actual or threatened death or serious injury, or a threat to the physical integrity of self or others' (American Psychiatric Association 467) that can result in post-traumatic symptoms.

Concrete suggestions that have been offered for extending current definitions of trauma include Type II traumas (Terr), complex PTSD or 'disorders of extreme stress not otherwise specified' (Herman), safe-world violations (Janoff-Bulman), insidious trauma (Root), oppression-based trauma (Spanierman and Poteat), postcolonial syndrome (Duran et al.), postcolonial traumatic stress disorder (Turia), and post-traumatic slavery syndrome (Poussaint and Alexander). These attempts to go beyond or diversify the DSM definition of trauma can assist in understanding the impact of everyday racism, sexism, homophobia, classism, ableism, and other forms of structural oppression. Even though post-traumatic symptoms may be exhibited, the chronic psychic suffering caused by such experiences does not qualify for the PTSD diagnosis if, as is most often the case, an overt threat or act of violence is absent.

Dominant conceptions of trauma have also been criticized for considering trauma as an individual phenomenon and distracting attention from the wider social situation, which can be particularly problematic in a cross-cultural context (Summerfield 1999: 1453–55; Wessells 269–71). After all, in collectivist societies individualistic approaches may be at odds with the local culture. Moreover, by narrowly focusing on the level of the individual psyche, one tends to leave unquestioned the conditions that enabled the traumatic abuse, such as racism, economic domination, or political oppression. Problems that are essentially political or economic are medicalized, and the people affected by them are pathologized as victims without agency, sufferers from an illness that can be cured through psychological counselling. The failure to situate these problems in their larger historical context can thus lead to psychological recovery being privileged over the transformation of a wounding political, social, or economic system. Insofar as it negates the need for taking collective action towards systemic change, the hegemonic trauma discourse can be seen to serve as a political palliative to the socially disempowered.[3]

The concerns about the PTSD construct expressed by psychologists and other mental health professionals, and the alternative paradigms which they have proposed, have received very little attention from within the field of cultural trauma research. The impact of different cultural traditions on the way trauma is experienced and on the process of healing is hardly acknowledged. Moreover, trauma theory continues to adhere to the traditional event-based model of trauma, according to which trauma results from a single, extraordinary, catastrophic event. It follows that the traumatic impact of racism and other forms of ongoing oppression cannot be adequately addressed within the conceptual frameworks which trauma theory provides.

Beyond Trauma Aesthetics[4]

I have argued that trauma theory needs to become more inclusive and culturally sensitive by acknowledging the sufferings of non-Western and minority groups more fully, for their own sake, and on their own terms. I will now address the textual inscription of such experiences and suggest that certain received ideas and assumptions about how literature bears witness to trauma may need to be revised. More specifically, I will challenge the notion that traumatic experiences can only be adequately represented through the use of experimental, modernist textual strategies. This notion, which can be traced back to Theodor Adorno's notorious pronouncements about poetry after Auschwitz, has become all but axiomatic within trauma theory. Trauma theorists often justify their focus on anti-narrative, fragmented, modernist forms by pointing to similarities with the psychic experience of trauma. An experience that exceeds the possibility of narrative knowledge, so the logic goes, will best be represented by a failure of narrative. Hence, what is called for is the disruption of conventional modes of representation, such as can be found in modernist art.

However, this assumption could lead to the establishment of a narrow trauma canon consisting of non-linear, modernist texts by mostly Western writers, modernism being a European cultural tradition. To quote the introduction to Jill

Bennett and Rosanne Kennedy's collection *World Memory: Personal Trajectories in Global Time* (2003), 'there is a danger that the field is becoming limited to a selection of texts that represent a relatively narrow range of traumatic events, histories and cultural forms, rather than engaging the global scope of traumatic events and the myriad forms that bear witness to them' (10). In *The Trauma Question* (2008), Roger Luckhurst similarly laments trauma theory's sole focus on anti-narrative texts and points out that the crisis of representation caused by trauma generates narrative *possibility* just as much as narrative *impossibility*. Beyond the narrow canon of high-brow, avant-garde texts, he reminds us, 'a wide diversity of high, middle and low cultural forms have provided a repertoire of compelling ways to articulate that apparently paradoxical thing, the trauma narrative' (83). In his book, Luckhurst explores this broad range of testimonial forms, studying popular trauma memoirs and novels—by Stephen King, for example—alongside canonical trauma texts.

I do not reject modernist modes of representation as inherently Eurocentric, nor do I advocate realism or indigenous literary forms as a postcolonial panacea. However, I do think it is important to check the rush to dismiss whatever deviates from the prescribed aesthetic as regressive or irrelevant. Rather than positing a necessary relation between aesthetic form and political or ethical effectiveness, trauma theory should take account of the specific social and historical contexts in which trauma narratives are produced and received, and be open and attentive to the diverse strategies of representation and resistance which these contexts invite or necessitate.

Aminatta Forna's *The Memory of Love*

What I have tried to do so far is to expose some of the limitations and blind spots which I think trauma theory will need to confront if it is to deliver on its promise of cross-cultural ethical engagement and stay relevant in the globalized world of the twenty-first century.[5] In the final part of this chapter, I will illustrate this argument with a case study of a literary text which seems to me to call for a more inclusive, materialist, and politicized form of trauma theory. Published in 2010 to great critical acclaim, *The Memory of Love* is the third book by the award-winning writer Aminatta Forna, who is the daughter of a Scottish mother and a Sierra Leonean father. Except for her latest novel, *The Hired Man* (2013), all of her work to date has explored the causes and consequences of war in Sierra Leone. *The Memory of Love* is set in the country's capital, Freetown, in 2001, in the aftermath of a gruesome civil war that lasted eleven years and left more than 50,000 people dead and an estimated 2.5 million people displaced. Instead of focusing on the war itself, the novel examines how those who survived the war cope with the physical and psychological scars of those years, as well as devoting considerable attention to exploring forms of complicity and collaboration that enabled the authoritarian regime of the 1970s, which paved the way for the rebel uprising in 1991, to come to and stay in power.

The Memory of Love tells the story of three men who come into contact with each other at a Freetown hospital. One of these is Elias Cole, an elderly history professor at the city's university who is dying of lung disease and who has led a life of compromise and complicity with authority. He relates his past to Adrian Lockheart, a British psychologist specializing in post-traumatic stress disorder who is volunteering with the city's stretched mental health services. Among those affected by this condition is Kai Mansaray, a young local orthopaedic surgeon whom Adrian befriends and who is haunted by terrible memories of the war. The lives of the three protagonists are linked—somewhat too neatly, many critics feel—by the love of a single woman, known as Nenebah or Mamakay. Unbeknownst to Adrian when he begins a relationship with her, Mamakay is his patient Elias's daughter and his friend Kai's former lover.

Of particular interest for my purposes is the role played by the British psychologist, who functions as a conduit through which we learn the stories of the Sierra Leonean characters. In fact, this character already appeared in the final story in Forna's debut novel *Ancestor Stones* (2006), where he served the same function, listening to a Sierra Leonean woman recounting her experience of the invasion of Freetown. Like the primarily Western readership of *The Memory of Love*, for whom he acts as a point of identification, Adrian is an outsider who does not fully understand the situation in which he finds himself and who moves from bewilderment to insight in the course of the narrative. He brings familiar Western ideas to the problems of the local population that he has been parachuted in to help solve. However, this strategy proves unsuccessful. The novel makes it quite clear that Adrian's approach is inadequate to the situation he is confronted with. True to his name, Lockheart, there is something remote and detached about Adrian when he first arrives in Freetown—an attitude shared by most international aid workers, as the novel repeatedly points out. Feeling uncomfortable and out of place, he initially fails to connect with his patients: 'Adrian's empathy sounded slight, unconvincing in his own ears' (Forna 2010: 21). These patients are for the most part traumatized survivors of the war, it is suggested: they suffer from physical pains that began '[s]ometime after the trouble,' so they tell him, yet 'the doctors could find nothing wrong' with them—which is why they referred them to Adrian (21). After describing to him what they have endured, at his insistence, all of his patients request medicines from him. When he does not oblige, explaining that he is 'not that sort of doctor' (21), they thank him and leave, and '[n]one of them ever return[s]' (22). As a result of the general scepticism surrounding therapy, and his ineffectiveness in administering it, he soon finds himself underemployed. When his patients have 'stopped coming,' 'more or less entirely,' and his medical colleagues have presumably 'stopped bothering to make referrals,' he reflects: 'He came here to help and he is not helping. *He is not helping*' (64).

The novel's critique of the application of Western therapeutic models in the Sierra Leonean context crystallizes in a dialogue between Adrian and Attila, one of the few local psychiatrists to remain in the country. As head of the city's mental hospital, Attila has allowed Adrian to also treat some patients there but has always kept his distance from him.[6] However, when Attila at one point takes Adrian to see a cramped, stinking shantytown built on a sewage dump on the outskirts of Freetown, the following conversation—which begins with Attila speaking—unfolds between them:

'A few years back a medical team came here. They were here to survey the population. ... Do you know what they concluded? ... They were here for six weeks. They sent me a copy of the paper. The conclusion they reached was that ninety-nine per cent of the population was suffering from post-traumatic stress disorder.' He laughs cheerlessly. 'Post-traumatic stress disorder! What do you think of that?'

Adrian, who is entirely unsure of what is expected of him, answers, 'The figure seems high but strikes me as entirely possible. From everything I've heard.'

'When I ask you what you expect to achieve for these men, you say you want to return them to normality. So then I must ask you, whose normality? Yours? Mine? So they can put on a suit and sit in an air-conditioned office? You think that will ever happen?'

'No,' says Adrian, feeling under attack. 'But therapy can help them to cope with their experiences of war.'

'This is their reality. And who is going to come and give the people who live *here* therapy to cope with this?' asks Attila and waves a hand at the view. 'You call it a disorder, my friend. We call it *life*.' He shifts the car into first gear and begins to move forward. 'And do you know what these visitors recommended at the end of their report? Another one hundred and fifty thousand dollars to engage in even more research.' He utters the same bitter chuckle. 'What do you need to know that you cannot tell just by looking, eh? But you know, these hotels are really quite expensive. Western rates. Television. Minibars.' He looks across at Adrian. 'Anyway,' he continues, 'you carry on with your work. Just remember what it is you are returning them to.'

(319–20)

Several criticisms and accusations that resonate throughout the novel come together in this excerpt. Attila's key objection is that the assumption underlying Western notions of trauma recovery that the patient is to be returned to a state of normality through psychotherapy ignores the reality of life in Sierra Leone, one of the poorest countries in the world. Living conditions there are still extremely hard now that the war has ended. For most Sierra Leoneans, the 'normal' experience is one of oppression, deprivation, and upheaval; freedom, affluence, and stability—the Western standard of normality—are actually the exception rather than the rule. 'You call it a disorder ... We call it *life*': what for privileged Westerners is only a momentary deviation from the normal course of their safe, valued, and protected lives is a constant reality for most Sierra Leoneans, who lead poor, vulnerable, and unprotected lives. What we have here, then, is an instantiation of the critique of the event-based model of trauma and the associated methods of treatment, which risk obscuring the chronic suffering and structural violence experienced by the Sierra Leonean population and, indeed, by much of the world. An exclusive focus on psychotherapy is a misguided response to the psychic suffering of the Sierra Leonean population, it is suggested, in that the normality to which people will be returned after therapy is one of enduring pain, whose root causes—which are socio-economic and political in nature—remain hidden and go unaddressed.

When Attila has left, Adrian admits to himself the rightness of the Sierra Leonean psychiatrist's views: 'The man is right, of course. People here don't need therapy so much as hope. But the hope has to be real—Attila's warning to Adrian' (320). Adrian has never had to give much if any thought to these kinds of questions while training and working as a psychologist in Britain, where the traumas he studied and treated neatly conformed to the event-based model. The novel points out that Adrian's interest in trauma started with the phenomenon of shell-shock, which he read about as a twelve-year-old boy (64). It also mentions a paper he wrote during his studies in the wake of an oil rig disaster off the coast of Aberdeen that killed 160 people and whose survivors 'struggled to return to their lives' (65). The paper, which was published and won him some acclaim, 'argu[ed] for a more proactive response from mental health professionals after major disasters' (65). This kind of response, intended to help survivors pick up the thread of their pre-disaster lives, loses its self-evidence in the Sierra Leonean context of unrelenting, generalized trauma.

In fact, Adrian now begins to develop a greater appreciation for local coping mechanisms such as the adoption of a fatalistic outlook on life. While Westerners he has met 'despise' such a response to trauma (320), Adrian comes to see it as entirely sensible in the absence of hope for any real change in people's living conditions. He reflects that 'perhaps it is the way people have found to survive' (320). This is just one of several moments in the text affirming the value of local coping strategies and methods, which tend to be summarily dismissed or looked down upon by Western aid workers. For example, while being shown around the mental hospital, Adrian learns that there are relatively few female patients, as families generally try to keep the women at home and 'seek treatment through local healers or religious leaders' (87). In response to his question, 'Do they help? The local methods?' he is told by Ileana, a colleague from Eastern Europe who has been working there for some time and who acts as his guide, 'It's just care in the community under another name' (87). Later on, she informs him that Attila has 'a lot of respect' for 'traditional healers,' who are 'really quite interesting': 'Some of the antipsychotic drugs we use they were on to hundreds of years ago' (276). When Adrian expresses his ignorance about this, Ileana, who does not seem to be surprised, adds: 'We call them witch doctors' (276). Thus, respect for local healing practices, which are presented as worthy counterparts to Western treatment methods, is instilled in Adrian and, by extension, the reader.

The supposed universal validity of Western traditions and experiences is further challenged by pointed remarks throughout the novel highlighting their situatedness or denouncing their imperialist pretensions. For example, Ileana, sounding like Allan Young, reminds Adrian that 'it was us Europeans who invented the talking cure. And most of the maladies it's designed to treat' (169), and Kai, annoyed at Adrian's assumption that Kai can easily understand his decision to leave home simply for the sake of something new, thinks to himself that '[t]his is the way Europeans talk, as if everybody shared their experiences' (182).

The novel suggests that local coping mechanisms may even trump popular Western ideas about trauma treatment by showing how silence plays a beneficial role in keeping trauma at bay. Silence is repeatedly put forward as a valid way of surviving the suffering inflicted by the war. This is how Mamakay points out its social prevalence to Adrian: 'Have you never noticed? How nobody ever talks about anything? What happened here. The war. Before the war. It's like a secret' (321). Trained to get patients to verbalize their trauma, to speak about their suffering, the British psychologist is troubled by these silences. He firmly believes in the benefits of directly confronting a traumatic experience and turning it into a story, which supposedly brings closure. At one point he wonders at how Kai and Mamakay 'both resolutely occupied only the present' and 'kept doors closed' (391). The fact that they both have 'places from which all others were excluded,' and about which they choose to remain silent, makes him distinctly uncomfortable: 'Even now the fear coiling around his heart is that in those closed-off places is something the two of them share from their past, some arc of emotion, incomplete, requiring an ending' (391). As Zoe Norridge points out, what he fails to understand is that 'there is no ending for those emotions ... even in peace the survivors live with the remains of the war' (196). Norridge reads Kai and Mamakay's silence as a viable and legitimate survival strategy, 'another manner of bounding pain—instead of seeking narrative closure, barriers are erected by not allowing the stories to circulate actively (even if they do unconsciously or implicitly) within the social space' (196). Adrian does in fact come to realize that his patients' 'reluctance to talk about anything that had happened to them' during the war is not simply to be 'put ... down to trauma,' as he initially thought, but that it is also part of 'a way of being that existed here' (321). Rather than merely a symptom of trauma, to be dispelled without a second thought, silence is also a coping mechanism, a conscious choice deserving of respect.

The novel's scepticism about the breaking of silence as an automatic or intrinsic good is also apparent from the fact that the only one of Adrian's patients to actively seek out his help (23) and to spontaneously unburden himself is Elias: 'Here in the land of the mute, Elias Cole has elected to talk' (327). After all, the reason why Elias wants to talk to Adrian, as it turns out, is to be able to construct a convenient narrative, concealing and excusing his past complicity with a repressive regime which had shielded him from harm and allowed him to thrive while men of greater integrity suffered persecution by the authorities. Thus, what initially looks like a bona fide instance of the Freudian talking cure reveals itself to be a parody of it, which drives home the point that supposed confessionals can serve morally dubious causes.[7]

However, the case which best shows the inappropriateness of Western attitudes towards silence in the face of massive suffering is that of a woman named Agnes, one of the patients Adrian treats at the mental hospital and in whom he takes a special interest. Hers is one of the most harrowing experiences of wartime suffering described in the novel. She witnessed her husband's beheading by rebel soldiers, lost two daughters, and returned home from a refugee camp after the war only to find that her only surviving daughter had unwittingly married her husband's murderer. Living under the same roof with her daughter and son-in-law, Agnes has to keep silent and pretend the horrors of the past never happened to make cohabiting with the perpetrator at all possible. However, she periodically loses her senses and wanders away from home, roaming from town to town in an unconscious effort to distance herself from the intolerable situation in which she finds herself. These bouts of temporary amnesia are the only respite she has from the brutal reality of her everyday life. Adrian becomes intent on breaking Agnes's self-imposed silences, convinced as he is that uncovering the event that he suspects caused her condition—which he diagnoses as a fugue[8]—will help relieve her suffering and bring healing. Agnes understandably refuses to play along, and Adrian will never hear her unbearable story—at least not from her mouth: eventually it is Kai who pieces it together from testimonies whispered by the other villagers and sends it to Adrian in a letter two years after the latter has left Sierra Leone to go back to England. For Kai, the most notable aspect of Agnes's story is 'the unbearable aftermath, the knowledge, and nothing to be done but to endure it. ... for Agnes there is no possibility of sanctuary' (325–26). As Norridge points out, the reader becomes aware that 'the story of Agnes hangs unresolved' by the novel's end, which makes him or her realize that 'narrating an impossible and enduring situation does not necessarily lead to resolution' (187).

Adrian's obsession with Agnes stems not only from a genuine desire to help her, but also from a desire to advance his career. Trying to convince a reluctant Agnes to return to treatment, he tells her daughter, 'I can help her' (204). However, another (unstated) reason why he would like to continue working with her is that she can help him achieve professional success: 'To prove the existence of fugue in a population would be a professional coup. But if he could also demonstrate a clear link to post-traumatic stress disorder? Well, that could make his name' (168). In fact, Adrian is repeatedly told by locals that his volunteering stint in Sierra Leone is probably more of an egotistical undertaking than an attempt to actually help the country's suffering people. Despite his friendship with Adrian, Kai views Adrian's mission with a suspicion bordering on contempt, comparing him to other Westerners who arrive in Sierra Leone to help but fail to stay for long—'tourists', he calls them (30). Kai questions the motivations of all Westerners who come to report on the war or to clean up in its aftermath, making no exception for Adrian: 'They came to get their newspaper stories, to save black babies, to spread the word, to make money, to fuck black bodies. They all had their own reasons. Modern-day knights, each after his or her trophy, their very own Holy Grail. Adrian's Grail was Agnes' (219). Kai's critique of the self-serving nature of Western involvement in Sierra Leone is echoed by Attila in the excerpt quoted above, where he mocks the medical team that had published a paper about the ubiquity of PTSD in Sierra Leone after briefly visiting the country. He scoffs at them for recommending extra funding for further research at the end of their report, research that he dismisses as redundant, paid for with money that would largely be spent on expensive hotel accommodation rather than on anything that would actually benefit the local population.[9]

It is worth noting, though, that, despite his sharp criticisms of Western aid practices, Attila ends the exchange with Adrian by advising the British psychologist to 'carry on with [his] work,' albeit in full awareness of his patients' living conditions (320). Just like the criticisms levelled by Attila that we have looked at, this piece of advice—of which Adrian notes that '[i]t is as close as [Attila] has ever come to praise' (320)—reflects a sentiment found throughout the novel. Indeed, for all its misgivings, *The Memory of Love* does not dismiss Western therapeutic models out of hand. Though Adrian makes a false start in Sierra Leone, he does eventually achieve some success in treating local patients using the expertise he acquired while studying and practising in England. He manages to get a group of male patients at the mental hospital 'to remember and write down or draw ... their experiences' after gaining their trust, '[a] small triumph' which makes him feel that he is 'making progress' (360), and gradually earns the respect of the hospital staff. Moreover, Adrian's diagnosis of Agnes's condition proves largely correct, and he eventually helps Kai deal with his personal war trauma, which is rendering him incapable of working, by getting him to talk about the core events. Indeed, that the therapy administered to Kai is successful is clearly suggested in the closing section of the novel, when, two years later, he is said to be driving across a bridge where one of his colleagues died and he himself was nearly shot, and which he had scrupulously avoided ever since that day.

It is such elements that lead Norridge to conclude that *The Memory of Love* is, 'in some ways, an elegy to the persistent appeal of Western-style narrative therapy' (175): 'The overarching message of Forna's novel appears to be that the past must be told if it is not to dominate our existence in the present' (184). It seems to me, though, that Norridge slightly overstates her case here: I would argue that the novel is marked by an unresolved ambivalence about the applicability and viability of Western treatment methods in post-Civil War Sierra Leone, and that the many reservations expressed throughout the narrative are not invalidated by a few apparent success stories. While there may indeed be a measure of closure for some characters, *The Memory of Love* also awakens its readers to the chronic, ongoing suffering endured in silence by whole swathes of the population, with which Western psychology is ill-equipped to deal. The novel makes audible these silences and fosters attunement to this quiet suffering, which, it is suggested, our Western trauma paradigm risks obscuring. It does so, moreover, without resorting to the kind of avant-garde experimentation or modernist pyrotechnics beloved of many canonical trauma writers and, perhaps especially, trauma theorists. In fact, Forna's intricately plotted novel is a fine example of literary realism, which does not derive its haunting power from the conversion of unspeakable suffering into broken, traumatized speech, but rather from its acknowledgement of the existence of vast silent spaces of unknown, ongoing suffering in the face of which narrative therapy—to the extent that it is on offer—is an inadequate response. Thus, *The Memory of Love* can be seen to pose a challenge to trauma theory to remove its Eurocentric blinkers—a challenge that, as I have argued, the field would be well advised to embrace.

Notes

1 This part of the chapter reprises the theoretical argument developed at greater length and in more detail in the first three chapters of my book *Postcolonial Witnessing: Trauma Out of Bounds* (2013).
2 To her credit, though, Caruth includes an essay by Georges Bataille in *Trauma: Explorations in Memory* (1995) titled 'Concerning the Accounts Given by the Residents of Hiroshima', which focuses precisely on the story that remains untold in *Hiroshima mon amour*.
3 These criticisms of the individualizing, psychologizing, pathologizing, and depoliticizing tendencies of the dominant trauma model were anticipated by Frantz Fanon in his pioneering work on the psychopathology of racism and colonialism: see his *Black Skin, White Masks* (1967 [1952]) and the last chapter of *The Wretched of the Earth* (1963 [1961]). On Fanon as a trauma theorist, see Craps 28–31; Kaplan; Kennedy 90–92; Saunders 13–15; and Saunders and Aghaie 18–19.
4 The title of this section is adapted from a book by Rita Felski called *Beyond Feminist Aesthetics: Feminist Literature and Social Change* (1989), which is almost twenty-five years old now but whose argument—about the need to leave behind attempts to construct a normative aesthetic for feminist literature—remains pertinent and can help us understand what is problematic about trauma aesthetics.
5 To some extent, of course, this is already happening. Though in the early stages of its development trauma theory focused predominantly on the Holocaust, in recent years the field has begun to diversify. It now also includes a still relatively small but significant amount of work addressing other kinds of traumatic experiences, such as those associated with not only 9/11 but also slavery, colonialism, apartheid, Partition, and the Stolen Generations. Moreover, there is a growing number of publications that adopt a cross-cultural comparative perspective. See, for example, Michael Rothberg's *Multidirectional Memory: Remembering the Holocaust in the Age of Decolonization* (2009), Max Silverman's *Palimpsestic Memory: The Holocaust and Colonialism in French and Francophone Fiction and Film* (2013), Sophie Croisy's *Other Cultures of Trauma: Meta-Metropolitan Narratives and Identities* (2007), Victoria Burrows's *Whiteness and Trauma: The Mother-Daughter Knot in the Fiction of Jean Rhys, Jamaica Kincaid and Toni Morrison* (2004), Sam Durrant's *Postcolonial Narrative and the Work of Mourning* (2004), and several collections, such as *World Memory: Personal Trajectories in Global Time* (Bennett and Kennedy, eds. 2003), *Trauma Texts* (Whitlock and Douglas, eds. 2009), *The Splintered Glass: Facets of Trauma in the Post-Colony and Beyond* (Herrero and Baelo-Allué, eds. 2011), and special issues of *Comparative Studies of South Asia, Africa and the Middle East* (Saunders and Aghaie, eds. 2005), *Studies in the Novel* (Craps and Buelens, eds. 2008), *Continuum: Journal of Media and Cultural Studies* (Traverso and Broderick, eds. 2010), *Yale French Studies* (Rothberg et al., eds. 2010); and *Criticism: A Quarterly for Literature and the Arts* (Craps and Rothberg, eds. 2011).
6 The brief interaction between Attila and Adrian when they first meet makes it clear that, as Attila sees it, he—and, by extension, his patients—need not be grateful for Adrian's offer of help; he is actually doing Adrian a favour by giving him permission to see patients at the mental hospital. Attila is quoted as saying: 'In whatever way we can help you, you're most welcome' (82). As we will see, this response is typical of the novel's general distrust of the motives behind Western aid initiatives, which, it is intimated, are primarily self-serving rather than altruistic.
7 Elias is hardly alone in manipulating the facts to make himself look better. As Mamakay explains to Adrian, history is being rewritten all over post-war Sierra Leone: 'People are blotting out what happened, fiddling with the truth, creating their own version of events to fill in the blanks. A version of the truth which puts them in a good light, that wipes out whatever they did or failed to do and makes certain none of them will be blamed' (351).
8 The novel gives the following definition of this condition, from *A History of Mental Illness*, an apparently fictional reference book owned by Adrian: 'Fugue. Characterised by sudden, unexpected travel away from home. Irresistible wandering, often coupled

with subsequent amnesia. A rarely diagnosed dissociative condition in which the mind creates an alternative state. This state may be considered a place of safety, a refuge' (325).
9 Forna has made no secret of the fact that she shares the distrust of Western aid efforts expressed by several of the novel's characters, echoing their scepticism in interview after interview. To give but one example, in an interview with the Sri Lankan *Sunday Times* newspaper in which she talks about this issue at some length, she is quoted as saying: 'I think aid is a complete misnomer actually. I've watched a billion pounds of aid being poured into Sierra Leone at one point. I saw that it was completely doomed to failure and a lot of people saw that. There's been a lot of anger in the community about how aid is used …' (quoted in Tegal). She voices her suspicion that the purpose of aid is mostly to buy control and influence; criticizes Western countries for refusing to open up their trade, which they would do if they had any real interest in helping; accuses Western aid projects of being poorly planned and unsustainable; and indicts non-governmental organizations for spending far more on overhead and (largely expatriate) staff costs than on providing aid: 'actually it's an industry that is feeding the west' (quoted in Tegal). Disillusioned with existing aid initiatives, Forna has set up various development programmes herself in her family village of Rogbonko, in central Sierra Leone. As she writes on her website, the Rogbonko Project, which focuses on education, health care, sanitation, and agriculture, has at its heart 'the belief that Africans already possess the knowledge, will and systems to transform their living conditions. Every project undertaken in Rogbonko is initiated, administered and entirely run by the village. We have found this works, because we think Africa has all the experts it needs—they're the people who live there' (Forna 'The Rogbonko Project').

Works cited

Adorno, Theodor. 'Commitment.' Originally 1962. Trans. Andrew Arato. In Andrew Arato and Elke Gebhardt, eds. *The Essential Frankfurt School Reader*. New York: Continuum, 1982. 300–18.
Adorno, Theodor. 'Cultural Criticism and Society.' Originally 1951. *Prisms*. Trans. Samuel Weber and Shierry Weber. Cambridge: MIT Press, 1984. 17–34.
American Psychiatric Association. 'Diagnostic Criteria for Posttraumatic Stress Disorder.' *Diagnostic and Statistical Manual of Mental Disorders*. 4th ed., text rev. Washington: American Psychiatric Association, 2000. 467–68.
Bataille, Georges. 'Concerning the Accounts Given by the Residents of Hiroshima.' In Cathy Caruth, ed. *Trauma: Explorations in Memory*. Baltimore: Johns Hopkins UP, 1995. 221–35.
Bennett, Jill, and Rosanne Kennedy. Introduction to Jill Bennett and Rosanne Kennedy, eds. *World Memory: Personal Trajectories in Global Time*. Basingstoke: Palgrave Macmillan, 2003. 1–15.
Bennett, Jill, and Rosanne Kennedy, eds. *World Memory: Personal Trajectories in Global Time*. Basingstoke: Palgrave Macmillan, 2003.
Brown, Laura S. *Cultural Competence in Trauma Therapy: Beyond the Flashback*. Washington: American Psychological Association, 2008.
Burrows, Victoria. *Whiteness and Trauma: The Mother–Daughter Knot in the Fiction of Jean Rhys, Jamaica Kincaid and Toni Morrison*. New York: Palgrave Macmillan, 2004.
Butler, Judith. *Frames of War: When Is Life Grievable?* London: Verso, 2009.
Caruth, Cathy. 'Trauma and Experience.' Introduction to Cathy Caruth, ed. *Trauma: Explorations in Memory*. Baltimore: Johns Hopkins UP, 1995. 3–12.
Caruth, Cathy. *Unclaimed Experience: Trauma, Narrative, and History*. Baltimore: Johns Hopkins UP, 1996.
Craps, Stef. *Postcolonial Witnessing: Trauma Out of Bounds*. Basingstoke: Palgrave Macmillan, 2013.
Craps, Stef, and Gert Buelens, eds. *Postcolonial Trauma Novels*. Spec. issue of *Studies in the Novel* 40.1–2 (2008).

Craps, Stef, and Michael Rothberg, eds. *Transcultural Negotiations of Holocaust Memory*. Spec. issue of *Criticism: A Quarterly for Literature and the Arts* 53.4 (2011).

Croisy, Sophie. *Other Cultures of Trauma: Meta-Metropolitan Narratives and Identities*. Saarbrücken: VDM Verlag Dr. Müller, 2007.

Duran, Edwardo, Bonnie Duran, Maria Yellow Horse Brave Heart, and Susan Yellow Horse-Davis. 'Healing the American Indian Soul Wound.' In Yael Danieli, ed. *International Handbook of Multigenerational Legacies of Trauma*. New York: Plenum Press. 1998. 341–54.

Durrant, Sam. *Postcolonial Narrative and the Work of Mourning: J. M. Coetzee, Wilson Harris, and Toni Morrison*. Albany: SUNY Press, 2004.

Fanon, Frantz. *The Wretched of the Earth*. Originally 1961. Trans. Constance Farrington. New York: Grove, 1963.

Fanon, Frantz. *Black Skin, White Masks*. Originally 1952. Trans. Charles Lam Markmann. New York: Grove, 1967.

Felman, Shoshana, and Dori Laub. *Testimony: Crises of Witnessing in Literature, Psychoanalysis, and History*. New York: Routledge, 1992.

Felski, Rita. *Beyond Feminist Aesthetics: Feminist Literature and Social Change*. Cambridge: Harvard UP, 1989.

Forna, Aminatta. *Ancestor Stones*. London: Bloomsbury, 2006.

Forna, Aminatta. *The Memory of Love*. London: Bloomsbury, 2010.

Forna, Aminatta. *The Hired Man*. London: Bloomsbury, 2013.

Forna, Aminatta. 'The Rogbonko Project.' Available online at www.aminattaforna.com/rogbonko.html (accessed 10 March 2013).

Hartman, Geoffrey H. *The Fateful Question of Culture*. New York: Columbia UP, 1997.

Herman, Judith Lewis. 'Complex PTSD: A Syndrome in Survivors of Prolonged and Repeated Trauma.' *Journal of Traumatic Stress* 5.3 (1992): 377–91.

Herrero, Dolores, and Sonia Baelo-Allué, eds. *The Splintered Glass: Facets of Trauma in the Post-Colony and Beyond*. Amsterdam: Rodopi, 2011.

Hiroshima mon amour. Film directed by Alain Resnais, with screenplay by Marguerite Duras. Argos Films, 1959. DVD: Criterion Collection, 2003.

Janoff-Bulman, Ronnie. *Shattered Assumptions: Towards a New Psychology of Trauma*. New York: Free, 1992.

Kaplan, E. Ann. 'Fanon, Trauma and Cinema.' In Anthony C. Alessandrini, ed. *Frantz Fanon: Critical Perspectives*. London: Routledge, 1999. 146–58.

Kennedy, Rosanne. 'Mortgaged Futures: Trauma, Subjectivity, and the Legacies of Colonialism in Tsitsi Dangarembga's *The Book of Not*.' *Postcolonial Trauma Novels*. Ed. Stef Craps and Gert Buelens. Spec. issue of *Studies in the Novel* 40.1–2 (2008): 86–107.

Kilby, Jane. 'The Future of Trauma: Introduction.' In Richard Crownshaw, Jane Kilby, and Antony Rowland, eds. *The Future of Memory*. New York: Berghahn, 2010. 181–90.

LaCapra, Dominick. *Representing the Holocaust: History, Theory, Trauma*. Ithaca: Cornell UP, 1994.

LaCapra, Dominick. *History and Memory after Auschwitz*. Ithaca: Cornell UP, 1998.

LaCapra, Dominick. *Writing History, Writing Trauma*. Baltimore: Johns Hopkins UP, 2001.

Luckhurst, Roger. *The Trauma Question*. London: Routledge, 2008.

Micale, Mark S., and Paul Lerner, eds. *Traumatic Pasts: History, Psychiatry, and Trauma in the Modern Age, 1870–1930*. Cambridge: Cambridge UP, 2001.

Norridge, Zoe. *Perceiving Pain in African Literature*. Basingstoke: Palgrave Macmillan, 2013.

Poussaint, Alvin F., and Amy Alexander. *Lay My Burden Down: Suicide and the Mental Health Crisis among African-Americans*. Boston: Beacon, 2000.

Radstone, Susannah. 'Trauma Theory: Contexts, Politics, Ethics.' *Paragraph: A Journal of Modern Critical Theory* 30.1 (2007): 9–29.

Root, Maria. P. P. 'Reconstructing the Impact of Trauma on Personality.' In Laura S. Brown and Mary Ballou, eds. *Personality and Psychopathology: Feminist Reappraisals*. New York: Guilford, 1992. 229–65.

Rothberg, Michael. *Multidirectional Memory: Remembering the Holocaust in the Age of Decolonization*. Stanford: Stanford UP, 2009.

Rothberg, Michael, Debarati Sanyal, and Max Silverman, eds. *Nœuds de Mémoire: Multidirectional Memory in Postwar French and Francophone Culture.* Spec. issue of *Yale French Studies* 118–19 (2010).
Saunders, Rebecca. *Lamentation and Modernity in Literature, Philosophy, and Culture.* New York: Palgrave Macmillan, 2007.
Saunders, Rebecca, and Kamran Aghaie. 'Mourning and Memory.' Introduction. *Comparative Studies of South Asia, Africa and the Middle East* 25.1 (2005): 16–29.
Saunders, Rebecca, and Kamran Aghaie, eds. *Mourning and Memory.* Spec. section of *Comparative Studies of South Asia, Africa and the Middle East* 25.1 (2005).
Silverman, Max. *Palimpsestic Memory: The Holocaust and Colonialism in French and Francophone Fiction and Film.* New York: Berghahn, 2013.
Spanierman, Lisa B., and V. Paul Poteat. 'Moving beyond Complacency to Commitment: Multicultural Research in Counseling Psychology.' *Counseling Psychologist* 33 (2005): 513–23.
Summerfield, Derek. 'A Critique of Seven Assumptions behind Psychological Trauma Programmes in War-Affected Areas.' *Social Science and Medicine* 48 (1999): 1449–62.
Summerfield, Derek. 'Cross-Cultural Perspectives on the Medicalization of Human Suffering.' In Gerald M. Rosen, ed. *Posttraumatic Stress Disorder: Issues and Controversies.* Chichester: Wiley, 2004. 233–45.
Tegal, Megara. 'A Story for Her Family and Sierra Leone.' Interview with Aminatta Forna. *Sunday Times Magazine* (Sri Lanka). 29 Jan. 2012. Available online at www.sundaytimes.lk/120129/Magazine/sundaytimesmagazine_01.html (accessed 10 March 2013).
Terr, Lenore C. 'Childhood Traumas: An Outline and Overview.' *American Journal of Psychiatry* 148 (1991): 10–20.
Traverso, Antonio, and Mick Broderick, eds. *Interrogating Trauma: Arts and Media Responses to Collective Suffering.* Spec. issue of *Continuum: Journal of Media and Cultural Studies* 24.1 (2010). Reprinted as Antonio Traverso, and Mick Broderick, eds. *Interrogating Trauma: Collective Suffering in Global Arts and Media.* London: Routledge, 2010.
Turia, Tariana. 'Tariana Turia's Speech Notes.' Speech to NZ Psychological Society Conference 2000, Waikato University, Hamilton, 29 Aug. 2000. Available online at www.converge.org.nz/pma/tspeech.htm (accessed 10 March 2013).
Watters, Ethan. *Crazy like Us: The Globalization of the American Psyche.* New York: Free, 2010.
Wessells, Michael G. 'Culture, Power, and Community: Intercultural Approaches to Psychosocial Assistance and Healing.' In Kathleen Nader, Nancy Dubrow, and Beth Hudnall Stamm, eds. *Honoring Differences: Cultural Issues in the Treatment of Trauma and Loss.* Philadelphia: Brunner/Mazel, 1999. 267–82.
Whitlock, Gillian, and Kate Douglas, eds. *Trauma Texts.* London: Routledge, 2009.
Young, Allan. *The Harmony of Illusions: Inventing Post-Traumatic Stress Disorder.* Princeton: Princeton UP, 1995.

4

AFFECT, BODY, PLACE

Trauma theory in the world

Ananya Jahanara Kabir

> The beautiful Laila of freedom is shining in her beauty
> The Talib is half-drunk for her, approaching like Majnun
> *Sadullah Sa'eed Zabuli*, 'A Time is Coming'

These lines from a poem written by a member of the Taliban *c*.1990 have now been made available to the world at large through its inclusion in a controversial edited and translated anthology (Linschoten and Kuehn 69–70). Embedded in a series of apocalyptical images, the poem's culminating reference survives diminution through translation by drawing on a trope beloved throughout the Islamicate world: the unrequited love of Laila and Majnun. Further troped through the moth's self-destructive passion for the flame, and replicated in other pairs of doomed lovers, this story is ubiquitous in a cultural zone that stretches from the former Ottoman lands to the eastern-most reaches of the Mughal Empire. To be culturally and affectively knowledgeable in this zone is to appreciate a mythopoesis of love that ends in self-annihilation, and is nevertheless exquisite and to be aspired for; to appreciate that anti-teleology can surpass all desires for a 'happy ending' (Kabir 2003); and to be captivated by the layering of one forbidden pleasure (wine) with another (the beloved). The full shock value of these lines then goes beyond any superficial unease with an aesthetic approach to an ideological outfit reviled by the liberal world (Nair); it is to realize that the incandescent, intoxicated power of this image, with its roots deep in an Islamicate affective genealogy, has been diverted from its usual realm of Sufi and Sufi-inspired poetics to express the feelings of an individual whose overt political affiliations would seem remote from that more benign face of the 'Muslim world'.

This rupture of expectations traces multiple traumas of the decolonized world caught up in the Cold War and its repercussions. The challenge to those of us interested in the 'future of trauma theory' is to find ways of analyzing these traumas that acknowledge the myriad modes of consolation, memorializing and reconciliation which are deployed by traumatized subjects who may never have heard of Sigmund Freud, psychoanalysis and, indeed, 'trauma theory'. Can we make the shining Laila and the half-drunk Majnun not merely the objects but also the tools of our analysis? The present essay suggests some directions for moving forward with this agenda. These suggestions arise from my own work, of over a decade, on the Partition of India in 1947 as a traumatic event, and in the first section of the essay, I retrace that journey and the learning curve it represents. In subsequent sections, I offer examples of cultural production under the sign of trauma, from different parts of the world: south-east Asia, southern Africa, and, via a return to this poem by Zabuli, the borderlands between Afghanistan and Pakistan. The overall aim is to pinpoint limitations in our current toolkit for the analysis of trauma—limitations that have largely to do with the evident cultural gaps and geographic disconnect between the contexts in which trauma theory has arisen, and the contexts of specific traumatic events that continue to unfold across the world. Yet as the theory's drive is to generate connections and paradigms that must work in, and despite, different contexts, the essay will attempt to recuperate existing theoretical premises within a global framework: an effort that we may even think of as 'provincializing' the 'Europe' (Chakrabarty) within the heart of trauma theory.

Lyric iterations

Several years ago, the editors of an influential collection of essays on the relationship between memory and trauma contended that 'comparisons with non-European societies are vital in order to reveal the outlines of cultural tropes and social forms that can serve to conceal or highlight memories and legitimate specific versions of the past' (Antze and Lambek xiv). Formulating my own methods for analyzing collective trauma in non-European contexts, I had found invaluable that admission of the then-existent lacuna in trauma studies: a widening of focus to include traumatic events outside the Euro-American framework, and an evolution of methodology appropriate to their analysis. Having begun to explore the memorial repercussions of the Indian Partition of 1947, my search for hermeneutic tools had led me to the significant scholarship on trauma that centred on the experience of the Holocaust as a 'limit-event' (LaCapra). Indeed, the first article I wrote on the Partition's memorial complications borrowed heavily from the critical language and assumptions of that literature, most notably the concepts of 'unrepresentability' (Haidu) and the consequent fracturing of language (Kabir 2002). Nevertheless, in subsequent examinations of Partition's traumatic legacies, I found myself struggling with what we may term (cautiously) a 'Holocaust-centric' apparatus grounded in a Euro-American experiential space. Part of the problem was this apparatus's very indispensability: analysis has to start from somewhere, and it cannot ignore the presence of an existing, sophisticated set of theoretical approaches. In my intellectual travels with the Partition of India, I continue to grapple with this duality. The book I am now writing is titled *Partition's Post-Amnesias*, in a simultaneous acknowledgement of, and distancing from, Marianne Hirsch's influential concept of 'postmemory': an approach to the transgenerational memorialization of trauma articulated through her engagement with Art Spiegelman's celebrated graphic novel, *Maus* (Hirsch; Spiegelman).

The privileging of Euro-American experiences of collective trauma, particularly those centred on the Second World War, was not, however, the main hurdle that I encountered while dealing with traumatic experiences in non-European spaces. A more persistent problem was the concomitant privileging of certain interpretative structures devolving around narrative. As I noted in the same article where I cited Antze and Lambek: 'Like the Holocaust, partition was a void that ultimately remains beyond the capacities of narrative to replenish … [h]owever, one senses that mourning on a collective level has to embark through radical, non-narrative works of the imagination that foreground that void's untranslatability into narrative' (Kabir 2005: 190). Ironically, perhaps, this coda came at the end of an analysis devoted to women's novels on the Partition. In my search for theoretical models that would help illuminate a large-scale traumatic event such as the Partition of India and its continuing memorial repercussions, I was constantly confronted by the ubiquity of the narrative mode, and, initially, I replicated this emphasis in my own choice of primary material. I took on board the axiom that 'telling the story' was necessary to heal the traumatized subject and/or society—a direct inheritance from the Freudian emphasis on 'the talking cure'. Freud's distinction between a harmful melancholia that arises when the psyche is trapped in a loop of repetitions, and a healthy mourning which moves through progressive stages in order to bring about closure, affirms itself by emphasizing the need to talk (Freud; for further developments see, for instance, Bal et al.; Caruth). With the emphasis on closure, the structures of narrative converge on to those of mourning in a mutual validation of the 'best' response to trauma. Telling the story sutures the psychic wounds caused by the traumatic event, which manifest themselves in aporias and 'latencies' in memorial recall (Caruth).

The form and structure of narrative genres such as the novel and the film make them ideal vehicles for articulating Freudian-derived responses to traumatic events. This compatibility was the reason why I and other scholars interested in studying the Partition as a traumatic event (e.g. Daiya; Kumar) initially privileged their analysis over that of genres that resist incorporation within theoretical approaches to trauma reliant on the apotheosis of narrative-driven closure. For me, however, it became impossible to ignore lyric poetry and song, particularly expressions for lost, pre-traumatic pasts articulated through vernacular mythopoeses (see also Nijhawan), which repeatedly erupt through the surface of modern and modernist genres. These fragmented, iterated lamentations, unassimilated into the teleology of narrative, and, in fact, culturally sanctioned in popular film through the device of interruptive song and dance, are not aberrations, but intrinsic to South Asian memory work in the face of trauma: or so I came to argue in an examination of 'song' vs. 'story' in Anita Desai's novel *Clear Light of Day*, which striates its modernist formalism with the affective resources of vernacular lyric (Kabir 2006).

This argument is consolidated by Kumkum Sangari's recent analysis of the post-Partition trajectory of 'viraha' or 'longing caused by separation', an affective complex arising from medieval Sufi and Bhakti cults which expresses, through song, the same anti-teleology of separation and unrequited love conveyed in the Laila–Majnun story (Sangari). Throughout the 1950s, such songs were inserted into films, where they sat tangential to the narratives. The makers and consumers of these film songs responded to the trauma of Partition by participating in a revived version of 'viraha'. Their deterritorialized transmission through radio to Pakistani listeners further created a cross-border community of subjects alive to coded lamentations folded into the heart of modern, post-Partition entertainment.

Sangari's work exemplifies a new trend in south Asian studies: sensitivity to multiple and contradictory messages that are the modern nation's compromised legacy. The resources for these contradictions lie in the formation of affect clusters around diverse language and image-worlds through competing print cultures in late colonial South Asia (Jain; Jalal; Orsini; Mir). The splintered yet reticulated vernacular ('bazaar') and Anglophone modernities which result, offer a genealogy for post-Partition cultural production that manipulates different expressive registers to cope with the traumatic emergence of the nation. In this context film, with its simultaneity of soundtrack, narration, cinematography, and, in the South Asian context, song and dance, continues to be a rich vein to mine, but the most innovative work on Partition has moved away from 'Bollywood' to examine film industries of territorially partitioned regions, such as Bengal (Sarkar), or linguistic traditions that were the epicentre of contestations over identity, such as Urdu (Mufti). This shift in critical scrutiny has necessitated a renewed focus on, rather than mere 'defense of the fragment' (Pandey), with self-consciously marginal, interruptive and peripheralized genres such as the short story, film song and regional film commanding centre-stage. Sangari's work on 'viraha' as well as Nukhbah Langah's exploration of 'moonjh' (longing) in contemporary Siraiki poetry of Pakistan (Langah 186–230) exemplifies scholarly recuperations of a vernacular affective vocabulary, aligned to 'our poetry and the Sufi gnosis' (Naqvi xxxi). These 'lyric iterations' exist alongside and seep into the Anglophone realms of the novel, juridical and constitutional discourse, and official pedagogy. The challenge then is to explicate the lyric dimension within narrative and juridical structures which converge with trauma theory's emphasis on witnessing and testimony, despite any discomfort caused by the roots of this emphasis in 'Judaic texts' and 'Western traditions'.

The Bodhi tree

I have argued elsewhere that the transformative capacities of non-narrative, even non-linguistic reparation, may be the best way out of the silence versus testimony binary (Kabir 2009). The future of trauma theory cannot lie in a rejection of structures which make available a common currency for reckoning, accountability and reconciliation; wherever their roots may lie, they are now part of global modernity thanks to the spread of European social structures and norms through colonializing processes (even in nations never colonized, such as Japan and Thailand). The subsequent processes of interpellation created uneven modernities (Dube), but the expectations of the modern subject have become universal (Benhabib): access to liberal education, a passport, justice delivered through courts of law, the penal system for those adjudicated as transgressors. The theorist of trauma has to recognize the dialogic co-existence of these expectations, which, indeed, have often failed to be realized after the first flush of decolonization, and a range of affective domains with pre-colonial genealogies that persist in the postcolonial world as vernacular remainders. As Bhaskar Sarkar notes, 'Partition marks a moment of rupture, a historical realization of the structural lack endemic to all bourgeois formations' (Sarkar 7). Trauma theory must explicate the meta-trauma of modernity's ruptures. But it is insufficient to insist that it should decouple the analysis of specific collective traumas from its established heuristic dependence on narrative, witnessing and testimony and speaking out. For these regulatory and expressive structures are arguably also endemic to bourgeois formations. Thus this dependence must be analyzed—indeed, 'provincialized' (Chakrabarty)—by attending to the local play of disenchantments and re-enchantments through which the traumatized subject attempts to re-member its relationship to pre-traumatic anterior states—personal and collective—and utopian futures. A specific example of post-traumatic cultural production will substantiate these suggestions.

Phnom Penh's Tuol Sleng Genocide Museum is a sombre yet popular tourist destination. Not unlike the former concentration camps dotted across Central Europe, this place of torture and detention now memorializes the horrors of the Khmer Rouge regime that systematically brutalized Cambodia during the period 1975–1979, when the communist dictator Pol Pot was in power (Williams). A former school building that was converted into a prison for thousands of people before they were dispatched to the regime's 'Killing Fields' (see the film of that name, directed by Roland Joffé), the museum today showcases material traces, descriptive signposting in Khmer and English that clarify the function of its different rooms during the Khmer Rouge, and tour guides whose family members had been detained here. Tuol Sleng demonstrates how universal a phenomenon memorialization through the museum has become. As an institution, it now invites native and international visitors to respond to the Pol Pot era as an abiding collective trauma for the Cambodian nation and for the modern world. Indeed, the museum appears to be a classic site of memory in Pierre Nora's sense: a space 'dedicated to preserving an incommunicable experience that would [otherwise] disappear along with those who shared it' (22). Nora distinguished between 'dominant and dominated' sites of memory where the former, 'spectacular and triumphant', are 'generally imposed from above' and the latter are 'places of refuge, sanctuaries of spontaneous devotion and silent pilgrimage, where one finds the living heart of memory'; he also differentiated 'memory', that 'attaches itself to sites' from 'history', that 'attaches itself to events' (22–3). These binaries have been blurred by scholars revising Nora's original formulation (Huyssen 96–7; Rothberg et al.). Nevertheless,

Tuol Sleng reminds us how Eurocentric paradigms, even in revisionist forms, prove inadequate for explicating trauma and its memorialization outside European spaces.

As in Cambodian society at large, the museum's source of consolation is Buddhism. Indeed, the Cambodian Buddhist altar added to the schoolyard defies the modernist separation of 'pilgrimage' from the secular spaces of nationalist commemoration and pedagogy. Even the capitalist move of situating a café opposite the museum for the harrowed visitor's recuperation-through-consumption is confounded by the tree-fringed café's very name, 'Bodhi': the tree under which Siddhartha Gautama, alienated from worldly life, sat and meditated his way to enlightenment and transformation into the Buddha. The museum and its surroundings neither replicate nor repudiate European modes of memorializing trauma, but suggest the confluence of divergent forms of memorialization-as-healing. The modern framework of the museum contains the overwhelming pain that Tuol Sleng, as a monument to the Khmer Rouge's cruelty, still evokes. This framework is fractured but irradiated by the Bodhi tree as a 'Buddhist site of memory' that folds a specific philosophy of detachment (Brazier) into the museum's management of trauma through the circuit of witnessing and testimony. Another aspect of Tuol Sleng challenges even more acutely Eurocentric analyses of trauma: the social realist-style paintings mounted on the walls of the rooms through which the visitor walks. The paintings depict the modes of torture that took place in these rooms by picking up physical details that the rooms preserve, and peopling the scene around them with painted images of victims and torturers 'in the act'. The scrupulous replication of the rooms' details on the picture plane creates an uncanny continuity through recognition; the viewer is pulled thereby into a participatory mode both 'pedagogic' and 'performative' (Bhabha 139–170). The striking brown-and-white chequered tiles of the floor on which we stand reappear on the paintings, forging a common ground between representation and reality.

Prompted by the scenes in the painting, viewers compulsively interact with the objects retained in the rooms to bring to life processes of torture. For instance, visitors plunge their hands in a now-empty barrel in mimicry of a painted scene, placed before the 'real' barrel, which shows it containing hot oil into which a soldier forces a prisoner's hand. However, these paintings are not the only representational mode in Tuol Sleng: ID photos of prisoners are blown up into monumental grids of faces recalling the photograph's indexical function; while the retention of objects in rooms draws on the iconic potential of metonymic association. Yet the supplementary nature of the paintings pulls objects and photographs into a set of viewerly responses at odds with the behaviour one might expect in such a museum. How do we assess this invitation to memorialize the Khmer Rouge through mimicry and repetition? The question emerges as particularly salient given that, as I have noted above, such aspects of post-traumatic behaviour are relegated to 'melancholia' rather than 'mourning' in Freud-derived trauma studies. Tuol Sleng thus asks us to widen these now-classic discourses on trauma, reconciliation and healing. It demonstrates the need to break out of the twin grip of juridical and narratocentric frameworks for thinking theoretically and affectively about trauma, without, however, jettisoning them completely. Into that frame, it inserts the possibility of alternative modes of collective response to trauma: the spiritual resources of Buddhism as well as what I have called 'lyric iterations', which mirror symptoms of a melancholia unacceptable to the Freudian casebook. The museological, the meditative and the iterative co-exist, pointing to new ways in which we may study culturally-specific mechanisms through which trauma is survived and surmounted.

The kudurista's body

May 2012: evening in Luanda, Angola. Under the open skies at the downtown Elinga Teatro, a session of kuduro, the Angolan electronic music-dance complex, is in full swing. Its aficionados, 'kuduristas', take over the mike and the floor. Mostly male, in their late teens and early twenties, they are dressed flamboyantly and eclectically, accessorized with exaggeratedly pointed shoes, extravagant hairstyles, often partially or fully bleached, and pop-coloured spectacle frames. Their furious live rapping in Portuguese-meets-Kimbundu cuts against kuduro's explosive rhythmic mix of Angolan, Caribbean and global electronic beats. The vocal energy is matched by spectacular dancing. The young boys who leap on and off the stage with breakneck speed demonstrate moves from

> at least three areas: a) popping and locking, break-dance, headspins and power moves from hip hop b) traditional Angolan and carnival dance movements c) graphic theatrical movements such as crawling on the ground as if in a battle, dancing on the thighs as if the legs were amputated, dancing with legs turned inwards as if on crutches, dancing on crutches with missing limbs or mimicking media images of 'starved Africans'.
>
> *(Alisch and Siegert 2011)*

The dancing is aggressive rather than sexual. This is no courtship ritual, but the male body showing off its kinetic power through egotism that verges on the homoerotic, in spontaneous competitions between individual dancers. It is also hardly the male 'body beautiful': gangly, awkward, maimed, contortionist, stretching kinaesthetic norms to snapping point. The kudurista's dance is fiercely competitive, incredibly swift, and breathtakingly unpredictable. The demands of 'global ghetto-tech' (Brown) and its computerized music programmes may subject polyrhythmic texture to a 4/4 rhythmic grid (Butler); but the dancing body, playing freely with syncopated contrasts, constantly mocks this temporality. Thus does kinetic virtuosity dodge the 'time of history' (Coetzee 146).

Cranes, looming up from a building site directly opposite the Elinga Teatro, and a tall modernist office block transverse to the cranes, frame the kuduristas. The Elinga, a slightly decrepit colonial-era building, painted a charming strawberry pink with red accents, is marked for demolition; the cranes threaten the present and the office block points to the future. But the kuduristas' bodies populate and distend the precarious moment of the 'now'. This is postcolonial, post-civil war Luanda. After the ravages of five hundred years of Portuguese colonialism, a brutal struggle for independence and a twenty-seven year long civil war which was also one of the Cold War's major proxy arenas, Angola has entered the global economy through its oil and diamonds. Luanda, its capital city, shows all the signs of a nation impatient to move on: frantic and excessive construction, ruthless demolition of colonial-era buildings and complex contestations over the control of public culture, particularly its manifestation in music and dance forms. As Marissa Moorman has comprehensively demonstrated (Moorman 2008), collective expression through popular music and dance was central to the transition from colonial to postcolonial Angola; furthermore, as she (Moorman under review) and others (Alisch and Siegert 2012) argue, this centrality continues in the contemporary moment through kuduro. That kuduro is an epicentre of competing claims to Angolan cultural capital was clearly revealed at a conference on kuduro in Luanda, of which the Elinga kuduro session was a closing party.[1] Members of the political elite claimed kuduro for the nation; kuduristas, denizens of the city's least privileged zones, resisted appropriation through dexterous language play, outrageous style statements, and names that drew on the two sources of power in contemporary Angola—oil and political status (e.g. Príncipe Ouro Negro, 'Prince Black Gold'; and Presidente Gasolina, 'President Gasoline').

There is a connection between kuduro's subversive power and Angola's traumatized past. But what is it? How do we map the 'anatomy of kuduro' (Moorman 2008) on to collective trauma? For a start, trauma theory would have to re-engage the psychosomatics of the body in dance, in conjunction with the material conditions out of which it arises and in which it moves. These conditions, including the weight of history, are drawn into dialogic combat with the kudurista's body. In a contribution to a volume (Bischoff and Van der Peer) that will broaden trauma studies by examining art and trauma in Africa, Alisch and Siegert assert that 'kuduro dancing responds to the emotional legacies of brutal wars in Angola, and potentially effects change… recall[ing] violent events while sustaining a contemporary form of dealing with turbulent urban living in Luanda' (2012: 50). The spectacular displays of masculinity and swagger are all the more poignant for the economic marginalization of the typical kudurista. Does the 'anatomy of kuduro' reveal a balancing act between exhilaration and melancholia, or does kuduro's hyper-energetic kinesis render redundant theoretical paradigms of melancholia and mourning? The 'bodily-performative practices' of kuduro challenges conceptions of traumatized societies through somatic remembering in 'the heroic mode than in the self-definition of a traumatized victim' (52, 58). Indeed, despite 'the Angolan neologism *desconseguir* (to not succeed; to be unable to do), which seemed to so neatly sum up much of life in the civil war torn Angola of the 1980s and 1990s, kudurista body politics 'emphasizes the doing, not the un-, or at the very least, the dialogic relation of the two, as the song "Colo Diskoló" by Presidente Gasolina and Príncipe Ouro Negro exhorts: "the dance sticks and unsticks. Let's stick and unstick"' (Moorman under review).

The kudurista's exuberant re-making of the fractured collective self cannot be extrapolated, as some commentators have idealistically suggested, into utopian electronic dance floors situated in a global anywhere (Brown). Its recuperative potential must be emplaced within its own frames of dialogue and reference: it is a vigorous riposte to acoustic plaints for a pastoral Angola performed in the more overtly nostalgic couple dances such as the revived semba and its music, exemplified in the work of Paulo Flores (Moorman 2008: 190–2). Yet even Flores's *oeuvre* complicates easy interpretation as 'the work of mourning' (whether deemed 'successful' or not). In his song 'Boda', for instance, syntactic ambiguities surround images of stalled plenitude, which, in turn, contrast with the upbeat rhythm and the song's function as the accompaniment to two people dancing in partner-hold. Angola's different music-dance complexes thus invite interpretation as composite kinetoscapes. Formed through the interplay of trauma, modernity and the will to survive through creative kinetic pleasures, they demand equally creative and agile theoretical moves that can recognize the necessary simultancity of suffering and joy. The dynamic suspension of antinomies animates the kinetoscape from the micro-level of the kudurista's play with stasis and elasticity to the macro-level contrast between Angolan couple dances and kuduro's solo shows of masculine virtuosity. To extract the full valence of these contrasts, we would need to execute a final move: to the wider Black Atlantic world of which Angola is a part, whose kinetic histories are shaped by the same contrasts in the relationship between dance, music and trauma (Kabir 2013a). This story is only partially told by Paul Gilroy, who used jazz and hiphop to theorize the Black Atlantic's syncopated rhythms as a response to modernity's 'double consciousness', but, ironically, left both Africa and the dancing body out of his analytical frame (Gilroy; Zeleza).

Embodied, embedded

If Phnom Penh's Tuol Sleng Museum solicits from its visitors a meditative and mimetic response towards the Khmer Rouge, Luanda's kuduristas reclaim the Angolan body through kinetic exhilaration. In the Cambodian case, it is Buddhism, and in the Angolan, a Black Atlantic kinetic repertoire, but both exist in complex relationship to the deep structural interventions of European colonization, as the means to re-root the traumatized subjectivity in place. A similar vector drives the poem with which I started, 'A Time is Coming.' Its apocalyptic images and esoteric signs, that demand effortful interpretation, tap into the mystic and charismatic space shared by Shia Islam and Sufism (which, paradoxically, is here invoked by the staunchly Sunni Taliban; see Devji); it recalls Karbala as the archetypal battleground flamboyantly and histrionically commemorated annually during Muharram (Hyder). The poem signals this trans-local space through Iraq's Euphrates River, but simultaneously honours local geography through the River Amu; it pays homage to the Maiwand Valley, scene of the Anglo-Afghan War of 1860, and Maiwand's Afghan heroine, Malalai, as well as the trans-local myth of Laila-Majnun. All three cases I have cited draw on wider affect-worlds within which the space of trauma is located and which provide the traumatized subjectivity with the resources for reconstituting the self, even if the result is to continue 'grooving on broken'. These affect-worlds are epidermal and haptic (Naficy). They can hark back to pre-modern routes of cultural transfer—such as the trans-Asiatic Silk Route or the Indian Ocean trade routes, through which religions, ideas and goods passed in equal measure before the onset of European expansionism; but they can also, like the Black Atlantic, be created through the displacements and deracination that European expansionism set into motion.

Analysis of cultural production arising out of spaces of collective trauma should be attentive to the presence of affect-worlds deployed by the cultural producers concerned. Cues to interpretation of these affect-worlds with a view to understanding better the work of trauma must be taken from corresponding 'rules of the game'— the premium placed on kinetic contrast in Black Atlantic rhythm cultures, for instance, or the anti-teleology of separation and unrequited love constantly cited all across the Islamicate world, or, indeed, the askesis of bodily meditation (Alter) and detachment promoted within Buddhism. Such emphases should not merely be noted, but woven into the texture of analysis through close reading that gets both into the grain of the cultural text under scrutiny and reads against it. Secondly, these affect-worlds are more often than not invoked through processes of embodiment. The body, therefore, must be returned to the centre-stage of analysis; the original meaning of 'trauma'—a bodily wound (Caruth 3–4)—must be revived in our considerations of how people cope with traumatic histories, even when those histories operate through transgenerational (post)memorialization (Hirsch). This is the message of Derek Walcott's poetics of the persistent yet 'radiant' wound that marks the ankle of his postcolonial Caribbean fisherman Philoctete, one of the characters in his epic *Omeros* (Walcott; see also Ramazani). The body, however, does not exist in a vacuum: its return to the space of trauma is an act of reclamation. The ways in which the work of trauma embeds the body in place, as well as the processes which have displaced it, demand attention. In this context, the detritus of the Cold War—'dreamworld' followed by 'catastrophe' (Buck-Morss; see also Genter)—points to a new arena for a non-Eurocentric trauma theory, as my examples drawn from Afghanistan, Cambodia and Angola confirm.

A useful model here would be Michael Rothberg's 'multidirectional memory' (Rothberg; Rothberg et al.), which calls for the recognition of co-existing, overlapping but non-competitive modes of memorializing events that were experienced as traumatic for different identity-groups. This broadening out of trauma studies cannot, however, do away with its foundational dependence on the structures and articulations of the Freudian unconscious, which was both contingent in its eventual triumph over other possible analytical models, such as the Jungian one, and firmly a part of the early twentieth-century zeitgeist. Part of the modern condition is psychoanalytical determinism, which in turn is perhaps part of the larger trauma of the modern condition. Modernity's handmaiden has been the development of a theory of the unconscious, and modernity being a global phenomenon, the unconscious can hardly be done away with within attempted nativist re-appropriations of trauma theory. This continued dependence on Freudian vocabulary is evident in our inability to move away from that vocabulary even when attempting a severance: the most radical we can get is to call for recognition of 'critical melancholia' (Khanna), or melancholia as a positive force—rather than abandon the word altogether. Far more productive, then, is to develop a non-Eurocentric trauma theory that can revivify existing paradigms for explicating the work of trauma, by returning to consideration an interconnected emphasis on affect, body and place. As I have suggested in this chapter, affect-worlds lead us, time and again, to the traumatized subject using the resources of the body to re-embed itself in place. In the words of Michael Ondaatje, closing his own exploration of the traumas of the Sri Lankan civil war in his novel *Anil's Ghost*, it is time to come alive to 'this sweet touch from the world' (Ondaatje 307).

Note

1 The First Kuduro International Conference, Associaçao Cultural e Recreativa Chá de Caxinde, Luanda, Angola, 23–25 May, 2012. I am grateful to Stephanie Alisch and Agnela Barros Wilper for making possible my attendance at this conference and its associated events, which form the basis of this section of the essay.

Works cited

Alisch, Stephanie and Nadine Siegert. 'Angolanidade Revisited: Kuduro.' *Norient: Network for Local and Global Sounds and Media Culture.* 6 June 2011. Available online at http://norient.com/en/academic/kuduro (accessed 13 June 2012).

Alisch, Stephanie and Nadine Siegert. 'Grooving on Broken: Dancing War Trauma in Angolan Kuduro.' In Lizelle Bischoff and Stephanie Van der Peer, eds. *Art and Trauma in Africa: Representations of Reconciliation in Music, Visual Arts, Literature and Film.* London: I. B. Tauris, 2012.

Alter, Joseph. *Yoga in Modern India: The Body between Science and Philosophy.* Princeton, NJ: Princeton University Press, 2004.

Antze, Paul and Michael Lambek. *Tense Past: Cultural Essays in Trauma and Memory.* London and New York: Routledge, 1996.

Bal, Mieke, Jonathan Crewe and Leo Spitzer, eds. *Acts of Memory: Cultural Recall in the Present.* Hanover, NH and London: University Press of New England, 1999.

Benhabib, Seyla. *The Claims of Culture: Equality and Diversity in the Global Era.* Princeton, NJ: Princeton University Press, 2002.

Bhabha, Homi. *The Location of Culture.* London and New York: Routledge, 1990.

Bischoff, Lizelle, and Stephanie Van der Peer, eds. *Art and Trauma in Africa: Representations of Reconciliation in Music, Visual Arts, Literature and Film.* London: I. B. Tauris, 2012.

Brazier, David. 'Buddhist Psychology and Trauma Work.' *Illness, Crisis and Loss* 15:2 (2007): 155–66.

Brown, Jayne. 'Buzz and Rumble: Global Pop Music and Utopian Impulse.' *Social Text* 28:1 (2008): 125–48.

Buck-Morss, Susan. *Dreamworld and Catastrophe: The Passing of Mass Utopias in East and West.* Cambridge, MA: MIT Press, 2002.

Butler, Mark. *Unlocking the Groove: Rhythm, Meter and Musical Design in Electronic Dance Music.* Bloomington: Indiana University Press, 2006.

Caruth, Cathy. *Unclaimed Experience: Trauma, Narrative, and History.* Baltimore, MD and London: Johns Hopkins University Press, 1996.

Chakrabarty, Dipesh. *Provincializing Europe: Postcolonial Thought and Historical Difference.* Princeton, NJ: Princeton University Press, 2000.
Coetzee, J. M. *Waiting for the Barbarians.* Harmondsworth: Penguin, 1980.
Daiya, Kavita. *Violent Belongings: Partition, Gender, and National Culture in Postcolonial India.* Philadelphia: Temple University Press, 2008.
Desai, Anita. *Clear Light of Day.* London: Heinemann, 1980.
Devji, Faisal. *Landscapes of the Jihad: Militancy, Morality, Modernity.* Ithaca, NY: Cornell University Press, 2006.
Dube, Saurabh. *Handbook of Modernity in South Asia: Modern Makeovers.* Delhi: Oxford University Press, 2011.
Freud, Sigmund. 'Mourning and Melancholia.' *The Standard Edition of the Complete Psychological Works of Sigmund Freud,* Volume XIV (1914–1916). London: The Hogarth Press, 1953. 239–60.
Genter, Robert. 'Cold War Confessions and the Trauma of McCarthyism: Alfred Hitchcock's *I Confess* and *The Wrong Man.*' *Quarterly Review of Film and Video* 29:2 (2012): 129–46.
Gilroy, Paul. *The Black Atlantic: Modernity and Double Consciousness.* Boston, MA: Harvard University Press, 1993.
Haidu, Peter. 'The Dialectics of Unspeakability: Language, Silence, and the Narratives of Desubjectivication.' In Saul Friedlander, ed. *Probing the Limits of Representation.* Cambridge, MA: Harvard University Press, 1992. 277–99.
Hirsch, Marianne. *Family Frames: Photography, Narrative, and Postmemory.* Cambridge, MA: Harvard University Press, 1997.
Huyssen, Andreas. *Present Pasts: Urban Palimpsests and the Politics of Memory.* Stanford, CA: Stanford University Press, 2003.
Hyder, Syed Akbar. *Reliving Karbala: Martyrdom in South Asian Memory.* Oxford: Oxford University Press, 2006.
Jain, Kajri. *Gods in the Bazaar: The Economies of Indian Calendar Art.* Durham, NC: Duke University Press, 2007.
Jalal, Ayesha. *Self and Sovereignty: Individual and Community in South Asian Islam since 1850.* Oxford and Delhi: Routledge, 2000.
Kabir, Ananya Jahanara. 'Subjectivities, Memories, Loss: Of Pigskin Bags, Silver Spittoons, and the Partition of India.' *Interventions: International Journal of Postcolonial Studies* 4:2 (2002): 245–64.
Kabir, Ananya Jahanara. 'Allegories of Alienation and Politics of Bargaining: Minority Subjectivities in Mani Ratnam's *Dil Se.*' *South Asian Popular Culture* 1:2 (2003): 141–60.
Kabir, Ananya Jahanara. 'Gender, Memory, Trauma: Women's Novels on the Partition of India.' *Comparative Studies of South Asia, Africa and the Middle East* 25:1 (2005): 177–90.
Kabir, Ananya Jahanara. 'Beyond Narrative? Song and Story in Contemporary South Asia.' *Moving Worlds* 5:2 (2006): 28–42.
Kabir, Ananya Jahanara. 'Double Violation? (Not) Talking about Sexual Violence in South Asia.' In Zoe Brigley Thompson and Sorcha Gunne, eds. *Feminism, Literature and Rape Narratives: Violence and Violation.* London: Routledge, 2009. 146–163.
Kabir, Ananya Jahanara. 'The Dancing Couple in Black Atlantic Space.' In Liamar Duran Almarza and Esther Delgado, eds. *Gendering the Black Atlantic.* London: Routledge, 2013a.
Kabir, Ananya Jahanara. *Partition's Post-Amnesias: 1947, 1971 and Modern South Asia.* Delhi: Women Unlimited, 2013b.
Khanna, Ranjana. *Dark Continents: Psychoanalysis and Colonialism.* Durham, NC: Duke University Press, 2003.
The Killing Fields. Film directed by Roland Joffé (1984).
Kumar, Priya. *Limiting Secularism: The Ethics of Coexistence in Indian Literature and Film.* Minneapolis: University of Minnesota Press, 2008.
LaCapra, Dominick. *Representing the Holocaust: History, Theory, Trauma.* Ithaca, NY and London: Cornell University Press, 1996.
Langah, Nukhbah Taj. *Poetry as Resistance: Islam and Ethnicity in Postcolonial Pakistan.* Delhi: Routledge India, 2012.

Linschoten, Alex Strick van, and Felix Kuehn. *Poetry of the Taliban.* London: Hurst Publishers, 2012.
Mir, Farina. *The Social Space of Language: Vernacular Culture in British Colonial Punjab.* Berkeley, CA: University of California Press, 2010.
Moorman, Marissa J. *Intonations: A Social History of Music and Nation in Luanda, Angola, from 1945 to Recent Times.* Athens, OH: Ohio University Press, 2008.
Moorman, Marissa J. 'Anatomy of Kuduro: Articulating the Angolan Body Politic after the War.' Article under review.
Mufti, Aamir. *Enlightenment in the Colony: The Jewish Question and the Crisis of Postcolonial Culture.* Princeton, NJ: Princeton University Press 2007.
Naficy, Hamid. *An Accented Cinema: Exile and Diasporic Filmmaking.* Princeton, NJ: Princeton University Press, 2001.
Nair, Supriya. 'The Drumbeats of War.' 8 June 2012. Available online at www.livemint.com (accessed 11 June 2012, no longer available).
Naqvi, Akbar. *Image and Identity: Fifty Years of Painting and Sculpture in Pakistan.* Oxford and New Delhi: Oxford University Press, 1999.
Nijhawan, Michael. 'Ambivalent Encounters: The Making of Dhadi as a Sikh Performative Practice.' In Kelly Pemberton and Michael Nijhawan, eds. *Shared Idioms, Sacred Symbols, and the Articulation of Identities in South Asia.* London: Routledge, 2009. 143–66.
Nora, Pierre. 'Between Memory and History: *Les lieux de mémoire.' Representations* 26 (1989): 7–24.
Ondaatje, Michael. *Anil's Ghost.* London: Picador, 2001.
Orsini, Francesca. *Print and Pleasure: Popular Literature and Entertaining Fictions in Colonial North India.* Delhi: Permanent Black, 2009.
Pandey, Gyanendra. 'In Defense of the Fragment: Writing about Hindu-Muslim Riots in India Today.' *Representations* 37 (1992): 27–55.
Ramazani, Jahan. 'The Wound of History: Walcott's Omeros and the Postcolonial Poetics of Affliction.' *PMLA* 112 (1997): 405–17.
Rothberg, Michael. *Multidirectional Memory: Remembering the Holocaust in the Age of Decolonization.* Palo Alto, CA: Stanford University Press, 2009.
Rothberg, Michael, Debarati Sanyal and Max Silverman, eds. *Noeuds de mémoire: Multidirectional Memory in French and Francophone Culture.* Yale French Studies 118/119 (2011). New Haven, CT: Yale University Press.
Sangari, Kumkum. 'Viraha: A Trajectory in the Nehruvian Era.' In Kavita Panjabi, ed. *Poetics and Politics of Sufism and Bhakti in South Asia: Love, Loss and Liberation.* Delhi: Orient Blackswan, 2011. 256–87.
Sarkar, Bhaskar, *Mourning the Nation: Indian Cinema in the Wake of Partition.* Durham, NC and London: Duke University Press, 2009.
Spiegelman, Art. *Maus I: A Survivor's Tale: My Father Bleeds History.* New York: Pantheon, 1986.
Walcott, Derek. *Omeros.* London: Faber and Faber, 1990.
Williams, Paul. 'Witnessing Genocide: Vigilance and Remembrance at Tuol Sleng and Choeung Ek.' *Holocaust Genocide Studies* 18.2 (2004): 234–54.
Zeleza, Paul. 'Rewriting the African Diaspora: Beyond the Black Atlantic.' *African Affairs* 104 (2005): 35–68.

5

TRAUMA TIES

Chiasmus and community in Lebanese civil war literature

Nouri Gana

الحكاية غالبا للمهزوم والتاريخ للمنتصر.
Al-ḥikāya ghāliban lil-mahzūm wat-tārīkh lil-muntaṣir
The story belongs usually to the defeated and history to the victor
Elias Khoury

In *Refractions of Violence*, Martin Jay contends that violence has become a constitutive function of today's world, structuring and sustaining our ways of existence and of socio-political and transnational intelligibility (Jay 3). Michael Hardt and Antonio Negri argue that contemporary warfare and violence have become 'a permanent condition', 'the primary organizing principle of society', and 'the general matrix for all relations of power and techniques of domination' (Hardt and Negri 12–13). Genocides, exterminations and massacres have become, in Jean-Luc Nancy's bleak aphorism, 'if not names properly speaking, at least *semantemes* of modernity' (Nancy 178). While it may be true that warfare and violence are compelling and foundational forces of our contemporaneity, it is incumbent upon us to discriminate carefully between the structural currency of violence and the historical grievances it produces and of which it is oftentimes the product. The rigorous task of exposing the entangled (foundational, objective, ideological or symbolic) domains of violence in contemporary societies ought not to override or discredit the still necessary critique of the more contingent and concrete forms of violence, and of their particular historical origins or precipitating causes. What is at stake in the very structural banalization of everyday violence is not only the foreclosure of human loss—and therefore the institutionalization of ungrievability, disposability and post-traumatic stress disorders as ineluctable conditions of human existence—but also the attenuation and marginalization of the very notions of justice, political redress and forgiveness, without which no meaningful sense of subjectivity, of community and of transnational solidarity, however precarious these might remain, could be instilled and nurtured in the survivors of extreme violence and in the generations to come, 'their' descendants and 'ours', the inheritors of histories of violence, inflicted and incurred.

The particular historical and largely colonial instigators of warfare and violence in Palestine, Iraq and Lebanon risk being displaced into ancient structural deficiencies or ethnic and religious exigencies that make the unnecessary, asymmetrical and unjust violence look inevitable, even if unfortunate. When it comes to studying the Arab world and the *status-turmoil* that continues to define it, analysts have too often given in to the lures of what might be called *licensed displacements* of the realities of war that serve not only the derealizing aims of actual warfare but also the legitimizing narratives that inaugurate and sustain military violence. What interests me in what follows is the counter-narratives—those that bear witness to the enduring impulse to make sense of war and to expose in the process its concrete traumatic demarcations, calculated structural denominations and profound derealizing effects. As James Tatum puts it, 'the one impulse that has proved as enduring as human beings' urge to make wars is their need to make sense of them' (Tatum xi), but this sensemaking impulse, it should be added, can easily slide into an ordering gesture of understanding. Making sense of war involves an engagement with the cruelties of memory and traumatic loss via the consolatory vistas of mourning, memorials, and artistic expression. Sensemaking as a hermeneutic process therefore risks conferring meaning on the meaninglessness of war, neutralizing the discontinuous chaos of the reality of warfare it wants to process, legitimizing the very structural dominion of violence it sets out to denounce.

Because of the increasing institutionalization of warfare and the decline of communitywide mourning practices, the literary (indeed, the aesthetic writ large) has become the most hospitable public space where the performance of memory and mourning takes place. Not surprisingly, if depressingly ironic, entire literary traditions have been facilitated by violence and warfare. This has, obviously, been the case with a good number of modernist and postcolonial national literatures as several new studies on trauma and mourning go to demonstrate.[1] While not boasting a comparable number of new studies, especially ones carried out through the theoretical lenses of trauma and mourning studies, this has also been the case with the national literatures of the Arab states, particularly in Algeria, Palestine and, more recently, Iraq, but, above all, in Lebanon, where the civil war (1975–92) has indeed acted as the midwife of post-modern Lebanese literature.[2] As Elias Khoury points out, 'In this city [i.e. Beirut] systematically ravaged by civil war, the only space left for memory is literature' (Khoury 1995: 139).

In what follows, I focus on Khoury's *City Gates*, one of the most experimental and abstract novels in post-modern Arabic literature, written in the midst of the Lebanese civil war and first published in 1981.[3] I shall examine the ways in which narrative bears witness to, protests against, and ultimately helps us gain empathic *access* to the devastating effects of war without entirely or necessarily proffering us consolatory reprieve or clear exit strategies. The more the narrative of *City Gates* clears a space for mourning, the more precarious becomes the search for emotional closure. While the novel comes to a literal full stop at the end of the narrative, it rhetorically resists throughout its formal texture any eventuality of narrative closure. By occluding narrative closure, the novel occludes, at least by implication, any corresponding emotional closure. As such, it exemplifies what might be called a *poetics of occlosure* in which the narrative unfolds within and through a chiastic oscillation between the announcement of the end and the pronouncement of its recessiveness or foreclosure. As will become clear, this poetics fans out through and across various tropes (particularly chiasmus and metonymy) and experimental narrative techniques ranging from a stylistic obsession with formlessness and fragmentariness to polyphony and, above all, repetition and plotlessness.

The nameless protagonist of Khoury's *City Gates*—'a man and a stranger' (*kāna rajulan wa kāna gharīban*) (6)—sets out on a journey home, back to the city from which he was exiled, but the lashing athletic elasticity and haunting lyricism of the prose—its economic admixture of excess and inadequacy, of indeterminacy and immanence, of literality and undecidability, of dream and hallucination, of semantic opacity and syntactic play, and of the reality and unreality of the city—combine to leave him (and us) practically stranded at the gates (also of meaning and truth), which, by the end of the novel, are nowhere to be found. In their tormenting hunt for meaning, readers are bound to fall under the shadow of the stranger's quest for the city, for the city square, for the suitcase and, above all, for the truth (of what happened) to which the stranger wants to bear witness.[4]

City Gates should be seen first and foremost as an attempt to forge a new language, a new type of writing and a new mode of critique that would not only respond to the licensed displacements of historical violence into structural violence, but also expose the material and immaterial aftereffects of warfare, particularly post-traumatic stress disorder. The novel is much less a mimetic representation of war-torn Beirut than an allegory of the traumatic demarcations of the war—not to say a foreboding prolepsis of the Sabra and Shatila massacre that would take place just one year after the novel's publication. Above all, *City Gates* charts the enabling contours for the emergence of a new type of subjectivity from within the constraints of extreme vulnerability—the traumas and trials of survival in the aftermath of catastrophe. Through the allegorically performative dramatization of trauma, the novel seeks to institute vulnerability as a condition of subjectivity and to redistribute human ties along trauma ties—ties that the traumatized (and trauma-tied) subject dreads but keeps rediscovering at a relatively removed experiential distance from the originating traumatic event.

In *City Gates*, chiasmus, metonymy, and repetition are among the tropological tools that Khoury deploys to register and simultaneously loosen up the hold of trauma on the psyche. Stylistically, the novel unfolds like a trauma whose cadence, rhythm and haunting lyricism match only its opacity, recessiveness or intricate evasiveness. The disrupted circular plotline of the story begins with a stranger who returns to an unnamed city, which is, most probably, the scene of the traumatic event:

> He was a man and he was a stranger,
> He didn't tell his story to anyone, he didn't know he was a story to be told. He thought, he used to think, the way we think, and he was like

everyone was, but he didn't tell anyone, because he didn't know that the things that had happened could be told to anyone.

He was a man and he was a stranger,

He doesn't remember how his story began, because he was busy with its ending. And when the ending came he found that he didn't know the ending either, because the ending can't be known, because the ending is an ending.

(3)

It is not for nothing that the style here is somewhat overwrought; it is expressive of the traumatic nature of the story and of the traumatized state of the anonymous protagonist (whose story reads, at least initially, as an unreadable report). Given that *City Gates* was published in 1981 (and was most probably written after 1977, the year when *Little Mountain* was published to great critical acclaim), this man and this stranger might easily dramatize the lived experience of a survivor of the 1976 siege and massacre of Palestinians in the refugee camp of Tel al-Zaatar in the suburbs of Beirut. He cannot tell his story partly because he does not know whether it can be *framed* as such and partly because he does not remember how it began, much less whether it actually reached an end. Because of the unwitting repetitive re-enactments of the traumatic event (on the threshold of experience), the story might never find the ending, at the end of which it could possibly be framed as a story to be told to others. This is the paradox of *City Gates*: it re-enacts the trauma whose story it wants to tell.

This performative élan does not seem to allow for the establishment of the kind of coherency and form constitutive of a story to be reconstructed through or read for its plot. Instead, a solid void starts building as soon as reading starts. That the stranger cannot tell his story means, in the final analysis, that he cannot frame it into a coherent narrative whose meaning and meaningfulness hinge on the development of a horizon of expectations for future potentialities; for the meaning of an event is, in the words of Ernst van Alphen, 'derived from an anticipation of events to follow' (Alphen 33). Clearly, from the very outset of the novel the stranger is unable to activate a narrative framework that would make it possible to anticipate coming events. What arises out of the lack of a narrative framework that normally makes possible the anticipation of future events is precisely a narrative (of that) lack. In no small measure, this is the *challenge* to *City Gates* (insofar as it seeks to inscribe that lack) and simultaneously this is the *challenge* of *City Gates* (insofar as it re-enacts that narrative lack in order to bear witness to it without inadvertently filling it out). Above all, this is *our* challenge—the challenge of reading the lack at the structural rib of *City Gates*.

City Gates treads the fine line between the structural and the historical dimensions of mourning, ensuring that the latter does not unwittingly slip into the former— that what we get is more than a structural poetics of narrative mourning. The narrator or storyteller here is not only the survivor of the *end* of the novel, or the mourner for the loss of the story in Hans-Jost Frey's sense of the fundamental 'sadness of the novel, whose story can never come to completion because its end is always followed by its narration' (76), but also the survivor of the traumatic event that the novel *presents* performatively: the survivor of a history of trauma whose psychic demarcations match only 'the very inaccessibility of its occurrence' (Caruth 18), and the very lack of a 'narrative framework that makes it possible to anticipate future events'(Alphen 33).

So far my discussion of the chiasmus between repetition and the search for psychoaffective closure and narrative end has relied on the somewhat loose relations I established between the traumatic triad: event, experience, and representation. Given that a traumatic event cannot be experienced during its actual occurrence, it bears reiterating here that repetition is the very experience of the traumatic event *for the first time*. This implies that living through a traumatic experience occurs only belatedly and through the work of remembering and/or compulsive repeating. Is it possible, however, one might ask, to experience *belatedly* an event that could not—in the first place—have been experienced when it happened? The impossibility of experiencing a traumatic event while living through it first-hand has more to do with the *discursive* nature of experience than with the extremity of the event itself. As Ernst van Alphen persuasively argues, the problem here 'is not the nature of the event, nor an intrinsic limitation of representation; rather, it is the split between the living of an event and the available forms of representation with/in which the event can be experienced' (27). For, an 'experience does not really exist until it can be named and placed in larger categories' (Kolk and McFarlane 488). To experience here is precisely to dispose of the traumatic in the realm of the discursive; it is to situate oneself at a safe remove or distance from the event. In short, 'experience is the transposition of the event to the realm of the subject. Hence the experience of an event is already a representation of it and not the event itself' (Alphen 27). *City Gates* attests to what happens when the traumatic event (here precipitated by the Lebanese civil war) cannot be channelled into experience 'because a distance from it in language or representation was not possible' (Alphen 27). If experiencing trauma is indissociable from representing it—from discursively locating it in the past and psychically integrating it into one's own past—how can a *failed experience* of trauma still be represented? A failed experience implies here that discourse has failed to bring about a timely experience of trauma or that the inextricable relationship between discourse and experience has been unsettled in such a way that, instead of experience, there follows a *collapse* of experience. *City Gates* should be seen as an intense dramatization of this collapse of experience in an abandon of repetition.

The politico-ethical wager of *City Gates* is to delve into the empowering potential of engaging (with) failure; this wager rests not only in its attempt to bear witness to a failed experience of trauma but also in its failure to bear witness to that very failure (without which it cannot impart an accurate sense of the failure it wants to represent). What better way to represent failure than by failing well! *City Gates* vacillates chiastically between the excess of the traumatic event—its narrative lack or unrepresentability—and the inadequacy of the novel to bring about the experience of the event except in the immanent play of repetition. The failure of the novel as a symbolic form to represent the event (a failure intrinsic to discourse) is inextricably tied to the overwhelming nature of the event (i.e. its unrepresentability and indeterminacy, which is in excess of discourse per se, and pertains rather, *pace* van Alphen, to the magnitude of the event). There unfolds a chiasmus then between inadequacy and excess, the inadequacy of the symbolic order and the excess of the traumatic event. This is a chiasmus that I find to be the master trope of narrative trauma par excellence. Far from thrusting forward dialectically, this chiasmus proceeds in reversible and oft-criss-crossing movements, reproducing the transformational generative play of repetition, by which the novel starts *in medias res* and *by* which rather than *toward* which it is driven. It is in this chiasmus that the highly experimental and postmodern venture of *City Gates* must be situated. I have already addressed two aspects of this chiasmus—repetition and the search of narrative/emotional closure—and will now address two final aspects: fragmentariness and the collapse of the narrative voice. My aim here is not to exhaust all the aspects of this chiasmus of inadequacy and excess; rather, it is to be more explicit and specific about how central chiasmus itself, as a trope, is to narrative trauma.

The fragmentariness of *City Gates* is the most daunting hurdle facing any reader or critic of the novel. What is perhaps more consolatory than revelatory is that the reason why the novel is very fragmentary seems simple: it wants to *literalize* the failed experience of trauma (i.e. the failure of representation to bring about an experience of the event at the moment of its occurrence). Here is another example:

> But … the truth is I didn't say anything, I wanted to say, but … no now I want to say, now after everything has happened I think that I wanted to say, or that I should've said. Now, I want to be there in order to say. But I'm not there, and I don't say anything.
>
> *(95–6)*

The man and the stranger here dramatizes the chiastic oscillation between the survival of trauma and the trauma of survival itself, between having lived through and having missed the traumatic, and between being there and not being there (even though still but not quite there). Were it possible to be transported back there to the scene of the traumatic event, it would have been possible to say, to represent and to experience the event at the moment of its occurrence. Above all, it would have been possible to distance oneself from it, but the fact that that did not obtain then precludes the possibility of making it happen now: Khoury's novel produces the lack of that distance (or would-be-discursive distance), the failure of representation, and the collapse of experience/witnessing the traumatic event at the moment it occurred.

City Gates reads and feels like a parable, a fable, a surreal or fantastic narrative—it proceeds allegorically, looking at the reality of violence awry. In the seven chapters that constitute its thoroughly dreamlike narrative, the man and the stranger meets with surreal creatures, including a thousand-year-old virgin with tiny worms coming out of her insides, who dreamt of making love to a stranger like him (25); a woman made of yogurt (33); a king in a grave of stone (36); a man eating salt and drinking water until he 'transformed into a lump rolling in the middle of the square' (47); a woman who splits in two (55); foul-smelling animals (80); 'women weeping over bloated corpses reeking of death' (83). Ultimately, the city to which he longed to return fades away in a cataclysmic fire and storm, and nothing remains of it 'except weeping voices coming from the entrails of the fish and rising to where no one can listen to them' (97). The events hardly resemble reality or the metonymies associated with reality; rather, they point at and toward reality in a more circuitous, urgent and enduring manner. Like the dizzying seriality of nightmares from which the man and the stranger keeps trying to awake throughout his journey into the 'black hole' of the traumatic encounter (Kolk), the reality of the war might not be properly apprehended if it cannot be discerned through the eerie and improbable events described in the novel. For one thing, neither can the reality of civil war be walked through first-hand nor can it be witnessed or experienced without recourse to free-wheeling fictional qualifiers or interjections such as 'surreal', 'preternatural', 'senseless', 'absurd', all of which could be aptly applied to *City Gates*. For another, the sense of sustained disorientation, formlessness and adventurousness that characterizes *City Gates* is not at all unwarranted if the novel is to be understood as a fierce representation of the failure of representation and of the collapse of the experience of trauma in the first place.

City Gates strives to stretch the limits of the re-presentable even while it is highly sensitive to its own inadequacy in front of the unpresentable trauma that paradoxically demands and defies representation. In its defamiliarizing and elusive style—simultaneously lyrical and post-elegiac, compelling and unyielding at every turn, elliptical at times and aphoristic or apocalyptic at others—*City Gates* clearly takes up the challenge of articulating (by means of a sustained and deliberate—even self-indulgent—inarticulacy) that failed experience and that failed representation: the encounter between its protagonist and the traumatic event (that is presumably the catastrophe of the Lebanese civil strife). This commitment to formal experimentation neither exists in a socio-political vacuum nor is it an aesthetic or meta-narrative end in itself; for, the postmodernist tendencies in modern Arabic literature arise out of profoundly presentist concerns: 'In societies in transition', says Khoury, 'you cannot separate what is political from what is literary… Literature, in our situation must put together two elements: seeing and inventing; it must tell the truth and lie; it must combine the real and the fantastic at the same level and at the same moment' (Khoury 1993: 131). In its allegorical venture, *City Gates* offers us a way to relate to the discontinuous chaos of war rather than a documentary and mimetic rendition of war's diurnal reality.

Having addressed the major formal and stylistic characteristics of the novel, I now want to conclude by addressing the collapse of the narrative voice, in order to stop at the ways in which *City Gates* presents us—in the final analysis—with the drama of depersonalization as a way of rethinking subjectivity in terms of vulnerability. Vulnerability becomes in turn a potential psychosocial concept for re-envisioning socio-political, communal and human ties (all of which can at any time be invoked or retreated from, particularly in contexts of everyday violence) along trauma ties. The narrative voice meanders jerkily between third and first person narration. The 'man and the stranger', the anonymous protagonist of the novel, splits—given the acute dissociative disorders from which he suffers and which are associated with PTSD—into the 'man', the 'stranger' and the 'storyteller', imparting thus a heightened sense of an authorless narrative, shading into anonymously and indistinguishably multiperspectival, protean and confusing narrative voices, including that of the frame narrator. First and third person narrative voices are continually fusing and collapsing into each other: 'I said I'll bend down and I'll lean over and I'll go to sleep. The stranger said I'll bend down and I'll lean over and I'll go to sleep' (19). At times, the first person narrative voice splits in two: 'The woman calls to me, I say to her, I am not me/I know you are not you, but she calls to me' (38). When the narrative voice finally reasserts its authority, it sounds far less than reassuring: 'And I say, I am the one who says, I am the one who' (89). The first example shows how the first person narrative voice identifies with the stranger. The second example shows how the first person narrative voice splits itself in two and disidentifies with one part of its own self. In the third example, the first person narrative voice clears any confusion caused by the chiastic vacillation between identification and disidentification and reclaims its authority over the narrative (even though it is clearly an attenuated form of authority). As a rule, however, whenever the narrative voice is the agent of a given action at the moment of trauma, it tends to identify with otherness (as in the first example); inversely, it tends to disidentify with all forms of otherness whenever it is the object of an action (as in the second example where the woman's call interpellates the first person narrator). It is as if the very subjective ambiguity of the experience of trauma—in which the traumatized subject experiences simultaneities of, or alternations between, deliberate *returns to* and disembodied *returns of* the traumatic event—dictates the economy of identification and disidentification here. It is as if the back and forth shifts from the first to the third person narration are expressive of the anonymous narrator's fantasy of mastery over a situation to which he is submitted. If such is the case, this fantasy of mastery is nothing more than an agentive fallacy. The traumatized subject is, in most cases, the object not the agent of the traumatic event. The protagonist of *City Gates* is no exception. One need not neglect, however, the role this fantasy of mastery plays not only in the process of experiencing and bearing witness to trauma but also in the formation of a new form of subjectivity.

The fantasy of mastery is first and foremost a symptom of the unmasterable character of trauma. Not only does this fantasy hold open the possibility of experiencing and representing trauma, but it also makes possible the endurance of the traumatized subject in the process of (processing) trauma. At the level of the failed experience of trauma that *City Gates* performs, this fantasy of mastery transforms and generates other fantasies, particularly the fantasy of storytelling: 'And I, I was speaking, I see and I don't speak. I said I won't tell my story to anyone. I don't know the story, so what's there to tell?' (69). It is ironic that the fantasy of storytelling throughout the novel repetitively announces the very foreclosure of storytelling except that the narrative voice had to live through that very foreclosure in order to announce it. It is ultimately through this repetitive announcement of narrative foreclosure that the novel inscribes the catastrophe it failed to represent:

> And the storyteller tells what he saw, and the storyteller bears witness to what he witnessed, and the witness dies as the victims die, and the witness knows no more than walls and doors and eyes in which hands burn, and hands that stretch out to smoldering eyes.
> And the one who witnessed writes about his eyes, and walks beside the man who walked and doesn't leave him alone and he will not be except where he found himself.
>
> *(5)*

This is the ending of the preamble, which is a compressed version of the entire narrative, except that it is at once inside and outside its circular structure. The ending of the preamble is a bit different from the ending of the novel, which puts forward a vision of the end in which nothing remains except 'weeping voices coming from the entrails of fish and rising to where no one can listen to them' (97). While both endings depict an apocalyptic destiny, the ending of the preamble injects a glimmer of hope for a different future provided that bold steps are taken. These do not even remotely amount to a blueprint for action (especially given the constant disorientation and abstractness of *City Gates*), but they revolve around an eclectic number of keywords that can be extracted from both endings. The first three keywords are explicit: *storytelling*, *witnessing*, *listening*. The other three are implicit; they include the notion of *vulnerability* (tacit in the description of victims that die and hands that burn), *solidarity* (latent in the determination not to leave the other man alone), and, finally, *subjectivity* (which is sufficiently encoded in the references to the conditions of being and selfhood). This is by no means a finite list, much less if it is to be taken, as I do here, to apply to the entirety of the novel. What is important here is to articulate the potential relations between these keywords that the novel itself points toward. I propose to do so by re-examining the fantasy of mastery and the fantasy of storytelling that propel the narrative voice in its self-professed mission: to listen, to tell and to bear witness.

While the fantasy of mastery over trauma may largely be a product of an agentive fallacy, it is nonetheless crucial to the process of coming to terms with a compromised subjectivity. Similarly, while the fantasy of storytelling is continually overridden by the foreclosure of storytelling, it nonetheless imparts a heightened sense of the urgency of the present (*al-ḥāḍir*) and the pressing need to put forward narrative acts—acts that are never more to be desired than at a time when not even the witness (i.e. the stranger) is (being) spared, as the passage above makes unequivocally evident, the fate of those *to* whom and *for* whom he seeks to bear witness. Both fantasies are, in point of fact, gestures of inconsolability, symptomatic not only of the experience of lonely suffering that the stranger lives through—'This has not happened before, it hasn't happened that everyone and I have not remained except alone' (90); 'The stranger said he was dying all alone' (97)—but also of the endurance of his subjectivity in the process. Above all, both fantasies are symptomatic of the ways in which the stranger attempts to redistribute solitary suffering into cultural and public memory, which is, after all, the foundational gesture of *City Gates* as a whole. This process, I argue, cuts across the private and public, the personal and communal, as well as the subjective and collective.

The fantasy of mastery is precisely the fantasy of bearing witness to one's own desolate experience of solitary suffering when no secondary and empathic witness can be found. In 'The Most Intimate of Creations: Symptoms as Memorials to One's Lonely Suffering', Paul Shabad deftly reveals the symptomatologic workings of witnessing—the logic whereby the symptom becomes the personal device of witnessing suffering. Accentuating the disjunctive temporalities between the occurrence of a traumatic accident and the psychic and affective response to it by the lonely individual who experienced it, Shabad explains how unwitnessed solitary suffering transforms into trauma and how only 'the transformation of experienced suffering into witnessed reality at the moment it occurs inoculates experience against traumatization' (200). In the absence of another person who can validate our solitary experience of suffering, however, 'we are forced into the awkward, involuted position of bearing witness to our own experience' (200). Individual consciousness becomes, as such, 'a powerful homegrown overseer' (198), or, in the words of Paul Russell, whom Shabad cites, 'a camera photographing its own imagery' (202)—really, a camera 'bearing the responsibility of remembering and testifying to the actuality of one's suffering' (201). It is as if the mind itself becomes an autowitnessing machine, or a post-traumatic shock recorder, converting the traumatic event into experienceable material.

In a provocative move that is partly reminiscent of Nicolas Abraham and Maria Torok's concept of encryption in *The Shell and the Kernel*, Shabad maintains that the conversion of a trauma precipitated by lonely suffering must pass through the intimate and creative path of symptomatology. Symptoms are self-invented 'communicative actions intended to build a lasting monument once and for all for one's experience of suffering' (207)—a 'monument that will be remembered and that will testify to the actuality of our own existence' (197). Shabad calls this also 'a moment in the sun', blurring thus the materiality of the symptom with its belated temporality (197). The dissolution of the symptoms is dependent upon the engineering of a 'credibly empathic witness' and 'of bringing the dignity of recognition, sometimes many years later, to a person's experience of lonely suffering' (210). As reiterative acts of lonely suffering generated by, or driven chiastically toward the traumatic event, trauma ties not only traumatize the survivor, but also become the animating impetus of communicative acts and optimal fostering ground for the formation of social intelligibility and communal ties. The protagonist of *City Gates* is estranged from, yet tied to, the anonymous city; his constant comings and goings between the city gates and city square present us with a poetics of relationality that is profoundly exiled and rooted at one and the same time—this is a chiasmus of exilic ties, which might be, in point of fact, at the very basis of an ethico-politics of relationality. As Kai Erikson argues, 'trauma has both centripetal and centrifugal tendencies. It draws one away from the center of group space at the same time drawing one back … estrangement becomes the basis for communality' (186). Estrangement allows for what Ricoeur calls, in a book of the same title, 'the course of recognition' (*parcours de la reconnaissance*) to unfold from 'self-recognition' to 'mutual recognition', from 'identity' to 'otherness', and along a 'background' 'dialectic between recognition and misrecognition' (248–9).

City Gates dramatizes throughout its narrative collapse this course of recognition, which is consistently expressed (in Khoury's, by now, routine indirectness) as an unremitting sense of estrangement, rootlessness and exile. For instance, the protagonist of the novel is called 'the stranger' (*al-gharīb*) and does, indeed, feel 'a stranger in his own city' (13). No wonder, then, that only toward the end of the narrative does he remember that he came to the city carrying a suitcase *and* a mirror which he also lost: 'I don't remember, I don't. I'm looking for my mirror that got lost and for my things that I lost' (71). The loss of the mirror (in the Lacanian sense) must have literally retarded the potentiality of misrecognition, but, given that the narrative is refracted through mirrors and through a continually split or splitting narrative voice, the stranger must have already confronted the spectral dimension of his subjectivity. This spectral subjectivity has to do more, though, with the historical magnitude of the warfare and violence than with the structural constitution of subjectivity, of which Lacan speaks in his famous essay on the mirror stage (3–9). What is important to stress is that the stranger's name (or lack of it) not only suggests that those around him fail to recognize him—and, therefore, recognize, or misrecognize him as a stranger, perhaps, even, less than human—but also, and more important by far, that he is himself alienated from himself and simultaneously from his surroundings. It is in the course of estrangement that a transformational and generative formation of subjectivity and community takes place, since, as Erikson argues, 'drifting away is accompanied by revised views of the world that, in their turn, become the basis for communality' (198).

Erikson goes on to argue that traumatized people, by virtue of their estrangement and alienation, 'calculate life's chances differently. They look out at the world through a different lens. And in that sense they can be said to have experienced not only a *changed sense of self* and a *changed way of relating to others* but a changed *worldview*' (194). The type of recognition that is furnished by estrangement and defamiliarization suspends the existing norms of intelligibility that determine the apportioning of recognition and open them up to the dynamics of empathy and epiphany—what I call *empiphany (Signifying Loss* 56). It is as if only by becoming totally unrecognizable to oneself and one's surroundings—only by undergoing, that is, a limit experience, such as trauma—does one aspire to be transformed and, more important, to transform the existing norms of intelligibility that grant and withhold recognition. Indeed, the ending of the preamble I cited above points toward a concept of recognition of empiphanic proportions, one that involves both cognitive insight and empathic reckoning, or, as Rita Felski argues, 'knowledge' and 'acknowledgement': 'The former is directed toward the self, the latter toward others, such that the two meanings of the term would seem to be entirely at odds' (30). It is, however, the bidirectional crosscutting of recognition that becomes obvious in the last passage in the preamble: 'And the one who witnessed writes about his eyes, and walks beside the man who walked *and doesn't leave him alone and he will not be except where he found himself* (*wa lā yatrukhu wahīdan wa lā yakūn 'illā haythu wajada nafsahu*)' (5; emphasis added). Recognition here cuts across all of the above keywords, particularly subjectivity, vulnerability, and solidarity. Only in solidarity with the vulnerability of the anonymous other—which is the flipside of our own exposure and vulnerability—can we become subjects.

Vulnerability here institutes and points toward a counterintuitive mode of subjectivity—a subjectivity that can no longer afford to harbour any illusions about its implication in and exposure to the vulnerability of the other anonymous man who walks beside. In no small measure, this is also the communal and sociopolitical dimension of vulnerability, whose force *City Gates* brings to the fore. Rather than reconcile us to its structural over-determination in an age of disaster capitalism, Khoury's novel puts us on trial before its historical trials. It points at and toward the crucial importance of form and style to any serious rethinking of trauma and politics in tandem. The vulnerability that the anonymous stranger lives through and endures materializes in the paradoxically formless form of the novel. It makes itself known more closely through the chiastic repetitions and insistences of trauma—really, through the intensities of survival in the aftermath of catastrophe. Chiasmus is the figure of traumatic survival and vulnerability. Above all, it is the figure of connectivity between an *emurgent* (urgent and emergent) sense of post-traumatic subjectivity and an apprehensive revival of community. The figure of chiasmus in the novel ties the stranger to the locus of trauma and simultaneously to the bounds and bonds of community (precisely, the community of traumatized and trauma-tied subjects, at the margins of a perfectible humanity and worldwide community).

The rehearsed approximations of trauma that *City Gates* stages point toward the urgency of continually reopening history to the story of the man and the stranger and to the stories of his fellow men and strangers. These stories, which for Khoury belong to the defeated ought, one day, to belong to the victors, to the champions of history, in the hope they awaken them to their contingent invulnerability, that is, to their structural and human vulnerability. Until then, however, the task at hand is to continually discriminate between historical (i.e. singular-plural) vulnerabilities *and* structural vulnerability (i.e. the primary vulnerability that inheres in our thrownness into the world, in the Heideggerian sense, of course). This is a task that I cannot overstress here—it is one of the most enduring preoccupations and lessons of post-modern Arabic literature provided that it is approached for no purely extra-literary motives. Trauma studies specialists may not find in this literature the satisfactions of European literature, and nor should they, but they may very well find in it the future of trauma studies.

Notes

1 The modernist studies include in particular Ramazani, Ricciardi, Spargo, Moglen, Flatley; the postcolonial studies include in particular Durrant, Khanna, Gilroy. For a good overview, see Rae.
2 In a lecture titled 'Sociology and the Novelist', Elias Khoury maintains that 'the Lebanese civil war novel was born with the birth of the war itself and, as such, it evolved into a unique social and literary phenomenon.'
3 I have elsewhere studied film and poetry. See, for instance, 'Reel Violence' and 'War, Poetry, Mourning'. This essay is a reworked version of 'Formless Form'. For a longer version, see my *Signifying Loss*.
4 Indeed, in Arabic, suitcase (*haqība*) could actually be a pun on truth (*haqīqa*)—both words are after all near-homographs as well as near-homophones.

Works cited

Abraham, Nicholas and Maria Torok. *The Shell and the Kernel: Renewals of Psychoanalysis*. Ed. and trans. Nicholas Rand. Chicago: University of Chicago Press, 1994.
Alphen, Ernst van. 'Symptoms of Discursivity: Experience, Memory, Trauma.' In Mieke Bal, Jonathan Crewe and Leo Spitzer, eds. *Acts of Memory: Cultural Recall in the Present*. Hanover: UP of New England, 1999. 24–38.
Caruth, Cathy. *Unclaimed Experience: Trauma, Narrative, and History*. Baltimore: Johns Hopkins UP, 1996.
Durrant, Sam. *Postcolonial Narrative and the Work of Mourning: J. M. Coetzee, Wilson Harris, and Toni Morrison*. New York: SUNY Press, 2003.
Erikson, Kai. 'Notes on Trauma and Community.' In Cathy Caruth, ed. *Trauma: Explorations in Memory*. Baltimore: Johns Hopkins UP, 1995. 183–199.
Felski, Rita. *Uses of Literature*. Oxford: Blackwell, 2009.
Flatley, Jonathan. *Affective Mapping: Melancholia and the Politics of Modernism*. Cambridge: Harvard UP, 2008.
Frey, Hans-Jost. *Interruptions*. Trans. Georgia Albert. New York: SUNY Press, 1996.
Gana, Nouri. 'Formless Form: Elias Khoury's *City Gates* and the Poetics of Trauma.' *Comparative Literature Studies* 47.4 (2010): 504–32.
Gana, Nouri. 'Reel Violence: *Paradise Now* and the Collapse of the Spectacle.' *Comparative Studies of South Asia, Africa and the Middle East* 28.1 (2008): 20–37.
Gana, Nouri. *Signifying Loss: Toward a Poetics of Narrative Mourning*. Lewisburg: Bucknell UP, 2011.
Gana, Nouri. 'War, Poetry, Mourning: Darwish, Adonis, Iraq.' *Public Culture* 22.1 (2010): 33–65.
Gilroy, Paul. *Postcolonial Melancholia*. New York: Columbia UP, 2004.
Hardt, Michael and Antonio Negri. *Multitude: War and Democracy in the Age of Empire*. New York: Penguin, 2004.
Jay, Martin. *Refractions of Violence*. New York: Routledge, 2003.
Khanna, Ranjana. *Dark Continents: Psychoanalysis and Colonialism*. Durham: Duke UP, 2003.
Khoury, Elias. *Abwāb al-madīna*. Beirut: Dar al-Adāb, 1981. Trans. Paula Haydar, *Gates of the City*. Minneapolis: U of Minnesota P, 1993. Reprinted as *City Gates*. New York: Picador, 2007.
Khoury, Elias. 'Politics and Culture in Lebanon.' *The Beirut Review* 5 (1993), 131–142.
Khoury, Elias. 'Sociology and the Novelist.' *AUB Bulletin Today* 5.5 (August 2004).
Khoury, Elias. 'The Memory of the City.' *Grand Street* 54 (Autumn 1995).
Kolk, Bessel van der and Alexander C. McFarlane. 'The Black Hole of Trauma.' In Julie Rivkin and Michael Ryan, eds. *Literary Theory: An Anthology*. Oxford: Blackwell, 2004. 487–502.
Lacan, Jacques. *The Four Fundamental Concepts of Psychoanalysis*. 1964. Trans. Alan Sheridan. New York: Norton, 1977.
Moglen, Seth. *Mourning Modernity: Literary Modernism and the Injuries of American Capitalism*. Stanford: Stanford UP, 2007.

Nancy, Jean-Luc. *Being Singular Plural*. Trans. Robert D. Richardson and Anne E. O'Byrne. Stanford: Stanford UP, 2000.

Rae, Patricia. 'Modernist Mourning.' In Patricia Rae, ed. *Modernism and Mourning*. Lewisburg: Bucknell UP, 2007.

Ramazani, Jahan. *Poetry of Mourning: The Modern Elegy from Hardy to Heaney*. Chicago: University of Chicago Press, 1994.

Ricciardi, Alessia. *The Ends of Mourning: Psychoanalysis, Literature, Film*. Stanford: Stanford UP, 2003.

Ricoeur, Paul. *The Course of Recognition*. Trans. David Pellauer. Cambridge: Harvard UP, 2005. 248–49.

Shabad, Paul. 'The Most Intimate of Creations: Symptoms as Memorials to One's Lonely Suffering.' In Peter Homas, ed. *Symbolic Loss: The Ambiguity of Mourning at Century's End*. Charlottesville: Virginia UP, 2000. 197–225.

Spargo, R. Clifton. *The Ethics of Mourning: Grief and Responsibility in Elegiac Literature*. Baltimore: Johns Hopkins UP, 2004.

Tatum, James. *The Mourner's Song: War and Remembrance from the Iliad to Vietnam*. Chicago: University of Chicago Press, 2003.

6

UNDOING SOVEREIGNTY

Towards a theory of critical mourning

Sam Durrant

> But we have more to say of the living vesicle with its receptive cortical layer. This little fragment of living substance is suspended in the middle of an external world charged with the most powerful energies; and it would be killed by the stimulation emanating from these if it were not provided with a protective shield against stimuli: its outermost surface ceases to have the structure proper to living matter, becomes to some degree inorganic and thenceforward functions as a special envelope or membrane resistant to stimuli. ... By its death, the outer layer has saved all the deeper ones from a similar fate—unless that is to say, stimuli reach it which are so strong that they break through the dead shield. *Protection against* stimuli is an almost more important function for the living organism than *reception of* stimuli.
>
> Sigmund Freud, Beyond the Pleasure Principle 299

> Let's face it. We're undone by one another. Or if we're not, we're missing something.
>
> Judith Butler, Precarious Life 23

Freud's paradoxical recourse to biological organisms such as the vesicle[1] in order to explain—or, more precisely, to image—the non-organic phenomenon of psychic trauma has often been noted. But in the passage quoted above, something particularly odd is taking place: the organic turns out to itself contain both an organic (living) interior and an inorganic (dead) exterior, an outer layer that has sacrificed itself for the greater good of the organism. The primary problem that concerns Freud at this juncture in *Beyond the Pleasure Principle* is not how human beings become traumatized through overexposure to certain powerful stimuli, but how it is that human beings are able to ward off the majority of such stimuli. Freud's analogy solves this conundrum by positing a primary vulnerability of the organism, a vulnerability that triggers an evolutionary process by which part of the organism becomes so deadened or 'baked through' (Freud 297) by stimuli that it becomes impervious, incapable of feeling. While his essay will famously conclude that 'the aim of all life is death' (311), here the reverse seems to be true: only by becoming partially dead or 'to some degree inorganic' does the organism ensure its survival.

Judith Butler returns us to a sense of our primary vulnerability in the wake of that breach in homeland security that we (all) refer to by the figures 9/11 (as if American time has now definitively become everyone's time). But Butler's agenda is very different from Freud's: far from marvelling at the subject's ability to protect itself against stimuli by surrounding itself with a layer of inanimate matter, Butler urges us to remain fully animate, open to stimuli, undone. Against the normative, psychoanalytic account of mourning as a reconstitution of the subject's borders, a withdrawing of the ties that bind or bound us to others, Butler argues that traumatic losses are occasions for a kind of ethical growth, whereby we come to understand that 'we' were never simply ourselves but were always part of others, that our 'common corporeal vulnerability' (Butler 2004: 42) is the very condition of our relationality, our very ability to love more than ourselves.

Precarious Life, with its explicit debt to the thought of Emmanuel Levinas, can be read as a late product of the so-called ethical turn in the humanities, and as a more politically urgent variant of the trauma theory established in the early nineties by the work of Cathy Caruth, Shoshana Felman et al. As the title of Butler's celebrated early work, *Bodies that Matter*, implies, a broadly deconstructive ethics leads us towards a materialism whose end or purpose is the end of the individuated human subject and the beginning of an attunement to the broader field of 'matter'; that is, a commitment to all material life forms in so far as each presents 'us' with a potentially equal and infinite claim to matter, to be of ethical weight or consequence. Although drawing on the insights of deconstruction, Butler's work has always been of a more immediately political—activist, feminist—nature than that of the Yale School critics. As such, Butler's work constitutes something of a limit case for a field that, shuttling between literature, deconstruction and psychoanalysis, has tended to produce ethical as opposed to political insights (assuming for the moment that the ethical and the political can indeed be opposed).

Trauma studies gains a more obviously political purchase in the shift from individual to collective trauma—a move that Butler herself makes even while she draws attention to the problem involved in theorizing the USA as a national subject: 'nations are not the same as individual psyches but both can be described as subjects, albeit of different orders' (2004 41). Rather than imagining a traumatized collective psyche, trauma studies is on surer ground when it theorizes the state's role in the process of subjectification, as Butler does in *The Psychic Life of Power*. The distinction between historical (event-based) and structural trauma would seem to have been eclipsed by the recent turn to the biopolitical.[2] Where once talk of structural trauma seemed to constitute a depoliticization of discrete or even 'unique' events such as the Holocaust, the work of theorists as diverse as Slavoj Žižek, Giorgio Agamben, Achille Mbembe, Jenny Edkins and Butler herself has emphasized the importance of understanding trauma as an inevitable part of our ideological construction as subjects, our subjection to the state and the myriad forces of modernity. While this biopolitical turn has, of course, taken its cue from the work of Michel Foucault, it also draws much from the Lacanian understanding of trauma as both constitutive of the subject's entrance into the social ('symbolic') order and as something that is re-experienced whenever the fabric of that social order is ripped. As Žižek in particular has revealed, Lacanian psychoanalysis was always already a political critique: the Lacanian Symbolic is another version of Freud's protective shield, but one which reveals the role of ideology not only in subject-formation but also in insulating the subject from the various forms of violence that simultaneously underwrite and threaten its existence.

Trauma studies' biopolitical turn is anticipated by the multiple invocations of the work of Walter Benjamin and his sense of the traumatic experience of modernity. His famous description of the 'tiny fragile human body' caught in a field of force of destructive torrents and explosions' (84) recalls Freud's account of the vulnerability of the vesicle 'suspended in the middle of an external world charged with the most powerful energies', an echo that reminds us that both works are concerned with the traumatic after-effects of the First World War. While critics such as Roger Luckhurst have historicized the rise of trauma as a medico–legal category that has its origins in the technological innovations of modernity (such as the train), Benjamin's sense of trauma is not so readily historicisable. His reading of Klee's Angelus Novus has become *the* figure for the traumatized witness, a witness not to one historically locatable event but to history itself, as one long catastrophe.

And it is not coincidental that postcolonial studies turns to Benjamin almost as frequently as it does to Frantz Fanon in its attempt to convey the traumatic nature of colonial and postcolonial experience. Homi Bhabha, for instance, cites Benjamin's description of the traumatic onset of modernity in order to prepare us for the doubly traumatic entrance of the postcolonial subject into a modernity that was never its own, the 'profound perplexity of the living' (Benjamin quoted in Bhabha 161) complicated by the fact that 'his migration is like an event in a dream dreamt by another' (Berger quoted in Bhabha 165). Interestingly, Bhabha's essay comes close to Butler's later work in attempting to make an inter or anti-nationalist virtue out of trauma, casting Gibreel, the schizophrenic migrant from Rushdie's *The Satanic Verses*, as the traumatic return of the history that happened overseas, as that which will rupture the ideological shield protecting the English national subject from knowledge of its irrevocable hybridity (168). Bhabha's essay, published in 1990, emanates from a different historical moment and a very different sensibility to Butler's post 9/11 work. Indeed, Bhabha's almost wilful misreading of *The Satanic Verses*, a novel which ends not with the hybridization of the English but with the suicide of Gibreel and the return home to India of his fellow migrant and reluctant travelling companion, prevents us from seeing the historical lines that might be drawn from *The Satanic Verses* and its hostile reception in parts of what suddenly became known as 'the Muslim world' through to the 'blowback' events of 9/11, the subsequent shoring up of national defences and the 'war on terror', more accurately phrased as a war on foreign bodies and migrant stimuli, a neo-colonial resumption (and denial) of the history that happened overseas.

Taking Butler's response to 9/11 as my guide to our bleak historical times, my argument will be that the end of trauma theory (its purpose, future, utopian horizon) is something like a shared consciousness of our common corporeal vulnerability. Rather than constructing yet another model of deconstructive ethics, my aim is to theorize a properly critical mourning, a mourning that works to undo not simply 'the idea of the sovereign subject' but sovereignty itself, property relations, and the human assumption of sovereignty over nature. Firstly, I explore David Lloyd's materialist critique of the way in which the memorialization of the Irish Famine is complicit with the drive of a 'therapeutic modernity' that teaches postcolonial subjects how to 'lose our loss' and thereby 'enter more lightly into the new world order' (222). Secondly, I return to Horkeimer and Adorno's famous reading of *The Odyssey* as the legitimation of modernity and of the not quite successful attempt to simultaneously record and suppress the memory of the traumatic violence involved in the process of (re)establishing settlement. Their reading of the epic suggests that literary form is another version of Freud's protective shield, that the ideology of form insulates the subject from consciousness of its own constitutive violence. And thirdly, I explore a cycle of poems on the Truth and Reconciliation Commission by the South African poet Ingrid de Kok, a cycle which works to recover a sense of our common corporeality precisely by being critical of its own mourning work, by undoing both its own lyric form and its ideological status as literature of, or 'for', reconciliation. Precisely because form is historically determined, or what Adorno describes as 'sedimented content', its auto-critique becomes a critical questioning of the terms of post-apartheid settlement. Throughout this essay, my interest will be in the relationship between mourning and property; the integrity of a term such as critical mourning forever depends upon its capacity to unsettle the claims of sovereignty, in its colonial and postcolonial guises alike.

The critique of postcolonial mourning[3]

David Lloyd begins his provocative essay, 'Colonial Trauma/Postcolonial Recovery?' by showing how colonized cultures manifest the clinical symptoms of individual trauma. However, the ease with which we are able to map the 'psychological effects of trauma onto the cultures that undergo colonization' (214), should give us pause for thought. The seemingly widespread assumption that a postcolonial culture of mourning offers a way of recovering from colonial trauma ignores the question of what sort of postcolonial subject is thereby 'recovered':

> The commemoration of the Famine becomes unhappily one with a set of current cultural and political tendencies in Ireland that are thrusting the country uncritically into European and transnational modernity ... If we allow commemoration of the dead to become a means to enter more lightly into the

new world order, are we not in fact reproducing the attitudes of the colonialism that destroyed them, as well as reproducing those attitudes in the present with regards to other postcolonial peoples that are undergoing the catastrophes of development? If the function of therapeutic modernity is to have us lose our loss in order to become good subjects, then the very process of mourning the dead is at once their condemnation, their devaluation.

(222)

The essay is distinct from many of the countless studies that reveal the counter-intuitively amnesiac effect of contemporary practices of memorialization in the way in which it urges us to think in particular about the relation between mourning and property. It is not simply that mourning prescribes a form of letting go, or reconciliation to loss, that is at odds with a postcolonial desire to reclaim or recover that which was lost/stolen. Instead, Lloyd seeks to recover the traces of a moral economy that would contest property relations per se. The essay ends by quoting a passage that is not about the Famine itself but its after-effects, namely a scene of eviction as recollected by a descendant. Having evicted the tenant farmers and their furniture, the British soldiers demand the key to the house:

> But god help us, there was no lock to the door. A hasp on the outside, and a bar of iron from wall to wall was used to make it fast on the inside, but it was never used, the door was always unbarred, and a sod always burned on the hearth, for the poor carriers to come in to light their pipes when passing, either day or night.
>
> The old man brought out the bar, and he said afterwards, what he'd like to have done with it was to give the soldier a blow of it. But he didn't he threw it towards him on the road.
>
> 'Yo damn swine' muttered the soldier, as he rode off with his men to the next house.

(226)

Earlier in his essay, Lloyd asks whether 'rage might not be a more proper response to those deaths and other sufferings for which our mourning is redundant now, rage even at the frustration that our mourning changes nothing?' (221), a question that is equally pertinent to post-apartheid South Africa, and the rage that its own culture of mourning suppressed. But here I simply want to note how Lloyd turns the old man's gesture into the symbol not simply of rage but also of 'incommensurable economies':

> what is thrown before the officer is the antithesis of the key that he demands: an item without use since there is no property to be protected and no barring of the door in the moral economy of the poor … Lying athwart the path of the soldier, the iron bar … marks, in a minimal gesture perhaps, the persistence of an ethos that escapes the logic of property and economic reason.

(227–8)

Like the early work of Gayatri Spivak,[4] Lloyd's essay is performative rather than simply descriptive of its 'postcolonial commitment' in so far as it provides us with an *image* of resistance that it seeks to suspend in time precisely in order to rescue it from its obliteration by the triumph of modernity, an image with which, pace Walter Benjamin, we might seek to redeem, or indeed unlock, the future. Lloyd's essay ends with an invocation:

> As for us, rather than lament the futility of that gesture or rush to trace in it the contours of a resistance that will emerge in more articulate forms, we should perhaps suspend for a moment the image of this iron bar cast on the road as the die turns in the air before it falls to the ground. In the very cusp of catastrophe, this turning bespeaks the memory of alternative possibilities that live on athwart the mournful logic of historicized events.
>
> *(228)*

What is both exhilarating and slightly troubling about this final flourish is the way in which the essay reads the archive[5] in such a way as to turn itself into the gesture which it has recovered. Lloyd cannot help but be complicit in the culture of memorialization that he seeks to critique. In asking his readers to 'suspend for a moment' the image of this falling bar, he almost seems to be asking us to suspend the rage of the evicted tenant as much as the time of capitalist modernity that will render such rage futile. Ultimately he leaves us with an appropriately unresolved image of a rage, owned and disowned, appropriated and sublimated, barely transmuted into the 'possibility of alternative possibilities of living on', an image that lives on precisely through its resistance to resolution, its refusal to reconcile incommensurable historical trajectories.[6]

Although he isn't quite explicit enough about what he is up to, Lloyd in effect reverses the formula that he sets out to question in his title; instead of postcolonial mourning as the cure for colonial trauma, the 'living on' of colonial trauma disrupts the therapeutic culture of postcolonial modernity. Like Butler, Lloyd is interested in how we might respond to trauma and loss in a way that doesn't simply serve to shore up the boundaries of the subject and the state:

> The discourse of the subject that I have been outlining here proposes that the overcoming of loss is achieved by the direction of the subject towards identification with the state (or with the aesthetic disposition that prefigures it) as the representation of a lost wholeness or harmony.
>
> *(218)*

In other words, postcolonial mourning problematically colludes in the production of an illusory moment of reconciliation:

> The claim to a correspondence between the form of a subject and the forms of the social must be seen, then, not as the grounds for therapeutic resolution

of the traumatic contradictions of colonial subjectivity, but as a constitutive element of the common sense of domination.

(216)

The question thus becomes how to imagine a recalcitrant, anti-therapeutic form of mourning that, rather than accommodating the subject to postcolonial modernity, would instead invoke a 'common sense of domination'.

The psychopathology of *nostos*

As we have seen, Lloyd's essay finds in the historical archive an image of the critical, unreconciled mourning he is after, but he doesn't meditate on the performative move he makes from theoretical analysis to lyrical evocation. I want to turn now to the work of Adorno[7] not in order to reinvoke his (in)famous remark about the dangers of such lyricism, but precisely in order to garner a fuller sense of how the aesthetic sphere might work to produce 'the common sense of domination'. The first point to make here is that the work of art must work *against itself* if it is to avoid the naturalizing function of the postcolonial memorializing practices that Lloyd sets out to critique. In Adorno's aesthetics we might say that the form of the artwork mimes the formation of the subject in so far as form is understood as 'sedimented content'. That is, the form of the artwork has a social history and is thus determined or 'preformed' by its specific historical moment. In this sense we might conceive of artistic form as another version of Freud's dead(ening) protective shield. But what makes Adorno's aesthetics interesting is that, beyond the oft-quoted critique of the numbing effect of the culture industry, Adorno also sees the aesthetic sphere as the one sphere capable of administering the kind of shock that would liberate us from our ideological insulation and awaken us to the fact of our domination (both of ourselves and of others).

Adorno is often critiqued, like the Yale School trauma theorists, for privileging modernist artworks, those 'anti-realist' artworks which insist on drawing attention to their own formal nature. But his analysis of *The Odyssey* makes it clear that all forms of art need to be read dialectically: on the one hand as forms of subjective expression that cannot but naturalize the subject's conceptual domination of the world, and on the other as works that flinch at the very process of domination in which they are implicated. David Quint's *Epic and Empire* has made it clear that epic is about the production of master narratives, that the form of epic is programmed to produce a feeling of awe before the spectacle of heroic might, an awe that prevents us from feeling any real sympathy for the losers, for those on the wrong side of history. Adorno's reading of *The Odyssey* concurs with this New Historicist analysis of epic in so far as both readings begin from the assumption that epic form constitutes an ideology that naturalizes domination. But, unlike Quint's book, Adorno's essay works to make epic conscious of its own violence by suspending the force of its *telos*, by suggesting, like Lloyd, the possibility of alternate historical trajectories. Odysseus's drive to return home to Ithaca is shown to be the self-alienating drive of the modern, patriarchal subject to escape his home in nature (in the mythical, pre-civilized forms of life that Circe and the lotus eaters offer him) and instead (re)install himself as lord and master of the private property that he mistakes for a homeland.

Adorno's critique of the concept of homeland is rather more far-reaching than Lloyd's suspended nostalgia for the pre-capitalist economy of the Irish poor:

> Precipitated in epic is the memory of an historical age in which nomadism gave way to settlement, the precondition of any homeland. If the fixed order of property implicit in settlement is the source of human alienation, in which all homesickness and longing spring from a lost primal state, at the same time it is towards settlement and fixed property, on which alone the concept of homeland is based, that all longing and homesickness are directed.
>
> *(60–61)*

Part of the reason why postcolonial mourning is not the answer to colonial trauma is that it retrospectively constructs the pre-colonial homeland as an ideal, non-alienated state. Critical mourning must recognize that nostalgia or homesickness is itself an alienated pathology, in so far as it fails to recognize that the origins of its malaise lie not in colonialism per se but in fixed property relations. The trauma that it seeks to address is not simply the historical trauma of colonialism, but the structural trauma that is the precondition of all settlement.

But Adorno's allegorical reading of *The Odyssey* as the birth (and annihilation) of the modern subject does more than simply recalibrate our historical conception of modernity. It is also a meditation on the dialectical process by which the artwork both conceals and reveals the traumatic violence it narrates. The long, last paragraph of the essay considers the excessive violence of Odysseus's homecoming, the putting to death not only of Penelope's suitors but also of the 'faithless maidservants who have sunk into harlotry':

> It is not in the content of the deeds reported that civilization transcends [the primeval world]. It is in the self-reflection which causes violence to pause at the moment of narrating such deeds. Speech itself, language as opposed to mythical song, the possibility of holding fast the past atrocity through memory, is the law of Homeric escape.
>
> *(61)*

This moment of self-reflection is the moment at which the epic becomes conscious of itself as ideology, and catches itself in the act of providing a protective shield that would neutralize the traumatic impact of the past atrocity that it nevertheless records. In his first move, Adorno suggests speech/language is opposed to the self-forgetful nature of mythic song (that song, for instance, sung by the sirens, wherein the subject loses its instinct for self-preservation) in its capacity to hold fast the memory of atrocity. However, this very capacity to remember constitutes 'the law of Homeric escape', Odysseus's capacity to escape from the clutches of myth into modernity and thereby into another form of self-forgetfulness. As in Lloyd's essay, memorialization turns out to be an alibi, a therapeutic mode of remembering in order to forget. But Adorno's dialectical critique also contains a redemptive moment: language contains within it the structural possibility (memory, even) of its own cessation, and it is in this cessation or pause that a different kind of memory arises.

> The cold detachment of the narrative, which describes even the horrible as if for entertainment, for the first time reveals in all their clarity the horrors which in song are solemnly confused with fate [i.e. supposed to be inevitable]. But when speech pauses, the caesura allows the events to flash up a semblance of freedom that civilization has been wholly unable to extinguish ever since.
> *(61)*

Adorno locates this pause or caesura as a kind of after-echo of language itself. The epic narrative describes the hanging of the maidservants with an 'unmoved composure', 'expressionlessly' comparing the victims to birds caught in a trap. However, the simile is followed with the remark 'For a little while their feet kicked out, but not for very long':

> The exactitude of the description, which already exhibits the coldness of anatomy and vivisection, keeps a record, as in a novel, of the twitching of the subjugated women, who, under the aegis of justice and the law, are thrust down into the realm from which Odysseus the judge has escaped ... But after the words, 'not for long' the inner flow of the narrative comes to rest. 'Not for long?' the narrator asks by this device, giving the lie to his own composure. In being brought to a standstill, the report is prevented from forgetting the victims of the execution and lays bare the unspeakable torment of the single second in which the maids fought against death.
> *(61–2)*

Like Lloyd, Adorno ends his essay with an image of suspension, not simply the literal suspension of the maidservants, but the suspension of the narrative itself as it becomes fleetingly conscious of the human cost of its narrative drive, its misguided *telos*, the homecoming that is in fact the guarantee of Odysseus's—and our own—alienation. The 'semblance of freedom' lies in the way that the narrative itself (dis)sembles, the way in which its own pause mimes the suspension of the hanged women and thereby betrays its secret affinity with their suffering.

As Adorno makes clear in his passing reference to the novel in the passage quoted above, all art forms are capable of recording and thereby forgetting suffering. Each art form has its own logic or *telos*, its own self-justificatory end. If Adorno champions certain works of art or aesthetic movements over others, he does so because of their tendency to reflect on their own form and, in so doing, momentarily suspend their internal logic. It is this mimetic capacity of art that Adorno champions in modernism: its ability to signal, via the suspension of its own form, an affinity with the suffering that it must thrust down into the realm of the forgotten through its very ability to record. By mimesis, Adorno means not the direct, content-based representation of the world—what in the above passages he refers to as reporting or recording—but rather the moment at which the artwork, through reflecting (on) its own form, suspends its own impulse towards domination. Thus Adorno argues on the one hand that 'the mimesis of works of art is resemblance to themselves' and on the other that this self-resembling produces an affinity with what lies outside the artwork: 'expression in art is mimetic, just as the expression of living creatures is the expression of pain' (Adorno quoted in Nicholsen 146). This last gnomic pronouncement makes it clear that the artwork operates by a form of *non-conceptual analogy*: *The Odyssey* is capable of registering (or more precisely, 'prevented from forgetting') the death of the maidservants only by its own 'twitching'. Critical or material mourning would be this empathic twitching or flinching of form, the refusal/inability of the artwork to maintain its own protective shield.

Post-apartheid literature and the critique of reconciliation

The Truth and Reconciliation Commission (TRC) represents a classic example of the equation that Lloyd positions himself against: the multiple traumas of the apartheid era were memorialized through a series of hearings in which both victims and perpetrators were called upon to testify, to serve as witnesses and confessors to a range of human rights violations.[8] Although the commission repeatedly attempted to reassure its audience that forgiving did not mean forgetting, its emphasis on the cathartic power of (re)telling painful stories in public, its power to grant amnesty in return for full disclosure of crimes committed during apartheid, and its tendency to absorb disparate—and disparately motivated—individual narratives into a national narrative of reconciliation had a similar effect to the Irish state's attempt to memorialize the Famine, namely the production (in theory at least) of 'good' or 'docile' citizens. To requote Lloyd: 'the overcoming of loss is achieved by the direction of the subject towards identification with the state' (218). The hegemonic force of the TRC is reflected in the reception of post-apartheid literature as literature of, or for, reconciliation, as if such literature's primary role was to replicate and extend, rather than critique, the TRC's mourning work. Critical Mourning thus names the recalcitrance of this literature, the way in which even those texts that set out to endorse the project of national reconciliation end up exposing its contradictions.

Here I have space to mention only two works. The first I mention briefly as an example of a text that attempts to endorse the project of reconciliation and the second I deal with more fully in order to show how its critical distance from the attempt to produce a unified national subject allows for a mimetic affirmation of corporeal community.

Sindiwe Magona's *Mother to Mother* explicitly addresses itself to the American mother of a white woman killed in a black township by the narrator's son, only to jeopardize its own reconciliatory impulse by jamming the TRC's narrative of personal responsibility: just as she refuses to claim responsibility either for her son's birth (figured as an immaculate conception) or his upbringing (disrupted by the long hours she was forced to work as a domestic servant), she pictures her son as 'only an agent, executing the long-simmering dark desires of his race' (210). Anger at the bleak conditions that determined her son's actions (in particular the family's forced removal to the bleak environment of the Cape Flats) outweighs the novel's ostensible impulse towards reconciliation: despite its best intentions, the novel is in secret accord with Lloyd's rhetorical question: 'would not rage be a more proper response to those deaths and other sufferings for which our mourning is redundant?' (221). During the TRC hearings mourning, far from being understood as redundant, was cast as the potential agent of reconciliation, a collective joining in condolence, as Mark Sanders describes it.[9] But as *Mother to Mother* reveals, the 'end' of grief may not be reconciliation but a rage that learns to redirect itself not, as in the normative psychoanalytic account, against the lost object but against the state itself. A decade and a half after the TRC submitted its report, the Khulumani Support Group, initially set up to provide psychological support for the bereaved, has found its vocation in holding the state to account.[10] In the absence of the structural economic reparations that the TRC initially promised, grief can operate to suspend rather than confirm the subject's submission to 'therapeutic modernity'.

The title of my second example, Ingrid de Kok's cycle of poems 'A Room Full of Questions', would seem to draw an analogy between the space of the hearings and the lyric space of witnessing that the poems themselves constitute. However, the title also intimates a critical doubling, a turning of tables, in which it is the Commission, rather than the witness, that is questioned, for the way in which trauma is 'transpose[d] into the dialectic of record' (Kok 'Parts of Speech'). Instead of reproducing the testimony and thereby turning the grief and/or guilt of others into elegiac (and thus consolatory) lyric, the poems testify to the pain of the testimonial process itself, establishing a mimetic or non-linguistic form of solidarity with the witness called upon to turn trauma into words. Critical mourning here amounts to the suspension of the memorializing function of the TRC, the refusal to become complicit in the therapeutic reproduction of a compliant post-apartheid subject.

Crucially, the poems are only able to open up this mimetic space of solidarity through a form of auto-critique, a critique of their own lyric form. The cycle of poems was first published as part of de Kok's 2002 collection, *Terrestrial Things*, a title taken from Hardy's famous elegy, 'The Darkling Thrush', in which the poet is perplexed by the thrush's 'ecstatic sound' because there seems to him 'So little cause for carolings … written on terrestrial things.' The ecstatic caroling of Hardy's thrush sings of 'some blessed hope' to which the poet himself does not have access. While lyric poetry is traditionally aligned with song, Hardy's elegy complicates this traditional association: song, hope, is now something outside the poem's orbit. In interview, de Kok responds to the suggestion that references in her poems to birds and birdsong are about 'challenging readers to redefine conventional understandings of freedom' with the counter-possibility that 'I am trying to redefine, for myself, aspects of the lyric as "song" or as imagined transcendence' (Kelly 35). As we shall see, in de Kok's poetry freedom is glimpsed not through transcendence but precisely through suspending the lyric poem's ability to transcend terrestrial things.

The last verse of Hardy's elegy forms the epigraph to de Kok's collection, and seems to announce the depths of the despair to which the poet has been brought by her witnessing of terrestrial things. This sense of a blasted, almost apocalyptic terrestriality is enhanced by the cover artwork, a photomontage by Jane Alexander featuring a mournful therianthropic creature in a bleak, recognizably South African landscape of scrubland and *koppie* (rocky outcrop). Its outsized, wide open eyes and ears render it hyper-receptive, while its sealed and shadowed muzzle indicate an inability to speak of what it has seen and heard.

This mute, naked figure is described in interview by de Kok as a 'strangely tender construction', an almost oxymoronic phrase that tells us much about the mixture of closeness and distance that marks the poems' relation to the 'common corporeal vulnerability', the common terrestriality, of those who come before the TRC. The poems respond mimetically to the spectacle of 'damaged life' (Adorno's phrase) by focusing on the physical impact of testimony, both on those who testify and on those who receive the testimony. Noting that, among the professionals engaged in TRC reporting, the highest turnover was apparently among reporters editing sound for radio, she even includes a poem in which the blood of a sound engineer 'drums the vellum of his brain' until he 'hears/ his own tympanic membrane tear'. The imagery used throughout is markedly anti-metaphorical in its refusal of abstraction, its insistence on the bodily, relentlessly terrestrial nature of hearing.

I have space to focus on just two poems in the cycle. If the first poem I turn to bears witness to how the TRC turned souls into things, the second bears witness to an animistic ritual that might reendow things, discarded corporeal matter, with souls.[11]

'Parts of Speech', which opens the cycle, does not concern a specific testimony, but is instead a meditation on a difficulty, perhaps even a core inexpressibility, at the heart of traumatic testimony:

> Some stories don't want to be told.
> They walk away, carrying their suitcases
> Held together with grey string.
> Look at their disappearing curved spines.
> Hunchbacks. Harmed ones. Hold-alls.

The poem countermands the TRC's cathartic slogan that 'revealing is healing', 'terrestrializing' the very possibility of revelation. Those who bring these untellable stories to the 'Room Full of Questions' are present only as their own baggage, as suitcases fragilely held together with grey string. The untellability of the stories is indicated by their materiality, first as suitcases and then as figures that lie somewhere between suitcases and human beings. As they walk away, defeated, weighed down by the burdens which they embody, we are invited to note their 'disappearing curved spines'; they exist somewhere between human hunchbacks and 'hold-alls', humans that have been transmogrified into objects not only by the inhuman, brutalizing force of apartheid but also by their need to 'hold-all' their pain, as if that pain has become so much a part of them that they cannot afford to share it. Like the cover figure, they have become mute, misshapen bodies lost in their own landscapes of despair.

The second stanza restates this impossibility/refusal of story but complicates it by suggesting that to tell their stories would have been a demeaning show or performance:

> Some stories refuse to be danced or mimed,
> drop their scuffed canes
> and clattering tap-shoes,
> erase their traces in nursery rhymes
> or ancient games like blindman's bluff.

The paradox here is that to speak, to verbalize their losses, would itself be a kind of dumb show, a tap-dance, a mime, at best a nursery rhyme or, most worryingly, a game of blindman's bluff (in which a blindfolded figure is spun around and made to search out comrades without the use of his or her eyes). To suggest that those who testify might in fact find themselves involved in this brutal child's game is to raise the question of whether the process of testimony might constitute a new kind of torture, a dark spectacle of groping in which the witness has once again become the victim.

The third stanza reinforces this suggestion, turning the public process of extracting testimony itself into an industrial process. Far from its promise of cathartic liberation, the TRC's version of therapeutic modernity is revealed to be complicit with the thingification of the human:

> And at this stained place words
> are scraped from resinous tongues,
> wrung like washing, hung on the lines
> of courtroom and confessional,
> transposed into the dialect of record.

The words of the stories that would not be told are nevertheless violently stripped from the body, as if they were membranes attached to the testifiers' tongues, and then 'wrung out like washing' and 'hung' out to dry. The sequence of near and full rhyme (tongues–wrung–hung) suggests an inexorable process, but also a continuing resistance: the words remain scraped rather than spoken, transcribed without ever being verbalized. The process of extracting the testimony seems almost akin to the ancient process of making vellum, paper derived from the split skin of animals.[12] Here it is as if the stories have been stripped from the bodies of the testifiers themselves, as if testimony were a process of flaying live bodies in order to produce a written 'record'.

The poem reaches its nadir at this point, with this vision of testimony as physical torture; the images work in an alarmingly anti-metaphorical way, in mimetic sympathy with the objectification of the witness. However, the last two stanzas shift our attention from the complicity of the TRC to the complicity of lyric poetry, its own potential betrayal of the witnesses' dumb materiality.

> Why still believe stories can rise
> with wings, on currents, as silver flares,
> levitate unweighted by stones,
> begin in pain and move towards grace,
> aerating history with recovered breath?
>
> Why still imagine whole words, whole worlds:
> the flame splutter of consonants,
> deep sea anemone vowels,
> birth-cable syntax, rhymes that start in the heart,
> and verbs, verbs that move mountains?

The question marks effect something like the pause or suspension that Adorno posits at the end of *The Odyssey*, putting on hold the lyrical tradition that would enact a flight from this moment of despair. But the auto-critical turn also allows for the possibility of a 'negated' faith in the poem's own formal nature. Even in the absence of the thrush's 'ecstatic carolings' language itself retains the memory of hope, a messianic motive, a faith in itself that, despite the poet's own crisis of faith, might still move mountains.

'Parts of Speech' thus announces the cycle of poems as witness to a testimonial impasse. A certain distance is maintained between the poet and those who testify before the Commission, a distance brought about by the (near) impossibility of verbalizing trauma. At the same time, a mimetic solidarity is affirmed in so far as the poem, like the disappearing spines, is also weighed down by the weight of the untold stories, also falls into despair at the inadequacy of language. And a secret line of sympathy is established that runs counter to the sympathy of the Commissioners, those who ask the questions and scrape the resinous tongues of those who testify: a sympathy with those who are unable to believe in the banners of the TRC, those who remain outside the ambit of a catharsis that might 'acrate history'.

Corporeal community here names a solidarity between a testimony that retains its silence and a poem that suspends, or at least puts on hold, its own lyric potentiality. The very corporeality of the testifiers becomes their testimony; grief takes on a material weight that, precisely because it remains unverbalized, resists abstraction and thus instrumentalization. The poem 'approximates' the TRC by restaging it as a dumb show, an extra-linguistic mime, that allows testimony to be or embody itself without being transposed 'into the dialect of record'. We might say that the poem, like the therianthropic creature of the cover, corporealizes mourning. In conventional Freudian terms, this refusal of verbalization, substitution and abstraction would be pathologized as melancholia, that state of stasis which refuses to be moved, which refuses the very temporality of mourning. But perhaps this pausing, this lack of movement, is precisely how the artwork resists the historical drive that would appropriate mournful testimony as national archive, and thereby achieve that separation which would allow the nation to move on. Like Benjamin's angel of history, the artwork remembers precisely by refusing the movement of history and the 'homogeneous empty time' in which Benedict Anderson locates the imagined communities of the modern nation state, organized around that universal abstraction of death, the tomb of the unknown soldier. Anderson argues that such tombs have to remain empty in order for the nation's powerful discourses of heroism and sacrifice to function. If, as Marc Redfield writes in a recent reconsideration of Anderson's thesis, 'the corpse may be read as the remainder, the excess that nationalism's official scene of mourning excludes' (68), then de Kok's poem, in its corporealization of testimony, disrupts the national imaginary and instantiates an alternative form of community.

I want to end, though, by considering the cycle's penultimate poem, so as to heed Butler's call to remember those non-national lives that the state has rendered ungrievable. 'Some there be' (32) gestures towards a scene of remembrance that is itself unremembered, an animistic time of remembrance that lies outside the time of the Truth Commission. Appropriately, the poem takes its cue from Apocrypha, from those books that were themselves forgotten, retrospectively excluded from the biblical account of the Jewish people's history because they were not originally written in Hebrew.

Some there be

'There be of them, that have left a name behind, that their praises might be reported. And some there be, which have no memorial, who are perished as though they had never been, and are become as though they had never been born; and their children after them.' APOCRYPHA

> Only the rustle of reeds
> thin pipe smoke
> a flickering paraffin lamp
> women in blankets bent over
> their faces lost to the light.
>
> And remnants:
> gate without hinges
> stones in a half circle
> afterbirths buried in silt.
>
> Can the forgotten
> be born again
> into a land of names?

The poem's opening line recalls Hardy's 'Only a man harrowing clods', the opening line of 'In Time of "The Breaking of Nations"' (1916) which turns away from the noise of war in order to affirm the quiet, restorative rhythms of agricultural labour, deliberate in its belief that these rhythms will 'go onward the same/ though dynasties pass'. De Kok's poem offers no such reassurance in her (anti-)pastoral scene of 'women in blankets' whose faces are 'lost to the light'. These are the unnamed, the unmemorialized, those whose losses will not be the subject of Truth Commissions. We cannot know for sure why these women are gathered, or what they are doing.

However, the second verse speaks of 'remnants' suggesting a rudimentary burial site that is only partially demarcated from the land, itself in danger of being forgotten: 'gate without hinges/ stones in a half circle/ afterbirths buried in silt'. Whether the women are performing their own rites of remembrance is not something which the poem allows us to make out, as if the poem is marking the limits of its own memorial power—even as it gestures beyond its own limits to the possible powers of conjuration demarcated by the women's half-circle, a 'damaged' version, perhaps, of the magic circle with which humans once endowed the world with spirit.[13] The poem contains the memory of a magical power to which, like the thrush's song, it no longer has access, an inner circle that, unlike Freud's protective shield, would leave open the possibility of exchange between self and world, the human and the non-human. One might say that the poem's very inability to name the scene is precisely what gives rise to a non-conceptual, non-verbal affinity between the poem and those who reside in the land beyond names.

And perhaps one should leave things there, except for the insistence of the final, questioning stanza. I do not think that much would be served by hauling such women before the TRC, by extending its remit of remembrance beyond the spectacular abuses of human rights to the realm of what Laura Brown has termed 'everyday' or 'insidious trauma'. This would be to recall the women to that particular 'land of names' that is the modern nation state, to recall them only to absorb them into a different form of anonymity and objectification. The challenge is to reimagine what 'a land of names' might consist of, and the clue lies in the poem's mention of 'afterbirths buried in silt'. For this burial site may not be a graveyard in the modern sense of the word, not a place of the dead. Alongside the forgetful temporality of modernity, alongside that alienated sense of belonging that comes with the idea of land ownership, cultures exist, in Africa and elsewhere, in which one buries a child's afterbirth in order to secure the future of the child, to protect it from harm, to prevent it from straying too far from the land in which that which once connected it to its mother, that corporeal evidence of its and our interconnectedness, is buried.[14] Such burial rites allow us to dream of a different land of names, a place where, to recall the mysterious ending of J. M. Coetzee's *Foe*, 'bodies are their own signs' (157).

From Freud's protective shield, that protects only by sealing the subject off from the external world, we have arrived at a very different conception of protection, whereby safety is ensured only by acknowledging corporeal connection. Might this poem, or rather the rites that it barely mimes, teach us a different form of *nostos*, a different sense of return that has to do with belonging but not with ownership? And does it matter that these women are forced to bury their afterbirths in silt, in shifting sands that can only provide an uncertain burial and thus an uncertain future for the women's children? Or is silt, in fact, the very proof that land itself is not fixed, that its very fertility is predicated on geological movement? Freud speaks of trauma as a point where 'there is no longer any possibility of preventing the mental apparatus from being flooded' (301). But perhaps, while not forgetting the many ways in which we are overwhelmed by 'external' forces that painfully remind us of our constitutive vulnerability, we should also learn to think of the self, trauma and flooding in a different light:

> You know they straightened out the Mississippi River in places, to make room for houses and liveable acreage. Occasionally the river floods these places. 'Floods' is the word they use, but in fact it is not flooding; it is remembering. Remembering where it used to be. ... Still, like water, I remember where I was before I was 'straightened out'.
>
> *(Morrison 199)*

Morrison begins her essay by wryly noting that her presence in an essay collection on autobiography and memoir is 'not entirely a misalliance' (185). She ends it by reminding us that the story of the singular, straightened, biopolitical subject, the story of houses, settlement and liveable acreage, is a story of dominance masquerading as a story of protection, a story no less mythical than the civilization it serves to legitimate.

Notes

1. The OED's primary definition of a vesicle reads: 'a small bladder-like vessel in an animal body; a cavity or cell with a membranous integument; a small sac or cyst'.
2. Nouri Gana nevertheless rightly reminds us, in his contribution to this volume, of the political dangers of assuming all trauma is structural and therefore inevitable.
3. This subtitle itself contains autocritical traces, insofar as my 2004 study, *Postcolonial Narrative and the Work of Mourning*, was indebted to the ethical turn and perhaps insufficiently attentive to the possibilities of a properly materialist mourning.
4. I am thinking of Spivak's essays on Mahasweta Devi as much as her more famous essay 'Can the Subaltern Speak', all three of which end with an image of a female body turned into an image of resistance in the instance of its obliteration. See Durrant, *Postcolonial* 16–17.
5. Lloyd is quoting from the records of the Irish Folklore Commission.
6. Lloyd is aware of the risk of mythologizing the virtue of some pre-modern state of nature: the moral economy of the poor is no more 'natural or primordial' than the capitalism that supplants it (228).
7. Without belittling the contribution of Horkheimer to the *Dialectic of Enlightenment*, it is reasonably well established that Adorno wrote the excursus on *The Odyssey*, and my analysis is informed by my reading of Adorno's later work.
8. TRC's Final report is accessible at http://www.justice.gov.za/trc/report. See vol. 1 for a detailed outline of the Commission's genesis, basis and rationale. I have no space here to rehearse the multiple debates surrounding the TRC. For a trenchant political critique see Mamdani. For an intricate deconstructive consideration, see Sanders.

9 'Mourning would make good for the violations of apartheid. As a system of social separation, apartheid would be undone through condolence' (49). The conditional mood of Sanders analysis indicates another mode of critical suspension; his book is partly a meditation on what the TRC might have been.
10 See the Khulumani group's impressive website at http://www.khulumani.net.
11 In the preface to *The Dialectic of Enlightenment*, Adorno and Horkheimer famously remarked: 'Animism had endowed things with souls; industrialism makes souls into things' (21).
12 Indeed a later poem uses the same image to focus on the reception of the testimony: the tympanic membrane of the sound engineer's inner ear is described as the 'vellum of the brain' (33).
13 'Art has in common with magic the postulation of a special, self-contained sphere removed from the context of profane existence. Within it special laws prevail. Just as the sorcerer begins the ceremony by marking out from all its surroundings the place in which sacred forces come into play, each work of art is closed off from reality by its circumference. The very renunciation of external effects by which art is distinguished from magic binds art only more deeply to the heritage of magic' (Adorno and Horkheimer 13–14).
14 For the amaXhosa, for instance, the burial of the cord and the placenta seals the baby's attachment to his/her ancestral lands and the same word, 'inkaba', is used to denote both the ceremony and this attachment.

Works cited

Adorno, Theodor and Max Horkheimer. *Dialectic of Enlightenment: Philosophical Fragments*. 1944. Trans. Edmund Jephcott. Ed. Gunzelin Schmid Noerr. Stanford: Stanford UP, 2002.
Anderson, Benedict. *Imagined Communities: Reflections on the Origins and Spread of Nationalism*. London: Verso, 1983.
Benjamin, Walter. 'The Storyteller' and 'Theses on the Philosophy of History'. In Hannah Arendt, ed. *Illuminations*. Trans. Harry Zohn. London: Continuum, 1970. 83–108 and 253–65.
Bhabha, Homi. 'DisemiNation: Time, Narrative and the Margins of the Modern Nation.' *The Location of Culture*. London: Routledge, 1994. 139–70.
Butler, Judith. *Bodies That Matter: On the Discursive Limits of Sex*. London: Routledge, 1993.
Butler, Judith. *The Psychic Life of Power: Theories in Subjection*. Stanford: Stanford UP, 1997.
Butler, Judith. *Precarious Life: The Powers of Mourning and Violence*. London: Verso, 2004.
Brown, Laura S. *Cultural Competence in Trauma Therapy: Beyond the Flashback*. Washington: American Psychological Association, 2008.
Coetzee, J.M. *Foe*. 1986. Harmondsworth: Penguin, 1987.
Durrant, Sam. *Postcolonial Narrative and the Work of Mourning: J. M. Coetzee, Wilson Harris and Toni Morrison*. Albany: SUNY Press, 2004.
Freud, Sigmund. *Beyond the Pleasure Principle*. 1920. In Angela Richards, ed. *On Metapsychology: The Theory of Psychoanalysis*. Trans. James Strachey. London: Penguin, 1991. 269–339.
Kelly, Erica. 'Strangely Tender: an Interview with Ingrid de Kok.' *Scrutiny 2: Issues in English Studies in South Africa* 8.1 (May 2003): 34–38.
Kok, Ingrid de. *Terrestrial Things*. Cape Town: Kwela/Snailpress, 2002.
Lloyd, David. 'Colonial Trauma/ Postcolonial Recovery?' *Interventions* 2.2 (2000): 212–28.
Luckhurst, Roger. *The Trauma Question*. London: Routledge, 2008.
Magona, Sindiwe. *Mother to Mother*. Boston: Beacon, 1998.
Mamdani, Mahmood. 'Amnesty of Impunity? A Preliminary Critique of the Report of the Truth and Reconciliation Commission of South Africa (TRC).' *Diacritics* 32.3–4 (2002): 33–59.
Morrison, Toni. 'The Site of Memory.' In William Zinsser, ed. *Inventing the Truth: The Art and Craft of Memoir*. Boston: Houghton Mifflin, 1987. 103–24.
Nicholsen, Shierry Weber. *Exact Imagination, Late Work: on Adorno's Aesthetics*. Cambridge MA: MIT Press, 1997.

Quint, David. *Epic and Empire: Politics and Generic Form from Virgil to Milton*. Princeton: Princeton UP, 1993.
Redfield, Marc. *The Politics of Aesthetics: Nationalism, Gender, Romanticism*. Stanford: Stanford UP, 2003.
Rushdie, Salman. *The Satanic Verses*. Dover: Consortium, 1988.
Sanders, Mark. *Ambiguities of Witnessing: Law and Literature in the Time of a Truth Commission*. Stanford: Stanford UP, 2007.
Spivak, Gayatri. *In Other Worlds*. London: Routledge, 1987.

PART II
Politics and subjectivity

7

'THAT WHICH YOU ARE DENYING US'

Refugees, rights and writing in Arendt

Lyndsey Stonebridge

> A life without speech ... is literally dead to the world.
> *Hannah Arendt,* The Human Condition

In 2002, the refugee inmates of Woomera detention camp in south Western Australia sewed their lips together in protest against their incarceration. It is hard to think of a more eloquent image of the pathos of traumatic speech than a mouth transformed into a wound. Equally, it is hard not to see the future of trauma theory as bound to the political fate of today's refugees. If trauma theory began with the memory of the camps of the Holocaust, we could claim that its contemporary relevance endures most pressingly in the detention centres of the twenty-first century. These histories are not unconnected. Hannah Arendt was among the first to point out that the legal limbo into which the Jews were thrown by the denial of legal citizenship was a prelude to the extermination camps; 'a condition of complete rightlessness was created before the right to live was challenged' (Arendt 1949: 29; 2004: 374). More recently Giorgio Agamben has claimed a 'perfectly real filiation' between the refugee, internment, concentration, and death camps (Agamben 21).[1]

With its unforgettable imagery and partial political success (the camp was closed in 2003), the Woomera protest generated much theoretical work in the then relatively new interdisciplinary field of critical refugee studies. Unsurprisingly, given the number of exiled artists and intellectuals in the camp, it also produced some remarkable poetry. The poem most often reprinted and cited in discussions of Woomera is Iranian Mehmet al Assad's sadly ironic protest 'Asylum'. In the poem's final stanza, al Assad pulls the association between the sutured mouth and rightlessness central to the protest together in an elegant admonishment to those looking through from the other side of the wire, the rights-rich nationals of the West:

> Through the wire
> one last time
> please observe
> I am sewing my lips together
> that which you are denying us
> we should never have
> had to ask for.[2]

In much of the commentary these lines are read, not unreasonably, as a plea that the speaker's humanity be observed and that his rights as a human being be recognized too: 'that which' he should never have had to ask for.[3] The refugee poet, in other words, is assumed to be a kind of testifying supplicant, a ghost person, or a lyrical person (after all, he is writing a poem), asking to be recognized as a legal person. See me, the human being through the wire, the poet says, and on the basis of that recognition—a recognition made possible by poetry—grant me my rights.

But while that 'that which' could be human rights, as its pronominal heaviness might suggest, equally it could be something more elusive. As much as the lines run to a conclusion that the speaker be granted something that, because it is self-evidently his (the poem shows us so), he should never have had to ask for, the line breaks introduce a series of hesitations, stops or stutters, into the passage from lyrical to legal personhood: 'that which you are denying us/ we should never have/ had to ask for'. What is revealed in these pauses is less (or at least not only) the person that the poem gives the illusion is there waiting to be granted his rights, than a voice far less sure of its ground. Note, for example, how the line 'we should never have' hovers for a moment, both on the end of its line and in grammatical time, resting on the possibility of an entire life without rights. An alternative reading of al Assad's lines might conclude that it is precisely the 'that which', of which he is denied, of which he should never have had to ask, that the speaker is calling into question by asking us to read 'through' the wire of his words.

I begin with al Assad's 'Asylum' because it suggests a direction for trauma theory through which the pathos of the open wound (a speechlessness always demanding to be spoken) might be reconnected to what I describe here as a more critical lyricism in refugee writing that emerged with the denial of national, civic and legal rights identified by Arendt in the 1940s. The emergence of new refugee populations over the past twenty years means that the continuities between generations of the rightless are now becoming apparent; indeed, al Assad could almost be talking directly to Arendt when he de-couples his human speaker from the 'human' rights he is claiming in his poem. 'The paradox involved in the loss of human rights', Arendt wrote famously 'is that such a loss coincides with the moment a person becomes a human being in general.' In recent theory this bitingly eloquent sentence has become one of the most frequently quoted passages from *The Origins of Totalitarianism* (1951). Arendt first wrote the lines, however, within ten years of her own internment (as an enemy alien) in Gurs detention camp in south-west France, her flight across the Spanish border, and eventual arrival in the United States

(Arendt 1949: 33). Now you don't see it, now you do: as in al Assad's poem, for Arendt the refugee and theorist of statelessness, the human person appears just as her human rights are withdrawn.

Frequently cast as a figure of pathos, this frail human remnant stalks contemporary rights discourses; a stubborn reminder that, while the fiction of human nature may have lost whatever juridical purchase it once had, its shadow still remains. Arendt's tremulous 'human being in general', we might say in the context of the project of this book, is what is left after trauma. This figure is as central to law as it is to theory: the United Nations' 1951 'Convention Relating to the Status of Refugees' defines a refugee not as a person who is entitled to rights that she has been denied, but as one who can demonstrate that she lives in fear for her life.[4] Pathos, to some extent, has become a legal requirement for today's asylum seekers (see Pupavec; Malkki). Writing from deep within the experience of statelessness, Arendt, however, refuses to consign the refugee to the position of a quivering supplicant before the law. That refusal, I argue in this essay, is both linguistic and political. For Arendt the refugee (she was to spend 17 years of her life classified as stateless person), as for al Assad later, to claim rights is first of all to criticize the linguistic and political mystifications upon which they rest.

'A new kind of human beings'

Crossing from continent to continent, moving between languages, disciplines and genres, Arendt understood more than most just how intimate the relation between writing and legal subjectivity could be, and just how fraught. She wrote frequently and furiously on her arrival in New York in 1942: on the war, Jewish politics, homelands wrecked, homelands future (she published 38 essays, articles and reviews alone between 1943 and 1947). The experience of statelessness is lived on the page in these pieces, not only in the intensity of the writing, but in Arendt's struggle to inhabit linguistically the political–legal paradox that she was at the same time beginning to recognize and theorize. In both style and substance, this early writing asks what it might mean to speak as a 'human being in general', without the protection of sovereign rights.

The first thing it means is that speech itself is cut loose, not only from the law but from its speaker. 'We lost our language', Arendt writes at the beginning of 'We Refugees', a 1943 essay first published in the *Menorah Journal* in the January of the year that news of the full horror of the camps first seeped through to the refugee community. Losing one's language is not only to be denied a linguistic anchorage to nation and tradition, it also means losing 'the naturalness of reactions, the simplicity of gestures, the unaffected expression of feelings' (Arendt 2007: 264).[5] We lost the right to lyrical ease we might almost read Arendt as saying here, to the unaffected representation of feelings and suffering in our mother tongue. In fact, Arendt's voice in this essay is not so much lost, as purposefully restless. For the Jewish refugee, losing the lyrical immediacy one feels in one's own language is to lose something you had never had in an uncomplicated way in the first place. 'To know how to play the role of what one actually was seemed the most important thing' (Arendt 1951: 81), she later quipped of the ontological predicament of middle-class Jews in Europe in the late eighteenth and early nineteenth centuries.

By 1943, the refugee has nothing more to gain from self-mimicry. It is thus not only with a sense of mourning, but liberated ironic bitterness that Arendt writes most of 'We Refugees' in free indirect speech, citing rather than inhabiting the experience of the 'we' of whom she speaks in the distancing irony that was to become her linguistic trademark. In 'We Refugees' we could not be further from the fearfully suffering human voice expected of much contemporary refugee testimony (see Szörényi). Ducking and diving between (in the famous terms she borrows from Bernard Lazare) the affectation of the parvenue who would attempt to assimilate into her host culture and language, and the protesting irony of the pariah, the essay is a controlled performance of the very linguistic un-housing she at the same time describes. The 'we' of the title turns out to be something of an unaccomodating pronoun. Watch it slide, for example, in this acerbic rendering of the self-deluding linguistic compliance of the parvenu:

> With the language, however, we find no difficulties: after a single year optimists are convinced they speak English as well as their mother tongue; and after two years they swear solemnly that they speak English better than any other language—their German is a language they hardly remember.
>
> *(Arendt 1943: 265)*

The distancing irony ('we' slides into 'they') is typical of the tone that will later so trouble readers of *Eichmann in Jerusalem* (1963). But what looks like loftiness here is also a complicated kind of identification. What the parvenue is struggling to forget in the conceit that she speaks perfect English is the new political and existential status that Arendt was discovering for herself. The very next paragraph reads:

> In order to forget more efficiently we rather avoid any allusion to concentration or internment camps ... how often have we been told that nobody likes to listen to all that ... Apparently nobody wants to know that contemporary history has created a new kind of human beings—the kind that are put in concentration camps by their foes and in internment camps by their friends.
>
> *(265)*

'A new kind of human beings', the kind that emerge at the very moment that so-called human rights are withdrawn. 'The paradox involved in the loss of human rights is that such a loss coincides with the moment a person becomes a human being in general': Arendt first rehearses (or perhaps even discovers) her famous paradox in a piece of writing in which she is, we could say, most biographically true to her own history. True in the sense that her linguistic ducking and diving speaks directly to the sense that the 'human' so unceremoniously dumped by rights law cannot magically re-authorize itself by speech alone, and true too in the sense that speech itself cannot comfortably accommodate these new strangers. 'A new kind of beings'; those who apparently nobody wants to know first emerge in her writing through an arresting grammatical awkwardness. Arendt's voice stutters in its new language.

'A new kind of human beings' is archaic rather than grammatically inaccurate. Most of us who have attempted to speak or write in another language (English was Arendt's third) have used awkward grammar. 'I still speak with a very heavy accent, and I often speak unidiomatically', she later said in an interview on German television with Gunter Gaus in 1964 (Arendt 2000: 13). She was talking about the distance she felt from her English voice, and how the traces of the mother tongue in the new language testify to a kind of linguistic survival. Traces, perhaps, such as you can hear rippling across the translation of cases from German— *eine neue Art Menschen*—into English—'a new kind of human beings'.[6] It is telling enough that this translation effect occurs just after Arendt has admonished her fellow refugees for pretending to forget their mother tongue. More significant for the critical tradition in refugee writing I want to uncover here, however, is the fact that her language hesitates, so to speak, on the very category that the parvenue is anxious to disguise in her new language: the new human beings created by contemporary history, the radically rightless, the refugee, the detention camp inmate, who are now equivocating, as it were, between German and English, pariah and parvenu, in the same way as they are suspended in legal and political limbo. As in the later more deliberate hesitations of 'Asylum', in 'We Refugees' in 1943, it is as if to be lost to the law is also to lose one's way in language.

Because it (almost by definition) claims rights denied, refugee writing frequently puts the relations between law, language and humanity in question in ways such as this. Conventionally, much human rights testimony insists on the humanity of its speaker by borrowing from lyric an emphasis on individual feeling and suffering (its 'testamentary whimper' in Avital Ronell's evocative phrase). Rights, in this sense, are rewarded for the ability to voice the human. In the granting of a common personhood, the rents (the traumas) in law and language experienced by the refugee are passed (and pasted) over. Arendt's ducking and diving and grammatical awkwardness, on the other hand, like al Assad's hesitations, suggests a far more uncomfortable and critical relationship between the voices of the rightless and the law.

The intimate, and often vexed, relations between lyric and law were first noted by the late Barbara Johnson in her brilliant discussion of the relation between the laws of genre and the laws of the US constitution. What is always at stake in both legal and lyric texts, Johnson argued, is 'the question: What is a person?' (Johnson 551). On the one hand, because they assume that the human can be defined, because they are supremely anthropomorphic, lyrical texts allow the law to presuppose what a person is 'without the question of its definition being raised as a question—legal or otherwise' (574). Hence lyric supports rather than challenges the assumptions law makes about humanity. But at the same time, the very anthropomorphism that lyric needs in order to work reveals that the 'person' it treats as somehow already known is linguistic before it is anything else and hence can be—must in the end be—questioned. Recasting that argument for Arendt's 'new kind of human beings', and for refugee writing in general, we might then next ask what happens when language kicks away that support and deprives the law of its human alibi—its 'that which' which it never wants to define, but which has to be assumed for human rights law to keep face? In other words: what does refugee writing do to the conventional relationship between literary and legal persons?

Of all genres, lyrical texts, Paul de Man famously argued (de Man is at the heart of Johnson's essay), are most homesick for the mystical permanence of the human; the lyric voice, he says, is a fallacious mourning for human persons, looking to forge 'eternity and temporal harmony as voice as song' in their absence (de Man 262). If we wanted to read refugee writing as a kind of post-nation state late lyric, which is one of the implications of my reading of Arendt, we might say that it instead follows de Man's austere prescription for a truer, more critical mourning for the human in its decoupling of humanity and language. No good will come of pathos, the best we can do with language, de Man advised, is to 'allow for non-comprehension' (262).

In much recent theory, that linguistic moment has been aligned with historical traumas, such that 'non-comprehension' has come to describe (often at once) both our response to atrocity and the inability of language to hold traumatic experience. Although concerned with the same problems of linguistic referentiality, the critical lyricism of refugee writing I am tracing here suggests a different approach to the understanding of trauma. If the experience of statelessness uncouples the voice from the human, and hence from human rights law, it does not follow that the connections between linguistic and legal life should forever remain a mystery. If Arendt has a contribution to make to the future of trauma theory, I would argue in this respect, it is because of the political emphasis she brings to the project of understanding trauma. 'Comprehension', she insisted in the preface to *Origins of Totalitarianism*, 'means the unpremeditated attentive facing up to, and resisting of, reality—whatever it may be' (Arendt 2004: xxvi). An attentive facing up to, and resisting of, a reality we do not, and possibly cannot, know (the prescription sounds far more psychoanalytic than she would have liked); Arendt is clearly neither making a simple claim about understanding, nor advocating a return to a moment before trauma. Neither, however, will she ever concede that the human persons so incomprehensibly lost to rights law are lost too to politics or language, particularly, as it turns out, literary language.

Instead, her new kind of human beings demand a new kind of political and linguistic home.[7] Back in the mid-1940s, at the very moment she finds herself a stranger in a new land, Arendt discovers a model for that new home in, of all people to bring into a discussion of human rights perhaps, Kafka.

Jew-stranger

Of course, it is not that surprising that Arendt should have turned to Kafka's fiction at precisely the same moment as she was wondering just what was left of the human in human rights. Kafka's writing is notoriously resistant to anthropological interpretations as her friend, Walter Benjamin, first pointed out. Few of us finish a Kafka novel knowing what a person is.[8] Kafka starts from within the very linguistic un-housing that Arendt identified as the lot of the refugee. Writing, as he put it famously in a letter to Max Brod, from the ashes of a German uniquely summoned to life by Jewish hands, his fiction provides the newly English-speaking Arendt with the literary correlatives for the 'new kinds of human beings' she first discovered in Gurs detention camp, and in the refugee communities of Paris and New York.[9]

Arendt published twice on Kafka in 1944 (one year after 'We Refugees' was first published), first as part of the essay 'The Jew as a Pariah', in *Jewish Social Studies*, and second, in more depth, in her 'revaluation' for *Partisan Review*, on the twentieth anniversary of his death (Arendt 1944, 1994).[10] Two years later she would help prepare an edition of his *Diaries* for Schocken Press (Brod's sloppiness apparently made this hard work) (Young-Bruehl 189).

It is in K of *Das Schloß* (*The Castle*), in particular, that Arendt discovers a fictional model for the paradox lived by the rightless. K, the everyman stranger, and like Arendt a Jew-stranger, pulls the anthropomorphic rug from beneath the feet of the law (or what passes for the law) simply by asking (as al Assad will later) that his rights be observed. Called to the Castle for what he thought was a job offer (as for many of today's migrants, mistaking an invitation to work turns out to be his first error), but stubbornly refusing to disappear when the job appears to vanish, K exemplifies the plight of the stranger in a bureaucratized nation state. As the landlady reminds him: 'You're not from the Castle, you're not from the village, you are nothing (*Sie sind nicht aus dem Schloß, Sie sind nicht aus dem Dorfe, Sie sind nichts*). Unfortunately, though, you are something, a stranger (*Leider aber sind Sie doch etwas, ein Fremder*), one who is superfluous and gets in the way everywhere, one who is a constant source of trouble.' (Kafka 1997: 69). J. Hillis Miller has recently written of Kafka's extraordinary prescience in anticipating the Holocaust. Pressed up close against that moment precisely as it unravelled, Arendt seizes on Kafka's similarly acute understanding of the connection between being deprived of rights and the horror of a future that cannot be resolved (Kafka could never bring himself to finish *The Castle*).

The political, as well as moral and human, urgency of that moment in the early 1940s might be why Arendt chooses to read K as a human rights activist, a sort of literary-fictional advocate for the new persons disclosed in her paradox. 'His desires are directed toward those things to which all men have a natural right. He is, in a word, the typical man of goodwill', she writes, demanding no more than 'every man's right' (Arendt 1944: 292). Unlike the timid and self-deceiving parvenues in her own essay, K speaks up 'for the average small-time Jew who really wants no more than his rights as a human being: home, work, family and citizenship' (292). But K's activism is not a straightforward claim to rights deprived. He conspicuously lacks the empathy of the humanitarian rights' worker and is unmoved by the stories of misery, suffering and injustice he hears from the villagers, the 'grim and ghastly tales', Arendt calls them, invested with 'that strange poetic quality so common in folk-tales of enslaved peoples' (295). This deaf ear to the poetic qualities of human suffering (which some critics would say is also her own) for Arendt is a refusal on Kafka's part 'to accept the "magic"' that turns narratives of political injustice at the hands of the Castle, into folktales about human fate; 'the nauseating conceit', as she later describes it, 'which identifies evil and misfortune with destiny' (Arendt 2004: 316). To this extent, *The Castle* is also an object lesson, perhaps before the world knew it needed it, in the inability of humanitarian sentiment to secure political rights.[11]

If K is in a unique position to expose the poverty of rights under the Castle's regime, this is not because of any particular human or moral sensibility on his part, he is no more or no less human than the next person, but simply because he has no other refuge other than in the idea that universal rights might actually exist. It is only because K attempts to become an 'indistinguishable' generic rights-bearing human person, Arendt argues, to do what the world wishes all strangers would do (as nineteenth-century Europe wished all Jews would do)—renounce his race and, culture, and stand, alone, among men—that he becomes such an enthusiastic advocate of universal human rights in the first place (Arendt 1944: 291). Like many refugees, then, K exposes the fiction behind human rights simply by having the audacity to believe that as a human person he is entitled to them. At the same time, however, K's status as a 'human being general' is conditional upon his prior difference – his strangeness – from the villagers; one might almost say that this difference (and hence his lack of human rights) defines his universality (as a general human being). If the paradox of the rightless is that the loss of human rights coincides with 'the moment a person becomes a human being in general', in *The Castle* the human being in general is the Jew-stranger, the outsider who exposes the paradox simply in his struggle to live it.

But it is not just K's advocacy for the rights of strangers that makes *The Castle* such an important text for both Arendt and, I would argue, for the history of refugee writing. As important is how Kafka answers, or more precisely refuses to answer, the question 'what is a person?' If lyrical and legal texts, to recall Johnson's argument, are tied together in their answer to that question, and if lyric sometimes appears to answer it for the law too effortlessly, uncritically, Kafka's writing changes the terms of that mutually supportive relation entirely. His characters are strange not (just) because they behave weirdly, or because they seem so insouciantly unaware of the rules governing the plausible behaviour of persons in novels, but also because they have none of that enigmatic humanity that modern literature, for de Man at least, appears to mourn. Arendt puts it more forcefully: Kafka's characters, she writes, have 'little to do with that modern complication of the inner life which is always looking out for new and unique techniques to express new and unique feelings' (Arendt 1994: 70). No ostentatious lyricism—no compelling performance of human feeling—in Kafka then. And for good reason, for to cast K as a complicated human character who voices his anguished claim for legal and political recognition on the basis of a unaffectedly felt inner life would be to miss the critique of the dubious anthropomorphism of rights that Kafka is making here. If K is a stripped-down kind of literary being, lacking, as Arendt puts it, 'the many superfluous detailed characteristics which together make up a real individual', this is because, like his maker, he is not of the world he lives in (75). And, again, for good reason; for to be 'real' in such a world would be to be complicit with a regime in which rights are but mystifications of power. In Arendt's boldly political reading, Kafka is building a different kind of home for the rightless.

> If a man builds a house or if he wants to know a house well enough to be able to foretell its stability, he will get a blueprint of the building or draw one up himself. Kafka's stories are such blueprints; they are the product of thinking rather than of mere sense experience.
>
> *(76)*

Kafka, the unacknowledged architect of the world of rights yet to come. Is Kafka's fiction, then, a place that Arendt's new kind of human beings can finally inhabit?

Or is this home a piece of late modernist architecture too austere for today's humanitarian sensibilities? Has K arrived too late? Arendt's Kafka pointedly thinks rather than feels; he is a maker of new kinds of modern persons, not a mourner for the human. Many of Arendt's critics have fairly commented that her attachment to political reason blocks her understanding of sense experience, of the emotions, of suffering, even of trauma itself. But while the demand for testimonies of human suffering keeps pace with the production of the barbed wire encircling ever larger, and ever more permanent, detention camps, while no amount of anguished testimony to the trauma of statelessness seems to have any impact on the conditions which create it, perhaps we could do worse than to attend once more to Arendt's critical, reasoned and dispassionate voicing of the trauma of rightlessness.

Jew-stranger, Arab-stranger

In this essay I have been arguing that Arendt's writing discloses the political and historical frailty of grounding rights in an injured or enigmatic humanity. Writing in the most intense period of her own statelessness, for Arendt to claim, rights in the name of a putative humanity is to leave intact a concept of rights that speaks only to the caprices of political power. On the other hand, it is because the refugee speaks from within the collapse of an anthropological grounding of rights that this bitter truth is exposed. It is because the castle is so unaccommodating to the stranger that K can build a prototype for an 'ideal of humanity' that doesn't have to suffer in order to be granted rights. One reason for welcoming the recent return to Arendt in the wake of trauma theory is her refusal to consign the stateless and rightless to pathos. In this, she does more than simply 'allow' for non-comprehension (the rest point of much trauma theory); her writing also 'faces up' to a reality in which the connection between language, rights, and the human needs to be rethought altogether.

The new kind of human beings that emerge from Arendt's writing will not shore up the ruins of anyone's castle with their suffering humanity. Neither, however, can they exist alone, unprotected. The right to have rights, Arendt will later claim, is not a right that derives from an assumed humanity, but is the right we all have to confer rights upon one another within a political community. The dilemma Arendt leaves us with finally, as did so many writers of her generation, is how that community might be imagined. 'More intensely even than in solitude, Kafka lived in the difficult situation of one who recognizes the temptations and terrors of saying "we"', writes Vivian Liska in her beautifully rich study of the difficulties of imagining communities in modern Jewish writing (25).[12] Arendt, too, lived at a moment when that situation had become intolerable. For her generation saying 'we' had become both necessary and, for many, truly terrifying.

'If we should start telling the truth that we are nothing but Jews it would mean that we expose ourselves to the fate of human beings who, unprotected by any specific law or political convention, are nothing but human beings' (Arendt 2007: 273). At the end of 'We Refugees', Arendt writes (finally we might feel) 'we' from a firmly collective and non-ironic sense of despair. Being nothing more than Jews, amounts to being nothing more than human: in this sense at least, 'we' commune as collective outlaws. 'A true human life cannot be led by people who feel themselves detached from the basic and simple laws of humanity', she similarly concludes her reading of Kafka. It was 'the perception of this truth that made Kafka a Zionist. In Zionism he saw a means of abolishing the "abnormal" position of the Jews, an instrument whereby they might become a "people like other peoples"' (Arendt 1944: 295).

For Kafka, there was finally no place forward other than back to the concept of nation state, to the very place that had proved itself as capriciously incapable, and often downright unwilling to legislate for universal rights in the first place. The irony of this return to the nation state was not lost on Arendt: 'far from solving' the problem of the stateless, she wrote in *Origins of Totalitarianism*, the foundation of Israel, 'like virtually all other events of the twentieth century … merely produced a new category of refugees, the Arabs' (Arendt 2004: 368). No solution to the plight of the rightless, without the production of new refugees. We too return here to where I began this essay, to an on-going history of rightlessness, of camps, castles and sutured mouths. If al Assad's 'Asylum' flips between making its speaker's humanity a ground for claiming rights, and questioning any existing association between speech, rights and humanity, this is not least because he is still living the paradox Arendt first identified in the 1940s.

'One of these days—when? It doesn't matter when, let's say at some point—I will be able to describe the actual domain political life, because no one is better at marking the borders of a terrain than the person who walks around it from the outside', Arendt wrote to her husband, Heinrich Blücher, in 1955 (Arendt 2000: 236). Walking around the outside, marking the borders rather than hurrying through them, possibly better describes the critical lyricism of refugee writing that I have been trying to trace here than the model of home building Arendt finally, if reluctantly, advocates in 1944.[13] As many contributors to this volume argue, contemporary trauma studies now needs to move its focus from models of European memory and towards the traumas that exist beyond, and increasingly on the frontiers of, the nation state. Following Arendt, and reading through the wire, that shift means being attentive not just to the voices of the new rightless, but also to the paradoxes—political, linguistic and legal—that these voices reveal. Human rights do not travel with human persons; the pained lyricism of the rightless will not always prop up a legally and politically impoverished humanitarianism: these are the messages of the refugees, Jew-strangers, Arab-strangers. 'That which you are denying us' turns out to be the very thing we question.

Acknowledgements

Versions of this essay were originally presented at a 'Colloquium of the Work of Cathy Caruth', at CRASSH, Cambridge University in March 2011, and as a keynote lecture at 'The Future of Testimony' conference in Salford in August 2011. I would like to thank the organizers of and participants in those events, and Cathy Caruth, Yasemin Yildiz and Dennis Kennedy for discussing it with me.

Notes

1 Agamben's claim about direct filiation has not gone uncontested. In an essay which reads the lip sewing at Woomera as an example of political action in Arendt's terms (and to which I'm indebted here), Patricia Owens points out that for Arendt the death camps differed from others because of their unprecedented anti-instrumentality (575).
2 Mehmet al Assad, 'Asylum', first published in *The Age* 18.9 (2002), republished in *Borderlands e-journal* 1.1 (2002). Available online at www.borderlands.net.au/vol1no1_2002/alassad_asylum.html (accessed 14 May 2012). I have not been able to trace any more poems by al Assad in English, and have not been able to ascertain whether the poem was first written in English, or translated. The poet, who repeatedly asked to be observed through the wire (the request to 'please observe' is in all three stanzas of 'Asylum'), seems to have slipped from public view, rather like the ghost person who is both there and not there, seen and not seen, in his original poem. The absence is unnerving, not least because (among other reasons) it echoes the very disappearance of the person of the refugee I trace in this essay.
3 See, for example, Rajaram (2003: 17–19). Rajaram, Jenny Edkins, and Véronique Pin-Fat have stressed how the poem implicates the reader/observer in the denial and recognition of the speaker's rights, a point echoed by David Farrier in his reading of the poem in terms of hospitality (see Farrier 150–52; Edkins and Pin-Fat 19–20; Rajaram 2004: 222–4).
4 Article 1 of the 1951 Convention on Refugees defines a refugee as someone who 'owing to a well-founded fear of being persecuted for reasons of race, religion, nationality, membership of a particular social group or political opinion, is outside the country of his nationality, and is unable to, or owing to such fear, is unwilling to avail himself of the protection of that country'. Available online at www.unhcr.org/protect/PROTECTION/3b66c2aa10.pdf (accessed 18 May 2012).
5 I also discuss the relationship between statelessness and Arendt's style in '"We Refugees": Hannah Arendt and the Perplexities of Human Rights' (Stonebridge 101–17).
6 Derrida has written of the way in which for Arendt (as for many refugees, migrants, displaced persons and exiles) the mother tongue becomes an ambivalent '*remains* of belonging'. As Yasemin Yildiz points out, however, just as Arendt is stating the primacy of German in the original TV recording of her interview with Gaus, 'she is suddenly at a loss for words and briefly switches into English'. The switch gestures towards the

'postmonolingual tensions' at the core of Yildiz's arresting study. In the case of 'a new kind of human beings' these tensions produce an indeterminate kind of 'third' language, the idiom, perhaps, which also best expresses the legal no-man's land of the refugee (see Derrida and Dufourmantelle 89; Yildiz 16).
7 Seyla Benhabib argues that the move between an existential and political account of homelessness is at the centre of Arendt's project (see Benhabib 35–61).
8 Arendt is directly referencing Walter Benjamin's 1934 essay in her own revaluation written ten years later. See Benjamin, 'Franz Kafka: On the Tenth Anniversary of his Death' and 'Some Reflections on Kafka' (see also Hamacher). Arendt's anti-anthropomorphic emphasis can be read as an anticipation of Deleuze and Guattari's celebration of linguistic unhousing in Kafka's writing (see Deleuze and Guattari).
9 '[I]n German ... the linguistic middle ground ... is nothing but embers which can only be brought to a semblance of life when excessively lively Jewish hands rummage through them. That is a fact, funny or terrible as you like' (Kafka 1977: 288).
10 'The Jew as a Pariah: A Hidden Tradition' (1944), reprinted in *The Jewish Writings* and 'Franz Kafka: A Revaluation' (1944), reprinted in *Essays in Understanding, 1930–1954: Formation, Exile and Totalitarianism*. Arendt's Kafka traverses categories and languages, much as his K moves through courtrooms, prison cells, inns, castles, villages and continents. The tensions between parvenu and pariah, refugee and Jew, for instance, so pointedly enacted in 'We Refugees', still echo one year on; in her first discussion of the text, *The Castle* is described as the only novel 'in which the hero is plainly a Jew' (Arendt 1944: 290), whereas in the *Partisan Review* essay K is more neutrally presented as the rightless stranger. The postmonolingual dilemmas at the heart of that earlier piece also continue. Arendt wrote, and later published, German versions of both Kafka essays. Indeed, the English version of the *Partisan Review* essay in Susannah Young-ah Gottlieb's recent collection of Arendt's writing on literature and culture is Martin Klebes's translation of *'Kafka von neuem gewürdigt'*; so you have a piece originally written in English, written again in German by its author, translated back by a second hand (see Ardent, 'Franz Kafka, Appreciated Anew').
11 Jacques Rancière has written of the way that Arendt's account of the decline of the rights of man is 'tailor-made' to describe the 'shift from Man to Humanity and from Humanity to the Humanitarian' over the past twenty years or so (Rancière 298–9).
12 See also Liska's concluding discussion on the differences between Kafka and Arendt, 'The Gap between Hannah and Arendt and Kafka' (Liska 207–12).
13 This passage perhaps also echoes Kafka's description of writing as 'an assault on the frontiers', which, 'if Zionism had not intervened, ... might easily have developed into a new secret doctrine (*zu einer neuen Geheimlehre*), a Kabbalah' (Kafka 1976: 399)

Works cited

Agamben, Giorgio. 'Beyond Human Rights.' In *Means Without End: Notes on Politics*. Trans. Vincenzo Binetti and Cesare Casarino. Minneapolis: U of Minesota P, 2000.
al Assad, Mehmet. 'Asylum.' *Borderlands e-journal* 1.1 (2002). Available online at www.borderlands.net.au/vol1no1_2002/alassad_asylum.html (accessed 14 May 2012).
Arendt, Hannah. 'The Jew as a Pariah: A Hidden Tradition.' Originally 1944. In Jerome Kohn and Ron H. Feldman, eds. *The Jewish Writings*. New York: Schocken, 2007.
Arendt, Hannah. '"The Rights of Man": What are They?' *The Modern Review* 3.1 (1949).
Arendt, Hannah. 'Franz Kafka: A Revaluation.' In Jerome Kohn, ed. *Essays in Understanding, 1930–1954: Formation, Exile and Totalitarianism*. New York: Schocken, 1994.
Arendt, Hannah. '"What Remains? The Language Remains": A Conversation with Gunter Gaus.' Originally 1965. In Peter Baehr, ed. *The Portable Hannah Arendt*. London: Penguin, 2000.
Arendt, Hannah. *Within Four Walls: The Correspondence between Hannah Arendt and Heinrich Blücher, 1936–1968*. Ed. Lotte Kohler. Trans. Peter Constantine. New York: Harcourt, 2000.

Arendt, Hannah. *The Origins of Totalitarianism*. Originally 1951. New York: Schocken, 2004.
Arendt, Hannah. 'We Refugees.' Originally 1943. In Jerome Kohn and Ron H. Feldman, eds. *The Jewish Writings*. New York: Schocken, 2007.
Arendt, Hannah. 'Franz Kafka, Appreciated Anew.' In Susannah Young-ah Gottlieb, ed. *Reflections on Literature and Culture*. Stanford: Stanford UP, 2007. 94–109.
Benhabib, Seyla. *The Reluctant Modernism of Hannah Arendt*. 2000. Lanham: Rowman & Littlefield, 2003.
Benjamin, Walter. 'Franz Kafka: On the Tenth Anniversary of his Death' and 'Some Reflections on Kafka.' In Hannah Arendt, ed. *Illuminations*. Trans. Harry Zohn. New York: Schocken, 1970.
Deleuze, Gilles and Félix Guattari. *Kafka: Toward a Minor Literature*. Trans. Dana Polan. Minneapolis: University of Minnesota Press, 1986.
de Man, Paul. 'Anthropomorphism and Trope in the Lyric.' *The Rhetoric of Romanticism*. New York: Columbia UP, 1984.
Derrida, Jacques and Anne Dufourmantelle. *Of Hospitality*. Trans. Rachel Bowlby. Stanford: Stanford UP, 2000.
Edkins, Jenny and Véronique Pin-Fat. 'Through the Wire: Relations of Power and Relations of Violence.' *Millennium: Journal of International Studies* 34.1 (2005): 1–24.
Farrier, David. *Postcolonial Asylum: Seeking Sanctuary Before the Law*. Liverpool: Liverpool UP, 2011.
Hamacher, Werner. 'The Gesture in the Name: Benjamin and Kafka.' In *Premises: Essays on Philosophy and Literature from Kant to Celan*. Cambridge: Harvard UP, 1996.
Johnson, Barbara. 'Anthropomorphism in Lyric and Law.' *Yale Journal of Law and the Humanities* 10 (1998): 549–574.
Kafka, Franz. *Diaries 1910–1923*. Ed. Max Brod. New York: Schocken, 1976.
Kafka, Franz. *Letters to Friends, Family and Editors*. Trans. Richard and Clara Winston. New York: Schocken, 1977.
Kafka, Franz. *The Castle*. Trans. J. A. Underwood. Harmondsworth: Penguin, 1997.
Liska, Vivian. *When Kafka Says We: Uncommon Communities in German-Jewish Literature*. Bloomington: Indiana UP, 2009.
Malkki, Liisa H. 'Speechless Emissaries: Refugees, Humanitarianism and Dehistoricization.' *Cultural Anthropology* 11.3 (1996): 377–404.
Miller, J. Hillis. *The Conflagration of Community: Fiction before and after Auschwitz*. Chicago: University of Chicago Press, 2011.
Owens, Patricia. 'Reclaiming "Bare Life"? Against Agamben on Refugees.' *International Relations* 23.4 (2009): 567–82.
Pupavec, Vanessa. 'Refugee Advocacy, Traumatic Representations and Political Disenchantment.' *Government and Opposition* 43.2 (2008): 270–92.
Rajaram, Prem Kumar. 'The Spectacle of Detention: Theatre, Poetry and Imagery in the Contest over Identity, Security in Contemporary Australia.' *Asia Research Institute, Working Papers* 7 (2003).
Rajaram, Prem Kumar. 'Disruptive Writing and a Critique of Territoriality.' *Review of International Studies* 30.2 (2004): 201–28.
Rancière, Jacques. 'Who is the Subject of the Rights of Man?' *South Atlantic Quarterly* 103.2–3 (2004): 297–318.
Ronell, Avital. 'The Testamentary Whimper.' *South Atlantic Quarterly* 103.2–3 (2004): 489–99.
Stonebridge, Lyndsey. *The Judicial Imagination: Writing After Nuremberg*. Edinburgh: Edinburgh UP, 2011.
Szörényi Anna. 'Till Human Voices Wake Us: Responding to Refugee Testimony.' *Life Writing* 6.2 (2009): 173–91.
Yildiz, Yasemin. *Beyond the Mother Tongue: The Postmonolingual Condition*. New York: Fordham UP, 2012.
Young-Bruehl, Elisabeth. *Hannah Arendt: For Love of the World*. New Haven: Yale UP, 1982.

8
TIME, PERSONHOOD, POLITICS

Jenny Edkins

> The tradition of the oppressed teaches us that the 'state of emergency' in which we live is not the exception but the rule.
>
> *Walter Benjamin*

Introduction

In earlier work I examined the notion of time in relation to practices of memory or commemoration and forms of sovereign authority, identifying a form of time I called *trauma time* that provided an opening to challenge sovereign power and its reliance for legitimacy in modern times on the production of *linear time* (Edkins 2003). In this essay I attempt to extend this notion to encompass a present where the state has, arguably, attempted to take control of trauma time, to operate through or in a permanent state of exception. Thinking politics or the political through notions of time enables productive parallels to be drawn across a series of accounts from different traditions, and opens out a dimension of political thinking that often remains unexplored but that proves vital if forms of political life are to be refigured.

In *The Time that Remains,* Giorgio Agamben draws our attention to the unforgettable, that which is 'irretrievably lost in the history of society and the history of individuals' and which is 'infinitely greater than what can be stored in the archives of memory'. He enjoins us to remain faithful to that which 'having been perpetually forgotten must remain unforgettable' (40). Trauma time, as I developed the notion, is a time where events that we call traumatic or unspeakable both expose the lack that underpins a sovereign political symbolic order and reveal the radical relationality of life. The unforgettable testifies to an unspeakable perhaps similar to what we call the traumatic, before or outside any particular social or symbolic order and yet inhabiting it at its core. This calls for a broader reading of the traumatic and the forms of temporality it entails in relation to Agambenian notions of the messianic.

In this short exploratory essay I begin to look at how such a broadening might be thought, taking as my starting point Agamben's analysis of messianic time and the forms of life and community to which such a time might gesture. Central to this discussion will be the place or the absence of the person in contemporary politics and Agamben's contrast between *chronological time*, which transforms us into 'spectators continually missing themselves,' and *messianic time*, or *operational time*, 'the time that we ourselves are' (Agamben 2005: 68).

My interest in these questions arises from a concern with the way in which life, or more narrowly what I want to call *'personhood'*, is commodified or instrumentalized in contemporary politics. It is an attempt to understand an aspect of contemporary social and political life that I find unacceptable and to explore what is objectionable about it and what other politics might or might not be possible. My instinct here is that the missing person may provide a site for the contestation of the very sovereign practices that produce the person as instrumentalized or commodified in the first place. In the same way in which I argued previously that trauma time and practices of memory are a crucial site of weakness for sovereign power, missing persons provide a locus at which the instability and vulnerability to challenge of current political formations become apparent.

It is important to note, in an aside, that I do not want to confine the notion of person here to what we currently call human persons; the instrumentalization or commodification with which I am concerned arises in part from the distinctions human–animal and animate–inanimate, which many political discussions fail to question. I do not rule out inanimate 'personhood' either, though the objectification or instrumentalization of the inanimate is rarely problematized. It is considered obvious that stones, for example, are objects and not 'persons'. However, in the meaning that I want to give to 'personhood', inanimate objects as well as animate or living entities (whether human or animal) might be considered as possessing a form of singular personhood as opposed to a socially produced 'role', or place as mere objects among other objects.

What this essay attempts, then, to summarize and to put it slightly differently, is to think of the question of trauma time and that of the missing person alongside each other. It begins by examining first what the phrase 'missing person' might mean. There are a number of ways in which the person is 'missing'. It then turns to the question of time and temporality, and in particular to the possibility of drawing parallels between notions of messianic time and trauma time. Finally, time and personhood are examined together. It turns out that an exploration of missing persons in contemporary politics proceeds productively by way of an examination of what remains. Just as, when exploring the challenge that trauma time poses to sovereign authority in my previous work, a study of the contested practices of memory and commemoration was helpful, so in looking at missing persons, a study of how we treat missing persons and what remains when the person is missing—photographs, dust, artefacts, memories, bodies, relatives—as sites of political contestation and emotional investment is productive.

In what ways is the person missing?

In contemporary politics we find that what for the time being I will call 'persons' are missing in a number of distinct ways. First, we find a number of instances where people go missing: cases of the disappeared in the totalitarian regimes in South America, for example, those missing in action during a war, people whose fate remains unconfirmed after what we call terrorist attacks, such as those of September 11, 2001 in New York or July 7, 2005 in London, and those who as a result of a range of circumstances lose contact with their families and are regarded as missing. We might call these instances where people are *ontically* 'missing': people move out of a context in which they are part of their recognized social or symbolic system. Those who are dead are not 'missing', generally, in this sense. They have corpses; their remains have been buried or cremated according to the rites and rituals that obtain; they have a resting place; their relatives can 'move on', or at least that is the common perception. Of course the dead are not infrequently referred to as 'lost', which disturbs this account; they remain a presence of some significance in the lives of those who survive them.

On the whole, though, the missing are different from the dead. They are not there, they cannot be found, but they are not yet confirmed as dead. They have no corpses, no death certificates (for the most part), and time for those who are their relatives or friends is in some sense suspended: life *cannot* go on. The missing are not alive, but nor are they dead. We might wonder whether they are between two deaths, a symbolic death and an actual biological death. However, they are neither symbolically dead (they still have a place in the social or symbolic order, as long as there are people who are searching for them), nor actually dead, or at least we do not know whether they are dead or not.

There is another sense in which persons are missing, a sense that we might call *ontological*. Any person, or indeed any 'being', is in some sense 'missing'. A person is always incomplete, the subject of a lack or an excess in Lacanian terminology. In this sense, what is missing is that which is unaccounted for in terms of the role or place which persons are allocated within a social or symbolic order. This is not just 'because we are not the authors of the social roles we are compelled to assume, but rather because these roles are in turn never fully identical with themselves, are inconsistent/incomplete, haunted by a void' (Santner 2005: 113). In Lacanian terms again, the place which persons are allocated in the symbolic order, their entry into the shared symbolic or linguistic world, always produces a gap—a lack or an excess—persons are always both more and less than the identity implied by their entry into symbolic space. The person is incomplete, lacking, 'missing', produced around a lack or an excess.

When we come to examine the person in *political* terms, in relation to orders of authorization or authority that delineate and make possible the social or symbolic field, we come across another sense of 'missing person'. In the Lacanian account, at least in that version of the Lacanian account that relates to the discourse of the Master, the symbolic order is produced in relation to a master signifier—a signifier that halts the shifting of signifiers and quilts the field of meaning to provide a temporary stabilization and produce a social or symbolic order articulated around that particular master signifier. The master signifier authorizes and organizes the symbolic field. In contemporary western politics, the social or political field is articulated around sovereignty or sovereign power, which stands in as the master signifier (Edkins and Pin-Fat 1999). In the biopolitical account provided by Agamben, persons are produced in relation to sovereign power. The Foucauldian account of biopolitics, upon which Agamben draws, argues that persons are no longer the focus of politics. Instead, politics is organized around populations. The body of the individual is not the site of political investment and authority, rather the location of politics as administration shifts and the spotlight is on the population as a whole—population is produced as a site of regulation, control and intervention. The person as such is missing.

Agamben's account of the way in which what I am calling the person is missing in contemporary politics is a particularly productive one. Although it is framed as a development of the Foucauldian account, contesting Foucault's argument that in modern times sovereign power has given way, as the organizing form of relation, to biopolitics, for me and for others—I am thinking particularly of Eric Santner here—it is nevertheless an account that has important resonances with Lacanian thought.

In Agamben's analysis (1998, 1999, 2005), under sovereign power what could otherwise become the person is produced as *bare life* or *homo sacer*, life with no political status, life removed to the sphere of the sacred, life taken out of use. The challenge to sovereign power in the name of personhood would be profanation: the reclaiming of the sacred, its re-introduction into the realm of use. Personhood is politically missing; it has no political significance or meaning. It has no place as such in the sovereign symbolic order. It can exist—it can be included in the symbolic or political field—only as bare life, something that is excluded from politics, and something that is no longer taken account of.

It is possible to point to particular instances where the person is symbolically and politically dead, but remains alive, physically. Instances where the person is, psychoanalytically, *between two deaths*. Agamben himself regards the *Muselmann*, inhabitant in extremis of the concentration camp, as missing in this way. Another, more specific illustration of this might be the case of Dr David Kelly, the UK biological weapons scientist, who, after the stand he took against the Blair government's dossier of intelligence prior to the Iraq war, was reduced to nothing but bare life, and whose suicide, if suicide it was, could perhaps be understood as a recognition of the way in which he had been deprived of a political voice (Edkins 2005). In humanitarianism we have a further example. Those whose lives are at risk are rescued—their lives are saved—by humanitarian action, but this is action that does not reinstate them as political beings, but only as bare life.

In Agamben's account, contemporary sovereign politics has reached or is reaching the point at which 'we are all virtually *homines sacri*' (Agamben 1998: 115). We are all bare life, *biopolitically* 'missing'. Importantly, and ironically, this missing life can become intensely and decisively political; the assumption of bare life as a task is a crucial site at which sovereign power is challenged. The irony is that, as Agamben puts it, 'in the state of exception become the rule, the life of *homo sacer*, which was the correlate of sovereign power, turns into an existence over which power no longer seems to have any hold' (153).

In summary then, the person is missing in contemporary politics in a number of ways that I have outlined: ontically, ontologically, politically and biopolitically. A series of questions can be raised at this point. *When* is the person missing? Or in other words, what notions of time are implied in these conceptions? And *what remains* when the person is missing? How might an examination of these two questions throw light on what is meant in the account I am attempting to put forward here by the terms 'missing person' and 'personhood'?

When is the person missing?

What are the forms of time and temporality that are implied in these notions of missing person, and how might they relate to forms of authority or politics? Notions of time and temporality are central to the Agambenian and Lacanian concepts of personhood and politics that I am working with here, and, of course, the notion of what I am calling the person as missing, or in some sense 'absent', implies a concept of presence, presence which inevitably has to be thought (and problematized) in relation to how we might think about time.

In my work on trauma, memory and politics (Edkins 2003), I proposed two forms or notions of time, which I called *linear time* and *trauma time*. The former was associated with the nation-state and sovereign authority, the latter with instances of traumatic encounter, instances where the sovereign social order falters—only to be rapidly re-instated, of course, alongside a resumption of linear time. This work used an examination of *ontic* trauma—the occurrence of events we call traumatic such as wars, famines, violence, abuse—to explore the political implications of the *ontological* trauma at the root of both subjectivity and social order.

In the Lacanian account of the subject and the social or symbolic order, both are constituted around a traumatic excess or lack. Both are inevitably incomplete. The subject's search for wholeness is initiated in what Lacan calls the mirror stage. At this point we are faced with an image of ourselves, either in a mirror, or, more likely, in the regard or gaze of others, that we misrecognize. We take its apparent wholeness as meaning that we ourselves are whole or complete. Other people take us as 'whole', and it pleases us to accept that vision, despite any uneasiness we may feel or any sense we may have that we are not as we appear. This sets in train a pursuit of wholeness that continues to motivate our desire and deceive us. The search for wholeness or ontological fullness haunts our thinking and our action.

The symbolic or social order—or in Slavoj Žižek's useful phrase 'what we call social reality' (Žižek 1989)—is also structured around a traumatic excess or lack. In the Lacanian account this is figured in relation to what Lacanians call the real: the entry into the symbolic produces a 'real' that lies outside or beyond the symbolic and yet is internal to it and constitutive of it. The symbolic is never complete, never all-embracing: the effort to produce a symbolic order produces at the same time the unspeakable, the unsymbolizable, that which lies beyond the symbolic, or, and at the same time, deep within it. Another word for this is the traumatic. However, the symbolic order, or what we call social reality, functions to conceal the impossibility of completeness. As 'fantasy', it provides 'answers' for the unanswerable questions that plague thought. It provides a context for action and hides the trauma at the root of subjectivity and social order.

In contemporary politics, the sovereign state provides a crucial point around which the symbolic order is constituted. The state, through its accounts of historical origin and its vision of continuity into the future, provides a location in relation to which subjectivity, and its imaginary wholeness, is produced. However, the wholeness, both of the state and of the subject, is fragile. When what we call traumatic events occur, the inevitable incompleteness of the symbolic order is revealed. Events such as wars, and the *ontic* trauma they produce, reveal the inevitable *ontological* trauma around which what we call social reality is constituted.

In the face of the trauma of war, there are two responses. The response of the state is to reassert its authority through heroic stories of continuity and origin and narratives of sacrifice. Those who have experienced trauma themselves are often more inclined to want to hold on to the insights that they feel they have gained. They contest the reinstatement of the stories the state wants to tell. Practices of remembrance and commemoration in the aftermath of a war become an important site of contestation and struggle. There are those who want to return as rapidly as possible to the security of the accounts of continuity and wholeness, and there are others who wish to recognize the impossibility of such comforts and acknowledge the radical and inevitable incompleteness of any attempts at symbolization.

Thus events we call traumatic are a point at which the structures of sovereign authority are particularly vulnerable to challenge. The smooth *linear time* of the state, and its stories of past and future, have been thrown into question by the intrusion of *trauma time*. Traumas, by definition, are events that are incapable of, or at the very least resist, narration or integration into linear narratives or, in other words, into homogeneous linear time. Trauma is not experienced in linear time; there are no words, no language, through which such an experience could take place. A traumatic event cannot be integrated into our symbolic universe, the very universe that has been called into question by the trauma. It cannot be narrated. It is re-encountered through flashbacks that return to the scene, or re-told in accounts where the trauma is re-lived, moment-by-moment. As Cathy Caruth puts it, in her account entitled *Unclaimed Experience*: 'In its most general definition, trauma describes an overwhelming experience of sudden or catastrophic events in which the response to the event occurs in the often delayed, uncontrolled repetitive appearance of hallucinations and other intrusive phenomena' (11). However, importantly, the power of trauma 'is not just that the experience is repeated after its forgetting, but that it is only in and through its inherent forgetting that it is first experienced at all … It is fully evident only in connection with another place, and in another time' (17). Traumatic events are only experienced, if we can call it that, when the past, which has not yet 'taken place', intrudes into the present and demands attention.

Agamben's discussion of the unforgettable is interesting in relation to this discussion of the traumatic. That which remains unforgettable 'refers to all in individual or collective life that is forgotten with each instant' (Agamben 2005b: 39); he emphasizes that 'the quantity of what is irretrievably lost … is infinitely greater than what can be stored in the archives of memory' (40). The unforgettable, like the traumatic, is not something that has been remembered and then forgotten. Like the traumatic also, the unforgettable is something that inhabits the symbolic histories and traditions that are constituted around it: it is 'a shapeless chaos' or 'unforgettable nucleus that [history and tradition] bear within themselves at their core'. It is something of which we are 'unaware'—we might say that it is something of which we are unconscious—and yet it has an effect, 'a force and way of operating that cannot be measured in the same way as conscious memory' (40).

Importantly, 'the determining factor is the capacity to *remain faithful* to that which having been perpetually forgotten, must remain unforgettable' (40; my emphasis). If we don't, the unforgettable 'will reappear within us in a destructive and perverse way' (41), as a return of the repressed through symptoms and disturbances, or what Santner calls 'symbolic torsion' or 'signifying stress'. According to Agamben, there is no point in trying to 'restore to memory what is forgotten by inscribing it in the archives and monuments of history, or in trying to construct another tradition and history of the oppressed and defeated' (40). However, there is, I would argue, something to be said for the attempt to construct monuments and memories of another sort, ones that do not incorporate the unforgettable, or what I have called the traumatic, into the narratives of history and its linear temporalities, but which attempt to encircle the trauma, the unspeakable, the unforgettable, and mark its presence as such. We can *acknowledge* the void, the lack or the excess at the heart of our symbolic universe—or what Agamben calls 'the unforgettable nucleus' (40)—without attempting to name or gentrify it. Such an acknowledgement, a marking, is a way of remaining faithful.

I began this section by looking at the contrasts that I draw between two forms of time, *linear time*, or the time of the state, and *trauma time*. The first of these, linear time, is what Benjamin calls *homogeneous, empty time* (XIII), a time that he associates with the damaging and oppressive notion of progress, and what Agamben calls *chronological time*, the time that turns us into observers, third persons, continually *missing* ourselves. The second form of time I identify, trauma time, is similar, as I will attempt to tease out now, to what Agamben refers to as *operational time*, 'the time that we ourselves are' (Agamben 2005b: 68), the messianic 'time of the now' in Benjamin (XIV).

In *The Time that Remains*, Agamben stresses the difference between messianism and eschatology, 'the time of the end and the end of time' (63). Messianic time is 'the time of the now'; problems arise, however, when we try to represent messianic time along the line of chronological time, in the form of a spatial image of time. Agamben argues that spatial representations make unthinkable the lived experience of time, and suggests the concept of 'operational time' as an alternative. This is an attempt to take into account the way in which there is a disjuncture or disjointedness in our efforts to represent time, which always seem to have to take a particular form—a spatial form that makes it look as if time were already in existence—which does not coincide with our lived experience of time in the making. Our attempts to produce a representation of time produce, according to Agamben, another time, one that 'is not entirely consumed by representation' (Agamben 2005b: 67). This is a familiar problem to Lacanian thought, one that arises with any attempt at symbolization: such attempts always produce a lack or an excess. They always fail, in that sense.

What efforts to produce a symbolic time give rise to is another time, the time in which those representations are produced. In Agamben's terminology this is operational time, or messianic time, '*the time that time takes to come to an end*, or, more precisely, the time we take to bring to an end, to achieve our representation of time.' He continues:

> This is not the line of chronological time (which is representable but unthinkable) nor the instant of its end (which is just as unthinkable); nor is it a segment cut from chronological time; rather, it is operational time pressing within chronological time, working and transforming it from within; it is the time we need to make time end: *the time that is left to us* [the time that remains].
> (68)

The messianic 'is a caesura that divides the division between times and introduces a remnant, a zone of undecidability, in which the past is dislocated into the present and the present is extended into the past' (74). There are similarities to what I have called *trauma time*, the time that renders linear time inoperative.

Importantly for my argument here, Agamben draws out the connection between forms of time and subjects or persons:

> Whereas our representation of chronological time, as the time *in which* we are, separates us from ourselves and transforms us into impotent spectators of ourselves—spectators who look at the time that flies without any time left, continually missing themselves—messianic time, an operational time in which we take hold of and achieve our representations of time, is the time *that* we ourselves are, and for this reason is the only real time, the only time we have.
> (74)

The person, then, is missing in linear, chronological time, the time of sovereign power, the time of the state of exception.

At the end of my study of practices of memory and questions of political authority, I noted that practices of the state in relation to traumatic events seemed to be changing, to the extent that there was a possibility that 'the state has taken charge of trauma time' (Edkins 2003: 233). It had been noticeable how rapidly the state had moved to practices of memory after terrorist attacks, to the extent that commemorative silences had been called while events were still unfolding. It was noticeable too how insecurity had been emphasized; the inability of the state to guarantee security, and the likely continuing presence of insecurity for the foreseeable future, became the validating story of state violence and oppression. It is unlikely that this was a change that took place suddenly in the early twenty-first century, but talk of 'unknown unknowns' seemed to bring to light a story that was not the familiar narrative of wars followed by victory celebrations and commemorations of heroism and sacrifice.

Is it possible that Agamben and Benjamin's assertions that the state of emergency is no longer the exception but the rule require a re-thinking of the place of the traumatic in political life? Is sovereign power, working through a permanent and all embracing state of emergency or exception, now working through and with trauma? In other words, is the traumatic void around which the social order is constituted no longer an impediment, something to be concealed at all costs, but an asset, to be played up and exploited?

It is perhaps the case that the state, in the permanent state of exception, has normalized or gentrified *ontic* trauma. This is where the broader notion of the unforgettable as a more expansive notion of *ontological* trauma might be helpful. Although the state may have narrativized events of trauma, it is still using these new accounts to provide a semblance of order and completeness, a semblance that cannot acknowledge the unforgettable. Indeed, what has been forgotten has to be brought into these accounts as something we remember having forgotten, rather than as the unforgettable.

What is the meaning of personhood in this account?

Eric Santner points out that the psychoanalytic account is an account of subjectivity under sovereign politics. The life that is of concern to psychoanalysis is *biopolitical* life, the 'life that has been *thrown by the enigma of its legitimacy*, the question of its place and authorization within a meaningful order' (Santner 2001: 30):

> to be thrown by the enigma of legitimacy is to be seduced by the prospect of an *exception* to the space of social reality and meaning, by the fantasy of an advent, boundary, or outer limit of that space that would serve as its constituting frame and power, its final, self-legitimating ground.
>
> *(30)*

Escape from capture by sovereign power would then be not an escape *from* ordinary life, but rather an escape *into* the ordinary, a giving up of the fantasy of an 'exceptional "beyond"' (31), the idea of an outside, a transcendental foundation.

Without the notion of exception, without the prospect of an outside, an enemy, sovereign politics fails. Psychoanalysis itself, as a clinical practice, can be seen in two ways. In one view, it is seen as a means of normalization of the subject of sovereign power, a reconciliation of the subject to its place in the symbolic order, to a more satisfactory assumption of the symbolic mandate that gives the subject identity. Alternatively, it can be regarded as a practice aimed at breaking with a 'culture of legitimization' and its violences (27), a practice that enables a traversing of the fantasy.

Santner develops his notion of an escape into the *ordinary*, into what he calls 'the midst of life' (23), through the notion of the neighbour and an analysis of the miracle (Santner 2005). In particular he explores the 'miracle' of the move from *homo sacer*, as the form of life produced by and captured in sovereign power in the state of exception, to the *neighbour*, a form of life closely linked to messianic time. In the case of the neighbour, the demand is for neighbour-love, an interaction based on the recognition of that in the neighbour that is non-identical to itself. In the Lacanian account, as we have seen, personhood is constituted around a lack or an excess, and is always incomplete. The person as neighbour develops a stance or a comportment towards this gap, a comportment that is specific to each person as singularity. It is the recognition of this comportment towards the lack in the neighbour, and the structurally similar but practically quite distinct comportment adopted by what Santner calls the 'self' as opposed to the 'personality', that constitutes neighbour-love.

In previous work, Véronique Pin-Fat and I developed the notion of the *assumption of bare life* as a mode of resistance to sovereign power and re-appropriation of *homo sacer* without a reclamation of citizenship as such: a profanation, if you like, or a re-entry of life into the realm of use and into a properly political power relation (Edkins and Pin-Fat 2005). We looked at the acts of asylum seekers who took to sewing together their lips and eyelids as a protest against their confinement in detention camps as an example of the assumption of bare life. This was, we argued, a direct 'taking on' of their own bare life, and a demand addressed to others. As we pointed out, the acts of lip-sewing

> are not carried out invisibly. They are a demand addressed directly to those who observe 'through the wire', not a demand made on the terms of sovereign power. In taking on their life as bare life, the protestors call for a direct, unmediated, visceral response, life to life.
>
> *(23)*

In other words, in Santner's terms, by making visible their wound, in the most obvious sense, they demand a response neighbour to neighbour.

Slavoj Žižek gives another example, the example of the *refusniks* in Israel, soldiers in the Israeli army who in 2002 refused to serve in the occupied territories. The Palestinians in the occupied territories were being treated as bare life or *homo sacer*. According to Žižek, 'what the *refusniks* accomplished is the passage from *homo sacer* to "neighbour": they treat the Palestinians not as "equal full citizens" but as neighbours', a passage or move that represents the ethical moment at its purest (Žižek 2002: 116). According to Santner, 'fidelity to what opens at such moments, the labor of sustaining such a break *within* the order of the everyday, of going on with what interrupts our goings on' sustains 'a gap between the flow of historical time—the time of the "nations"—and that of the "remnant" ... It is precisely in this gap that the gesture of the *refusniks* transpires' (Santner 2006: 106). It testifies to trauma time, the trauma of what has to be repressed—the lack or the gap that has to be covered over—for life as *homo sacer* to be maintained.

What Santner's account brings out is the relation of the demand for a neighbourly response to the psychoanalytic account of the state of exception, an account that usefully builds on Agamben's work. What the psychoanalytic account provides is a reading of the hold that sovereign politics has over us—an explanation of what is seductive about it and what we must give up if we are to contest it. It enables us to see sovereign power not as some abstraction that oppresses us, but as a fantasy that we are simultaneously trapped in, implicated in and responsible for.

In Santner's account, trauma time, the messianic 'time of the now', is the time of the miracle. A traumatic encounter is an encounter with the real, an encounter normally prevented by the structure of fantasy or what we call social reality, which is sustained by sovereignty as master signifier. For Lacan, Santner argues, 'the possibility of experiencing miracles lies in suspending the hold of this structure of fantasy or at least of entering into a new kind of relationship with it' (Santner 2006: 198), or, in other words, encountering the real. In the context of sovereign power and its state of exception become the rule, the miracle, the trauma, is not the exception. On the contrary, 'a miracle signifies not the state of exception but rather its suspension, an intervention into this peculiar topological knot—the outlaw dimension internal to law—that serves to sustain the symbolic function of sovereignty' (103).

The neighbour is *the personhood that is missing in sovereign politics*—and yet available in everyday life. The neighbour is the *missing person* in my account: it is precisely the lack or gap between the neighbour-person and the social role he or she is supposed to play in the social or symbolic order that constitutes the neighbour as loveable. And it is precisely the excess of neighbourly personhood over social personality that has to be concealed or at least disregarded for sovereign authority to be legitimized. Sovereign power cannot take account of persons as neighbours; indeed sovereign symbolic order exists, is produced, precisely so that persons do not need to acknowledge their own personhood, the traumatic gap around which they are constituted, but can take refuge in personality or social role.

The neighbour as person must of course remain missing. Any attempt to produce a wholeness or completeness is impossible; such an attempt, which would be an attempt to bring the person to presence, would destroy the neighbour-person as such, producing in its place the *homo sacer*, the subject of sovereign power, 'a figure who is *included* within the sphere of political existence by virtue of his radical *exclusion*, whose *presence* within the order of the human is paid for by his deprivation of any symbolic *representation*' (Santner 2005: 100).

In conclusion

My work is both a call for the 'missing' person to be recognized and accorded a place in contemporary politics, and an insistence that the person as such must remain 'missing' in this context. How then can the person remain *ontologically* missing, and yet be re-introduced into *politics*? Clearly what is at stake here is a reintroduction of the person *as missing*, as profane perhaps, into something that goes under the name of politics. This would not be a sovereign politics, with its reliance on sets, distinctions, and location, but another politics, a politics of the neighbour perhaps. A politics not as a denial or covering over of the incompleteness of the symbolic order but as a recognition at least, maybe even a celebration, of that incompleteness. It would operate locally, on a small scale, face-to-face. *But we already have such a politics. It is called everyday life.* It is in everyday life, including the everyday lives of those we call politicians, that authority and power relations are negotiated and take place, in the here and now. It is in everyday life that the missing person is recognized and accommodated, by other 'missing persons'.

The final question then is how we can envisage a form of life (or perhaps form-of-life in Agamben's terms) where the person remains missing, but, importantly, without the instrumentalization or commodification of life that missing personhood entails in contemporary politics. The notion of the person as neighbour is very helpful here. The neighbour embodies, as we have seen, a form of personhood that relates to other persons precisely in terms of *ontological* lack. Santner points out that 'with respect to human being ... what is irreducible there pertains to a *constitutive*, rather than merely *contingent*, dimension of trauma .... this trauma is a function of our finitude, our subjection to death' (Santner 2005: 95). Neighbourliness is an interaction based on an acknowledgement of finitude, and of what is missing—an acknowledgment of the impossibility of completeness and a recognition of the trauma around which each person constitutes a fantasy of subjectivity. It is a taking on, or assumption of, the lack or exception at the heart of what we call social reality, a traversing of the fantasy, and a recognition in self and neighbour of a form-of-life other than that available through sovereign power.

Although Agamben enjoins us to 'attempt to understand the meaning and internal form of ... "the time of the now"', and maintains that 'only *after this* can we raise the question of how something like a messianic community is in fact possible' (Agemban 2005: 2; my emphasis), I would want to suggest that to wait as he proposes would be to remain trapped in too linear a view of the flow of time. The messianic community *is*, now, already. What we can do is look at *where* it is taking place—or, should we say, *when* it is taking time. We can begin to look for such community in the realm of the everyday, in the lives of the oppressed, the missing, the formerly disappeared, the survivors of betrayals ... in anything and everything that escapes the attention or capture of sovereign power. In the persons that sovereignty misses.

Acknowledgements

The arguments developed here build on earlier work with Véronique Pin-Fat, and I am greatly in her debt for continuing discussions on these and other topics.

Works cited

Agamben, Giorgio. *Homo sacer: Sovereign power and bare life*. Trans. Daniel Heller-Roazen. Stanford: Stanford UP, 1998.

Agamben, Giorgio. *Remnants of Auschwitz: The witness and the archive*. Trans. Daniel Heller-Roazen. New York: Zone, 1999.

Agamben, Giorgio. *State of exception*. Trans. Kevin Attell. Chicago: University of Chicago Press, 2005a.

Agamben, Giorgio. *The time that remains: A commentary on the letter to the Romans*. Trans. Patricia Dailey. Stanford: Stanford UP, 2005b.

Benjamin, Walter. *Walter Benjamin: Selected writings: 1938–1940 vol. 4*. Eds Howard Eiland and Michael W. Jennings. Cambridge: Belknap Press of Harvard UP, 2006.

Caruth, Cathy. *Unclaimed experience: Trauma, narrative, and history*. Baltimore: Johns Hopkins UP, 1996.

Derrida, Jacques. 'Force of law: The "mystical foundation of authority".' In David Gray Carlson, Drucilla Cornell and Michel Rosenfeld, eds. *Deconstruction and the possibility of justice*. New York: Routledge, 1992. 3–67.

Edkins, Jenny. *Trauma and the memory of politics*. Cambridge: Cambridge UP, 2003.

Edkins, Jenny. 'Ethics of engagement: Intellectuals in world politics.' *International Relations* 19.1 (2005): 64–69.

Edkins, Jenny and Véronique Pin-Fat. 'The subject of the political.' In Jenny Edkins, Nalini Persram and Véronique Pin-Fat, eds. *Sovereignty and subjectivity*. Boulder: Lynne Rienner, 1999. 1–18.

Edkins, Jenny and Véronique Pin-Fat. 'Through the wire: Relations of power and relations of violence.' *Millennium: Journal of International Studies* 34.1 (2005): 1–24.

Lacan, Jacques. 'The mirror stage as formative of the I function as revealed in psychoanalytic experience.' In Jacques Lacan, ed. *Ecrits: The first complete edition in English*. New York: Norton, 2006. 75–81.

Santner, Eric L. *On the psychotheology of everyday life: Reflections on Freud and Rosenzweig*. Chicago: University of Chicago Press, 2001.

Santner, Eric L. 'Miracles happen: Benjamin, Rosenzweig, Freud, and the matter of the neighbor.' In Slavoj Žižek, Eric L Santner, and Kenneth Reinhard. *The neighbor: Three enquiries in political theology*. Chicago: University of Chicago Press, 2005. 76–133.

Santner, Eric L. *On creaturely life: Rilke, Benjamin, Sebald*. Chicago: U of Chicago P, 2006.

Žižek, Slavoj. *The sublime object of ideology*. London: Verso, 1989.

Žižek, Slavoj. *Welcome to the desert of the real*. London: Verso, 2002.

Žižek, Slavoj, Eric L Santner, and Kenneth Reinhard. *The neighbor: Three enquiries in political theology*. Chicago: University of Chicago Press, 2005.

9
THE BIOPOLITICS OF TRAUMA

Pieter Vermeulen

Biopolitics and trauma after 9/11

The popularity of the signifier 'trauma' in the wider culture indicates the continuing relevance of the study of extreme violence and suffering. At the same time, the currency of the term in strongly politicized contexts is a strong reminder that designating certain events and experiences as traumatic, far from being a mere academic exercise, not only reflects but also shapes contemporary power relations. Contemporary identities are increasingly being articulated around experiences and memories of what Wendy Brown has called 'insistently unredeemable injury'. One consequence of this state of affairs is that trauma studies' principled commitment to instances of suffering and woundedness may very well end up contributing to 'a politics of recrimination that seeks to avenge the hurt even while it reaffirms it' (Brown W. 406). Nor is this danger a matter of identity politics alone: the first decade of the new millennium witnessed how the events of 9/11 fuelled new forms of violence that could not avoid perpetuating cycles of violence and resentment that were already at the basis of those events. Here also, the drive to eradicate the effects of suffering ends up reaffirming the logic of violence.

In her book, *Precarious Life: The Powers of Mourning and Violence* (2004), Judith Butler investigates this proximity between 'injurability and aggression', and wonders whether 'the experiences of vulnerability and loss have to lead straightaway to military violence and retribution' (xii). Butler's obvious answer is that they do not: when the reaction to the loss of certain (say, American) lives takes the form of massive aggression against other (say, Iraqi or Afghan) lives, this reaction is fostered by complex mediating processes that qualify certain forms of life as worthy of recognition and affective investment, even as they render other lives both 'unthinkable and ungrievable' (xiv). The juncture of trauma and violence, in other words, is always undergirded by multiple acts of 'framing', an aspect Butler foregrounds in her later book *Frames of War: When is Life Grievable?* (2009), which in many ways complements the project of *Precarious Life*. Still, if *Frames of War* mainly focuses on how the mass media 'frame' different experiences and events in very different ways, it also implicitly interpellates trauma studies. The 'framing' of 9/11 as a traumatic event, and of cultural and artistic responses to it as reflections of a post-traumatic condition, has become a popular academic occupation in the last decade in the fields of literary, cultural, as well as social studies. As such, trauma studies can hardly avoid the question whether the current state of the world does not belie its commendable ethico-political commitment, monumentalized in Cathy Caruth's foundational (and easily ridiculed) assertion in one of the field's inaugural texts that '[i]n a catastrophic age ... trauma itself may provide the very link between cultures' (Caruth 11).

Butler's emphasis on 'precarious' or 'grievable' life suggests one reason why trauma studies' ethico-political agenda has proven harder to substantiate in the new millennium than Caruth could have anticipated in 1995. It testifies to a widespread shift in the analysis of power from the domain of culture to the problematic of life, or from a politics of recognition to a discourse of biopolitics. Of course, the notion of life that is at stake in this shift is notoriously unstable, maintaining (while subverting) multiple relations to notions such as the (non)human, death, individuality, and the body. This instability is illustrated in Butler's attempts to theorize the idea of 'vulnerability'. At one point, she points to 'a primary and unwilled physical proximity with others', 'a condition of being laid bare from the start' that precedes the formation of the 'I' (Butler 2004: 26, 31). At other moments, she links this vulnerability and exposure to processes of globalization (xiii). And while this 'primary vulnerability to others' is said to define our humanity as such (as we 'cannot will [it] away without ceasing to be human' (xiv)), at other moments she declares that this 'common human vulnerability ... emerges with life itself' (31). While Butler seems to be unable to make up her mind about whether the contemporary vulnerability to trauma is an index of global connectedness, or rather of life or human sociality as such, she strongly affirms that it is a liability that '[n]o security measure', nor any 'radical forms of self-sufficiency and unbridled sovereignty' can defend us from (xii–xiii). A failure to adequately mediate the aftermath of trauma only perpetuates cycles of violence or retraumatization, yet our exposure to trauma is inescapable.

Butler's work invites us to locate trauma in relation to the inevitability of encroachment and contagion, on the one hand, and the task of securing life from such exposure on the other. By foregrounding this tension, trauma, and discourses of trauma, are resituated within the context of biopolitics. While the biopolitical tradition can be traced back as far as 1920 (Esposito 2008: 16–17), current discussions usually refer back to a series of lectures that Michel Foucault delivered at the Collège de France between 1974 and 1979, in which he deployed the term to 'designate what brought life and its mechanisms into the realm of explicit calculations and made knowledge-power an agent of transformation of human life' (Foucault 1979: 143).[1] Biopolitics names the processes and apparatuses through which life itself has increasingly become a target of power since the eighteenth and nineteenth centuries. Foucault famously developed an analytic of disciplinary power to make up for the insufficiency of the traditional framework of sovereignty to account for the operations of power since the eighteenth century. This disciplinary power in its intensified form becomes biopolitics; while disciplinary power (which emerged from the seventeenth century on) already differed from sovereign power in that it did not presuppose 'the physical existence of a sovereign' but rather 'a closely meshed grid of material coercions' (Foucault 2003: 36), biopolitics, rather than *replacing* disciplinary power, instead 'dovetails into [disciplinary power], integrate[s] it, modif[ies] it to some extent, use[s] it by sort of infiltrating it' (242).[2] Biopolitics does not depend on overt displays of power—that was (or, as Butler and others maintain, remains) the prerogative of sovereign power—but rather on the apparatuses of 'governmentality', which Foucault defines as 'the ensemble formed by institutions, procedures, analyses and reflections, calculations, and tactics that allow the exercise of this very specific, albeit very complex, power that has the population as its target …' (Foucault 2007: 108). Biopolitics and governmentality are dedicated to the care of life: they 'endeavor to administer, optimize, and multiply [life], subjecting it to precise controls and comprehensive regulations' (137). Biopolitics, in other words, also consists in a policing of trauma. By situating trauma within this biopolitical horizon, this chapter makes clear that trauma not only names a threat to life, but also functions as a technology that sustains and optimizes it.

Agamben: biopolitics as sovereignty

Biopolitical institutions such as safety measures, insurance, and hygienic regulations address the vulnerability that is an essential aspect of (especially modern) life in order to equilibrate and regulate the accidence and contingency that afflict life. Still, in the current critical theoretical climate, the articulation of trauma and biopolitics tends to evoke less such decidedly unspectacular governmental technologies than lurid images of torture, genetic surveillance, or the horrendous plight of stateless refugees. These images are compiled, and connected through a re-thinking of Foucault's work on biopolitics, in Giorgio Agamben's academic blockbuster *Homo Sacer: Sovereign Power and Bare Life* (1998). *Homo Sacer* not only famously theorized the camp as the 'biopolitical paradigm of the modern', it also decisively enriched the critical imagination by launching figures such as the *homo sacer* and the *Muselmann* as iconic instances of traumatized subjectivity. Agamben's influence on discourses of trauma and biopolitics cannot be overestimated; still, the differences between Foucault's and Agamben's accounts of biopolitics make it possible to bring into relief a number of limitations of Agamben's intervention, which resonate with recent developments in the field of trauma studies.[3] Before I start sketching out a more productive account of the juncture of biopolitics and trauma, I briefly focus on three such limitations.

Near the beginning of *Homo Sacer*, Agamben remarks that Foucault's work on biopolitics 'never dwelt on the exemplary places of modern biopolitics: the concentration camp and the structure of the great totalitarian states of the twentieth century' (4). Agamben's own project theorizes biopolitics by departing from a number of exemplary sites and figures,[4] yet this emphasis on the intermittency and extremity of biopolitical phenomena distorts one of the key aspects of Foucault's account. For Foucault, biopolitics counts as an 'intensification' of disciplinary power because it is no longer linked to specific locations—such as the asylum, the prison, or the hospital—but rather manages to infiltrate every aspect of our private lives; it is a capillary power that disguises itself as mere management or bureacracy and regulates populations by imperceptibly saturating the field of everyday life (Nealon). By reconnecting biopolitics to sovereignty, and by understanding the sovereign (following Carl Schmitt) as 'he who decides on the exception',[5] Agamben obscures the fact that biopolitics operates by eschewing the displays of power that are the prerogative of traditional sovereignty, and is instead dispersed through the different realms of everyday life. It obliterates, in other words, the fact that biopolitics, and the traumas it generates, have become a vital structure of contemporary existence.

A second problem with Agamben's reterritorialization of biopolitics (to the camp) is that it ends up reinstating the centrality of the Holocaust for the analysis of trauma. In his book *Remnants of Auschwitz* (2002), the third part of the *Homo Sacer*-project, Agamben perfects the fit between the biopolitical tradition and the Holocaust by launching the figure of the *Muselmann*, which he picks up from the work of Primo Levi, as 'the final biopolitical substance to be isolated in the biological continuum', that is, as an emblem of the closest that life can come to death (85). By borrowing the figure of traumatized subjectivity from Levi's account of the bare life of exhausted, stunted, and stuporous camp inmates, *Remnants* cements the association between the Holocaust and trauma. Even if this association is not problematic in itself, and can even function as a catalyst for the comparative imagination and for a better understanding of terror and suffering (Rothberg), it does run the risk of impoverishing accounts of the workings of trauma if it obscures the ubiquity of extreme violence and suffering in other domains. Achille Mbembe, among others, has insisted that the plantation and the colony are two such sites that tend to be overlooked by critical theories that focus on the Holocaust, and that slavery 'could be considered one of the first instances of biopolitical experimentation' (21). Agamben's 'extreme European exceptionalism' pre-empts a consideration of the role of colonial encounters and racial violence in the production of biopolitical trauma (Rothberg 62–3).

Agamben's Eurocentrism and his exclusive reliance on peculiarly lurid instances of biopolitical violence also—and this is a third limitation—contribute to a consolidation of a limited understanding of trauma that recent critical work has increasingly begun to challenge. Trauma studies have long been dominated by the idea—which can be traced back to the psychoanalytical tradition that informed this field—that trauma is essentially a sudden and punctual event that afflicts the subject from without. This notion all too easily assumes a solid and stable sense of self that is simply not available to many disenfranchised groups, and thus fails to account for the detrimental effects of the 'ongoing and sustained dynamics of social injury and deprivation' that affect the lives of non-dominant groups suffering from social injuries such as 'racism, mysogyny, homophobia and economic exploitation' (Moglen 151, 159). Already in Caruth's seminal collection *Trauma: Explorations in*

Memory (1995), Laura Brown coined the notion of 'insidious trauma'—a term that conjures biopolitics' capillary and invisible mode of operation—to refer to 'the traumatogenic effects of oppression that are not necessarily overtly violent or threatening to bodily well-being at the given moment but that do violence to the soul and spirit' (Brown L. 107; see Craps and Buelens 3–4).

While attention to such 'incessantly quotidian trauma' (Cheah 196–200) has primarily informed attempts to articulate trauma studies with postcolonial realities, an account of trauma that recognizes the pervasiveness of invisible biopolitical operations in everyday life can take this decolonizing tendency one step further, and also bring into focus the extent to which structural trauma undergirds contemporary metropolitan life. Mika Ojakangas has argued that the exemplary subject of biopolitics is not the *Muselmann* or the *homo sacer*, but rather 'the middle-class Swedish social democrat' (27), whose life is imperceptibly molded by statal as well as non-statal apparatuses that strive for that life's maximization and optimization. In the rest of this chapter, I propose an account of the interrelations between trauma and biopolitics that finetunes the widely accepted idea that trauma emerged with the advent of modernity by locating its emergence in nineteenth-century Europe—in a time and place, that is, that also saw the consolidation of biopolitics. When Roger Luckhurst notes that trauma is a concept that emerged 'as an effect of the rise, in the nineteenth century, of the technological and statistical society that can generate, multiply and quantify the "shocks" of modern life' (19), he underlines the concept's involvement in the infrastructures of biopolitics. In order to explain how this involvement not only mobilizes trauma as a technology for the optimization of life, but also threatens to fuel cycles of retraumatization, I turn from Foucault to the work of the contemporary Italian philosopher Roberto Esposito. In a trilogy that consists of *Bíos: Biopolitics and Philosophy* (2008), *Communitas: The Origin and Destiny of Community* (2009), and *Immunitas: The Protection and the Negation of Life* (2011), Esposito both adjusts Foucault's account of biopolitics and locates it in a larger frame by presenting biopolitics—and, implicitly, trauma—as modern instantiations of a fundamental tension between the dynamics of community and immunity.[6] Reading Esposito's account of biopolitics as a theory of trauma makes it possible to bring into focus the biopolitical challenge to contemporary trauma studies, one of the institutions that modulate the circulation of the signifier 'trauma' and assure (or proscribe) the attunement between that signifier and particular events and experiences. As I show, it reminds trauma studies that, especially in an age of globalization, they always risk strengthening 'immunitary' tendencies that perpetuate rather than minimize trauma.

Foucault: the birth of trauma out of the spirit of govermentality

Near the end of *Society Must Be Defended*, from his lecture series at the Collège de France from 1976, Foucault (2003) notes that biopolitical apparatuses and strategies emerged in order to safeguard the health and the productivity of the population. By shifting perspective from the individual to the people, they dissolved idiosyncrasies and deviations in a calculus of probabilities that allowed them to strive for 'overall states of equilibration or regularity' and to provide compensations for inevitable individual variations (246). Biopolitics, Foucault writes, is 'not individualizing, but, if you like, massifying ... directed not at man-as-body but at man-as-species'—man, that is, as a mass or a multitude (243). In order to optimize the health and productivity of the people, biopolitics deploys two closely connected kinds of technologies. First, there are provisions and measures that attempt to *prevent* the loss of vital capacities, and that install 'security mechanisms ... around the random element inherent in a population of living beings so as to optimize a state of life' (246). Still, the massive processes of mobilization, dislocation, and industrialization that define modernity render a foolproof prevention of accidents and injuries impossible. This is why biopolitics counts on statistical measures to 'tame' these contingencies by making them part of a calculus of probabilities. This project has been described as an '*archiving [of] the future*,' a process which 'subject[s] the future's contingency to the order of a calculable and intelligible archive' (Athanasiou 144), so that we can 'note constants and regularities even in accidents' (Foucault 2007: 74). On the basis of such knowledge, biopolitics can more surreptitiously influence and optimize the lives of the people—not by disciplining bodies, but by regulating populations (Foucault 2003: 250).

That biopolitics is 'massifying' rather than individualizing does not mean that it does not intervene in the construction of modern subjectivities. In *Security, Territory, Population*, from his lecture series from early 1978, Foucault (2007) traces the biopolitical concern with the health and the well-being of the population back to a Christian tradition of what he calls pastoral power. He notes that the Church's concern with individual salvation relied on 'knowing the insides of people's minds ... exploring their souls ... making them reveal their innermost secrets' (Foucault 1982: 214). Depending on analyses and techniques of reflection and supervision to acquire 'a knowledge of conscience and ability to direct it', pastoral power 'is linked with a production of truth—the truth of the individual himself' (214). In a secularized world, such power and care are no longer mobilized in order to acquire salvation, but morphs into a—collective as well as individual—concern for 'health, well-being, ... security, protection against accidents' (215). Biopolitics can be understood as a pastoral power that has 'spread out into the whole social body' and has taken the form of 'individualizing "tactic[s]"' deployed by institutions such as the family, medicine, education, and psychiatry' (215). The pastoral genealogy that Foucault traces for modern power signals that biopolitics not only operates through the biological life of the population, but also through technologies of subjectivation, both individual and collective. Biopolitics mobilizes the institutions of governmentality to produce both 'technologies of the self' and 'political technologies of individuals'; while the former concern 'the ways in which subjects relate to themselves as ethical beings', the latter shape the ways individuals recognize themselves as parts of society (Lemke 9–10).

Foucault's elaboration of biopolitics as a crucial dimension of modern power makes it possible to fine-tune the familiar connection between trauma and modernity and to situate trauma within a biopolitical horizon; his emphasis on the pastoral dimension of biopolitics, moreover, sheds light on the functioning of trauma in contemporary technologies of subjectivation. The emergence of trauma is famously linked to advances in industrialization that produced machines that, in their turn, led to the proliferation of train and factory accidents. Trauma emerged as part of a (biopolitical) vocabulary to map, predict, and regulate the proliferation of physical accidents and psychological damage that modernity incited. It was part of a discourse of shocks and sudden excitations that, even if they had no ostensible physical cause, manifested themselves in the psyche. Trauma was from the beginning a 'medico-legal' problem, as early medical theories of nervous shock were closely connected to the issue whether sufferers with no palpable bodily injuries could yet demand compensation (Luckhurst 24). Importantly, such compensation did not depend on the ability to assign guilt or responsibility, as trauma was soon given over to 'an insurance system where responsibility was not an issue' (25). Trauma, Roger Luckhurst writes, 'develops from the rise of the statistical society', which, as Foucault's account of biopolitics elaborates in great detail, abstracts 'larger orders and regularities of behaviour' and makes the notion of trauma a vital part of a systematic endeavour to take care of the life of the people (25–6). Already in the nineteenth century, trauma was part of the bureaucratic management of the life of the people; it served to name some of the calamities that befall modern life in order to be able to secure the productivity of that life. This emphatically does not mean that biopolitics always aims to *avoid* individual traumas at all cost: what matters is that vital capacities can be mobilized, even if this maximization of capacities goes at the expense of individual bodies; reduction of individual trauma counts for less than the massifying management of trauma (Goldberg and Willse 280–81).[7]

Foucault's work also indicates the ways in which trauma figures in contemporary technologies of subjectivation. His analysis of pastoral power, as a comprehensive guidance of individual life that is intent on securing knowledge of the inner truth that defines the self, resonates with the place of trauma in what Mark Seltzer has called contemporary 'wound culture'. In this wound culture, the self's relations to itself as well as to (certain sectors of) society are increasingly determined by infinitely rehearsed and strongly cathected experiences of woundedness. Seltzer writes that '[t]he notion of the public sphere has become inseparable from the collective gathering around sites of wounding, trauma, and pathology … to the extent that trauma serves as another name for the subject in wound culture, it holds the place of a sociality premised on the wound' (24). The crypto-pastoral urge to discover the truth about one's life by locating an individuating trauma is then complementary with the drive to publicly confess that trauma: both reflect a condition in which trauma mediates the self's relation to itself as well as to society.[8] Institutions such as psychotherapy and psychoanalysis—but also a vast library of self-help books or, why not, literature—have come to assume a pastoral role by allowing the contemporary self to take care of its well-being by managing its relation to certain traumas.[9] This deployment of trauma is continuous with the nineteenth-century bureaucratic and statistical codification of trauma. Anticipating Roberto Esposito's account of biopolitics, to which I turn in the next section, we may well wonder whether the recent rise of trauma as a technology of subjectivation has not spread an increasing sense of vulnerability, to the point where it begins to counteract the ability of biopolitical technologies to secure life against accidents and suffering. Esposito's work explains how such a sense of excessive exposure and powerlessness may incite further violence *against* life rather than offer a protection *of* life.

Esposito: biopolitics, community, immunity

While Foucault's work helps to put the emergence of the notion of trauma into perspective, it fails to explain how the biopolitical regime in which this emergence is located ends up subverting its goal of optimizing life and begins generating further traumas. Roberto Esposito's *Bíos* takes Foucault to task on precisely this point. His critique takes off from the hesitation in Foucault's work between an understanding of biopolitics as a set of technologies of subjectivation (a politics of life) and the idea that biopolitics limits and consumes life (a thanatopolitical assault on life) (31–2). For Esposito, Foucault fails to reconcile his silent conviction that 'life is stronger than the power that besieges it' with the reality of the modern 'mass production of death', and his work does not explain how it is possible that 'a power of life is exercised against life itself' (39). Esposito proposes a different account of the link between politics and life that at the same time establishes biopolitics as a quintessentially modern phenomenon. His key conceptual operation consists in folding politics and life back into the foundational tension between the notions of *communitas* and *immunitas*. For Esposito, community is emphatically not a substance that is 'the ethnic, territorial, and spiritual property' of its members (Esposito 2009: 3): he notes that the Latin *communitas* refers to something 'public' that begins precisely where the proper ends; it has, moreover, three further meanings that are all associated with the term *munus*, which indicates the idea of obligation. In the last of these meanings, which Esposito considers crucial, *munus* signifies a gift, and more specifically a gift that demands an exchange in return (4–5). In the last analysis, *communitas* points to a gift that never properly belongs to anyone and that asserts itself as a relation of mutual obligation. It is a relation of reciprocal exposure that constitutes the self *as* such a relation.

For Esposito, modernity is the name of the project that countered *communitas* by developing a massive apparatus of immunization. *Immunitas* is that which de-activates the mutual obligation that characterizes *communitas*; the subject who enjoys *immunitas* has received a *dispensatio* and is exempt from the obligation incurred through the gift. Esposito traces a philospical genealogy of the ways in which modern thought has mobilized notions such as sovereignty, personhood, property, and liberty in order to shield the individual from the risk of contagion by the unpredictable effects of *communitas*.[10] These notions make it possible for individuals to be 'bordered in such a way that they are isolated and protected', and that they are freed from 'the "debt" that binds them one to the other … exposing them to the possible conflicts with their neighbor, exposing them to the contagion of the relation with others' (13). Esposito recognizes that processes of immunization are crucial for the preservation of life; unlike Butler, for instance, who seems to envision a response to contemporary trauma through the recognition of a shared bodily vulnerability, he is aware that such intensified exposure will only end up inciting further—and potentially more violent—calls for immunization (Campbell xiii). The notions of community and immunity are properly inseparable, yet it is only in modernity that immunization begins to constitute society's 'most intimate essence' (Esposito 2008: 55). Modernity emerges with the diminishment of natural and transcendental protection, and this 'tear … in that earlier immunitarian wrapping … determines the need for a different defensive apparatus of the artificial sort that can protect a world that is constitutively exposed to risk' (55).

It is remarkable to what extent the account of the constitutive tension between *communitas* and *immunitas* dovetails with the common understanding of trauma as, in Roger Luckhurst's words, 'a piercing or breach of a border that puts inside and outside into a strange communication' (3)—even if Esposito's work already indicates that such a breach is the very condition of the (impossible) separation between inside and outside. The *munus* that defines Esposito's notion of *communitas* is described as 'loss, subtraction, transfer' (Esposito, *Communitas* 5); it is a 'violent loss of borders' that is not perceived 'as painless' (8). *Communitas* generates subjects that are 'cut by a limit that cannot be interiorized', as this limit signals their 'exposure to what interrupts the closing and turns it inside out: a dizziness, a syncope, a spasm in the continuity of the subject' (7); it is 'a contagion provoked by the breaking of individual boundaries and by the reciprocal infection of wounds' (xxx). This comes remarkably close to Freud's seminal assertion, in *Beyond the Pleasure Principle* (1920), that '[w]e describe as "traumatic" any excitations from outside which are powerful enough to break through the protective shield'. Freud continues that such an event 'is bound to provoke a disturbance on a large scale in the functioning of the organism's energy and to set in motion every possible defence measure' (quoted in Luckhurst 9). Reading Esposito from the perspective of trauma studies, we can see that he grafts his account of biopolitics (to which I turn presently) onto a dynamic (the relation between *communitas* and *immunitas*) that is structured very much like the scenario of traumatic encounter. A better understanding of the relations between this dynamic and its modern instantiation as biopolitics can make crucial adjustments and additions to our customary understanding of trauma and biopolitics.

Importantly, immunization does not consist in the outright exclusion or negation of community. In order to master the excessive and contagious dimensions of community, the process of immunization 'homeopathically' includes what it excludes; it 'reproduces in a controlled form exactly what it is meant to protect us from' (Esposito 2011: 8).[11] Immunity and community are 'at the same time juxtapose[d] and connect[ed]', in a relation in which the latter is 'the object and content' of the former (9). The process of immunization is 'a strategy … of outflanking and neutralizing' the expropriative effects of the trauma of community

(8). This interconnectedness of the expansive power of community and the limiting operations of immunization also accounts for Esposito's response to the unresolved hesitation in Foucault between an 'affirmative and productive' notion of biopolitics, on the one hand, and a 'negative and lethal' one on the other (Esposito 2008: 46): for Esposito, biopolitics names the attempt to protect and contain the expansive powers of life in order to secure it against the vulnerability and exposure that defines it. In biopolitics' immunizing operations, the negation of life 'doesn't take the form of the violent subordination that power imposes on life from the outside, but rather is the intrinsically antinomic mode by which life preserves itself through power'; biopolitical immunization 'subjects the organism to a condition that simultaneously negates or reduces its power to expand' (46).

The immunitary nature of biopolitics makes it possible to reread Freud's classical scenario of traumatic encounter. For Freud, the traumatic disturbance of the organism leads to what he calls 'the problem of mastering the amounts of stimulus which have broken in and of binding them, in the psychical sense, so that they can be disposed of' (quoted in Luckhurst 9). This 'binding' of traumatic stimuli famously takes the form of a 'repetition compulsion', in which the subject constantly relives traumatic scenes in the hope of belatedly processing unassimilable experiences. While this phenomenon famously led Freud to posit the existence of a death drive, a biopolitical reading makes it possible to understand repetition compulsion as a homeopathic strategy through which life manages to contain—rather than deny— its self-defeating drive toward excess and expansion, even as it continues to depend on that drive.[12] It illustrates 'the structurally aporetic character of the immunatory process' which, 'unable to directly achieve its objective, … is forced to pursue it from the inside out' (*Immunitas* 8–9). Repetition can only develop into the healthy process of 'working through' if working through (*durcharbeiten*) is understood as a more productive and more successful way of containing—rather than cancelling— trauma. This biopolitical perspective also makes it possible to see trauma discourses (and trauma studies) themselves as technologies that mobilize the negativity of trauma in a mitigated form for the sustainment of life.

Esposito's work also enables us to pose the question of the ethico-political stakes of trauma studies in a new way. Why is it that the immunization strategies that organize modern life—and to which trauma, as my account of Foucault's work in the previous section suggested, is inescapably linked—have so fatefully led to excessive violence against life? And why is it particularly the last two decades that have seen such destructive cycles of violence and traumatization? Esposito notes that the events following 9/11 can be defined as 'immunitary crises', as 'an explosion of the mechanisms of the victimary sacrifice that extends like a spill across the entire society, inundating it with blood' (Esposito 2009: 17). Esposito's immunitary framework substantiates Butler's (and others') intuition that the post 9/11-upsurge of trauma constitutes a displaced response to globalization. For Esposito, 'that global contamination that is globalization' maintains a 'structural as well as symbolic affinity with the features … [of] the originary community' (Esposito 2013a: 6; 2009: 15). It 'isn't so much a space as it is a non-space in the sense that, coinciding with the entire globe, there is no outside and therefore no inside either' (Esposito 2009: 15). Globalization deactivates the immunization process that separates inside from outside, and ceaselessly exposes the subject to communication, contagion, and contamination. The ensuing perception of vulnerability incites a violent upsurge of immunization measures that upsets the tenuouos homeopathic equilibrium that previously managed to mobilize trauma *for* life, and now unleashes it *against* life.

The process of globalization not only occasions immunitary crises, it is itself also a consequence of an inversion in the biopolitical dynamic. For Esposito, globalization 'expresses the decisive closure of the immunitary system on itself', as it is 'the immunization driven to a sole principle of the regulation of individual and collective life in a world made identical with itself' (Esposito 2013b: 14). It reflects a condition in which immunization no longer works to shield life from accidence and contingency, but in which immunitary technologies have begun to generate danger and risk in order to perpetuate themselves: 'It is no longer the presence of risk that demands protection, but the demand for protection that artificially generates the sensation of risk' (Esposito 2009: 14). In a society-wide generalization of the standard procedures of insurance companies, 'risk is artificially created in order to control it', and 'this mechanism of reciprocal strengthening between risk and insurance' ends up reinstating the contagious and violent logic of *communitas* (in the guise of globalization), thus inciting an uncontrollable immunitary reaction (Esposito 2013b: 8). Immunization technologies have begun to generate the traumas they were meant to contain. Esposito's work powerfully suggests that contemporary trauma studies must locate their ethico-political commitments within this biopolitical horizon.

Conclusion: trauma studies as an immunitary technology

In her book *Trauma and the Memory of Politics* (2003), Jenny Edkins draws on the example of Foucault to argue that trauma needs to be considered as a 'situated social practice': 'what experts or academics do when they analyse, categorise and write about memory and trauma', she writes, 'has just as much of a practical effect as other forms of social action' (44). Foucault's and Esposito's accounts of biopolitics have made clear that trauma studies ponders, negotiates, and circulates trauma in a context that is inevitably affected by biopolitics. This tradition guides the inscription of trauma in contemporary subjects' relations to themselves and to society, while it also explains how a concern for violence and suffering always risks inciting a further escalation of terror and pain. The dynamic Esposito lays bare explains that a denial of the need for security and defense is the surest way to provoke an inflation of immunitary violence. One of the defining features of trauma studies in the last two decades has been its consistent avoidance of such a denial. While different postmodernist, poststructuralist, and postcolonial discourses tend to prescribe and celebrate the sufficiency of a rhetoric of contagion, singularity, exposure, irruption, and so on, trauma studies underlines how this vocabulary is implicated with suffering and pain. As such, it insists that a position of unprotected exposure to contagion and contamination is not a livable option, and that life requires care if is not to undo itself.

Near the end of *Immunitas*, Esposito notes that it is possible to conceive of immunity not as an apparatus that ruthlessly defends the self against anything that befalls it from the outside, but rather as a technology that regulates the self's multifarious relations to the outside that defines it and that always crosses it. In this broader conception of a 'common immunity', tolerance and defense both count as strategies for managing the self's involvement in the outside world. The immune system, in other words, can be conceived as 'an amplifying box of a difference that involves us' (Donà 65). It is the task of the immune system to modulate the self's experience of alterity in a way that prevents an explosion of immunitary violence. The immune system is reconceived as an instrument of alteration that operates in an 'open system of self-definition' (Tauber quoted in Esposito 2011: 169), and that regulates the self's relation to its outside. Esposito gives the example of the relation between mother and foetus—an emblem which can serve as a powerful correction of the tendency to read the *homo sacer* or the *Muselmann* as the sole icons of biopolitical trauma. During pregnancy, the mother's immune system not only helps to protect the foetus, it also protects the mother's body against its tendency to immunize itself against the foetus. Here, it is precisely the difference between foetus and mother that allows the foetus to grow, and that at the same time protects the mother against autoimmune diseases during pregnancy.[13] This example shows that 'difference and conflict are not necessarily destructive' (171), and that the immune system is a strategy for managing the destructive *and* productive aspects of the self's relation to its world. From this biopolitical perspective, trauma studies can be considered as an immunitary technology—a technology that can manage the self's relation to the world and that aims to provide a position of sustainable exposure. As an immunitary device, trauma studies is a form of memory work that is crucially involved in preventing the future repetition of disaster in the service of a life that cannot be abandoned to itself.

Notes

1 Foucault uses the terms 'biopolitics' and 'biopower' without systematically differentiating between them. Michael Hardt and Antonio Negri do introduce a systematic distinction when they argue that biopolitics mobilizes the powers *of* life to resist biopower's attempt to gain power *over* life (Lemke 3–5).

2 The historical and conceptual relations between the different forms of power Foucault distinguishes remain a matter of debate. Wendy Brown notes that Foucault does not mean to imply that governmentality (which is one dimension of biopolitics) 'chronologically supersedes sovereignty and rule' (quoted in Butler, *Precarious* 60), as if the sovereignty of law was no longer a matter of concern. In an analysis on which I draw here, Jeffrey Nealon has recently theorized biopolitics as an 'intensification' of disciplinary power, and has underlined that biopower today is less the domain of the state than of global finance capitalism. See especially the second chapter in Nealon. For the unstable place of sovereignty in Foucault's account of biopolitics, see Esposito (*Bíos* 32–44).

3 There is no shortage of comparative studies of different accounts of biopolitics—often focussing on Foucault and Agamben, but also comparing their positions to those of, especially, Hardt and Negri and Deleuze. For Agamben's reading of Foucault, see especially Genel; Ojakangas.
4 For Agamben's discussion of such a 'paradigmatic' mode of thinking, in which historical phenomena are deployed in order to enlighten an encompassing historical and theoretical context, and which he explicitly links to Foucault, see the first chapter in Agamben, *The Signature*.
5 Butler's account of Foucault and Agamben (Butler, *Precarious* 50–67) also ends up reasserting the claims of sovereignty, and reducing governmentality to a name for those aspects of sovereign power that cannot be reduced to the law.
6 Esposito's *Bíos* was published in Italian in 2004, *Immunitas* in 2002, and *Communitas* already in 1998.
7 If we emphasize biopolitics' targeting of vital capacities rather than its focus on either the individual or the people, it becomes possible to understand biopolitics as a phenomenon that radically ruptures the horizon of the individual, the social, and the human. For Donna Haraway's work as a critique of the residual humanism of Foucault's emphasis on the body as a biological fact rather than a field for the inscription of sociocultural codes, see Esposito, *Immunitas*, 203–10. My focus on trauma highlights the individualizing complement to this radically de-individualizing tendency of biopolitics. See, however, Goldberg and Willse for an exploration of the interface of trauma and such a more radical understanding of biopolitics.
8 As has often been noted, the codification of post-traumatic stress disorder in the American Psychiatric Association's *Diagnostic and Statistical Manual of Mental Disorders* in 1980 cannot be told apart from 'an essentially political struggle by psychiatrists, social workers, and others to acknowledge the post-war suffering of the Vietnam War veteran' (Leys 5). PTSD is essentially a 'socio-political category' (Luckhurst 62) that, as Ruth Leys remarks, creates a type of person that people can imagine themselves to be and on the basis of which they can claim certain benefits (6). Again, trauma appears to be a crucial biopolitical category.
9 In his alternative geneology of trauma, Fritz Breithaupt traces trauma back to eighteenth-century German and Austrian empirical psychology, which he sees as 'less a science for understanding the human mind than a technique for transforming human beings' through the development of technologies of 'self-observation' (80, 82). Breithaupt's angle, like the biopolitical perspective that I adopt, makes it possible to see that contemporary trauma, far from being 'the wound that prevents the self from being a self', is the very 'condition of the possibility of the self' (98).
10 For Esposito, Foucault's work on biopolitics not only oscillates between a productive and a lethal understanding of the term, it also suffers from an inability to decide whether biopolitics constitutes a return to the paradigm of sovereignty or rather only emerges at the disappearance of the sovereign model (*Bíos* 40–41). For Esposito, sovereignty is to be understood as a manifestation of the tension between *communitas* and *immunitas*, a tension that, as I emphasize below, is inherent in life itself; therefore, sovereignty is simply 'the most powerful response to the modern problem of the self-preservation of life' (57).
11 Massimo Donà calls this a relation of 'excluding inclusion' or 'including exclusion' (58). This risks confusion with Agamben's notion of the 'inclusive exclusion', which names the relation between the sovereign decision, on the one hand, and bare life as the object of the sovereign decision that excludes it, on the other.
12 To phrase this differently, the biopolitical perspective suggests that Freud's thermodynamic conception of the living organism is inadequate to account for the modern politics of life, in that it is unable to grasp that life depends on the interiorization of something external. As Goldberg and Willse note, biopolitics addresses life 'not as a closed, homeostatic system, but rather as an open, turbulent system' (281).
13 Near the end of *Bíos*, Esposito in a very comparable way opens a number of suggestive trajectories that should make it possible to break with the 'thanatopolitical' tendency of

biopolitics: Merleau-Ponty's notion of the 'flesh', which breaks with the imagery of the body in order to reveal 'the tissue of relations between existence and the world' (160); the notion of birth; and finally the idea of the norm as 'the immanent impulse of life' (194) that Esposito borrows from Spinoza and Deleuze.

Works cited

Agamben, Giorgio. *Homo Sacer: Sovereign Power and Bare Life.* Stanford: Stanford UP, 1998.
Agamben, Giorgio. *Remnants of Auschwitz: The Witness and the Archive.* New York: Zone Books, 2002.
Agamben, Giorgio. *The Signature of All Things: On Method.* New York: Zone Books, 2009.
Athanasiou, Athena. 'Technologies of Humanness, Aporias of Biopolitics, and the Cut Body of Humanity.' *Differences* 14 (2003): 125–62.
Breithaupt, Fritz. 'The Invention of Trauma in German Romanticism.' *Critical Inquiry* 32.1 (2005): 77–101.
Brown, Laura. 'Not Outside the Range: One Feminist Perspective on Psychic Trauma.' In Cathy Caruth, ed. *Trauma: Explorations in Memory.* Baltimore: Johns Hopkins UP, 1995. 100–12.
Brown, Wendy. 'Wounded Attachments.' *Political Theory* 21.3 (1993): 390–410.
Butler, Judith. *Precarious Life: The Powers of Mourning and Violence.* London: Verso, 2004.
Butler, Judith. *Frames of War: When is Life Grievable?* London: Verso, 2009.
Campbell, Timothy. '*Bíos*, Immunity, Life: The Thought of Roberto Esposito.' Roberto Esposito. *Bíos: Biopolitics and Philosophy.* Minneapolis: University of Minnesota Press, 2008. vii–xlii.
Caruth, Cathy. 'Introduction.' *Trauma: Explorations in Memory.* Ed. Cathy Caruth. Baltimore: Johns Hopkins UP, 1995. 3–12.
Cheah, Pheng. 'Crises of Money.' *Positions* 16.1 (2008): 189–219.
Craps, Stef and Gert Buelens. 'Introduction: Postcolonial Trauma Novels.' *Studies in the Novel* 40.1–2 (2008): 1–12.
Donà, Massimo. 'Immunity and Negation: On Possible Developments of the Theses Outlined in Roberto Esposito's *Immunitas*.' *Diacritics* 36.2 (2006): 57–69.
Edkins, Jenny. *Trauma and the Memory of Politics.* Cambridge: Cambridge UP, 2003.
Esposito, Roberto. *Bíos: Biopolitics and Philosophy.* Minneapolis: Universiy of Minnesota Press, 2008.
Esposito, Roberto. *Communitas: The Origin and Destiny of Community.* Stanford: Stanford UP, 2009.
Esposito, Roberto. 'Community and Violence.' Carolina Lectures in Critical Thought (University of North Carolina at Chapel Hill, 15 April 2009).
Esposito, Roberto. *Immunitas: The Protection and Negation of Life.* Cambridge: Polity, 2011.
Esposito, Roberto. 'Immunitarian Democracy.' Available online at www.biopolitica.cl/docs/Esposito_immunitarian_democracy.pdf, 2013a (accessed 6 January 2013).
Esposito, Roberto. 'Immunization and Violence.' Available online at www.biopolitica.cl/docs/Esposito_Immunization_Violence.pdf, 2013b (accessed 6 January 2013).
Foucault, Michel. *The History of Sexuality, Vol. 1.* London: Allen Lane, 1979.
Foucault, Michel. 'The Subject and Power.' In Hubert Dreyfus and Paul Rabinow, eds. *Michel Foucault: Beyond Structuralism and Hermeneutics.* Chicago: University of Chicago Press, 1982. 208–26.
Foucault, Michel. *Society Must Be Defended.* London: Allen Lane, 2003.
Foucault, Michel. *Security, Territory, Population.* Basingstoke: Palgrave Macmillan, 2007.
Foucault, Michel. *The Birth of Biopolitics.* Basingstoke: Palgrave Macmillan, 2008.
Genel, Katia. 'The Question of Biopower: Foucault and Agamben.' *Rethinking Marxism* 18 (2006): 43–62.
Goldberg, Greg and Craig Willse. 'Losses and Returns: The Soldier in Trauma.' In Patricia Ticineto Clough and Jean Halley, eds. *The Affective Turn: Theorizing the Social.* Durham: Duke UP, 2007. 264–86.

Lemke, Thomas. 'Biopolitics and Beyond: On the Reception of a Vital Foucauldian Notion.' Available online at biopolitica.cl/docs/Biopolitics_and_beyond.pdf (accessed 30 June 2010).
Leys, Ruth. *Trauma: A Genealogy*. Chicago: University of Chicago Press, 2000.
Luckhurst, Roger. *The Trauma Question*. Abingdon: Routledge, 2008.
Mbembe, Achille. 'Necropolitics.' *Public Culture* 15 (2003): 11–40.
Moglen, Seth. 'On Mourning Social Injury.' *Psychoanalysis, Culture & Society* 10 (2005): 151–67.
Nealon, Jeffrey. *Foucault Beyond Foucault: Power and its Intensifications Since 1984*. Stanford: Stanford UP, 2008.
Ojakangas, Mika. 'Impossible Dialogue on Bio-Power.' *Foucault Studies* 2 (2005): 5–28.
Rothberg, Michael. *Multidirectional Memory: Remembering the Holocaust in the Age of Decolonization*. Stanford: Stanford UP, 2009.
Seltzer, Mark. 'Wound Culture: Trauma in the Pathological Public Sphere.' *October* 80 (1997): 3–26.

10
FUTURE SHOCK
Science fiction and the trauma paradigm

Roger Luckhurst

> How do you cope with tomorrow when (a) it may not be like the real tomorrow but (b) it's arrived when you weren't ready for it?
>
> *John Brunner,* The Shockwave Rider *(228)*

>SEARCHING...

In 1970, the American journalist Alvin Toffler published *Future Shock,* which became a bestseller and helped define an era. The book, mixing political commentary and summaries of psychological research, was a response to the violence and unrest of the 1960s. It argued that the social turmoil and a divided American polity that had produced assassinations, student demos, hippy dropouts, and conservative counter-reactions were all the products of an unprecedented 'accelerative thrust' in technology in advanced capitalist countries (11). Toffler pointed to the exponential expansion of cities, the increasing speed and complexity of transport and communication systems, and guessed that just-emerging computer automation would be likely to produce even greater revolutionary changes in the immediate future. Without a plan, he prophesied, humans were 'doomed to a massive adaptational breakdown' (11). In later chapters, using the latest psychological studies, Toffler came to define future shock as 'the distress, both physical and psychological, that arrives from an overload of the human organism's physical adaptive systems and its decision-making processes … Its symptoms … range all the way from anxiety, hostility to helpful authority, and seemingly senseless violence, to physical illness, depression and apathy' (297).

For biological authority, Toffler cited many studies that analyse the detrimental effects of persistently raised levels of catecholamines such as adrenaline on the nervous and endocrine systems. Readers today might note that this is not – as yet – framed in the language of 'trauma'. Hans Selye's metaphor of stress on these systems, first theorized in the 1950s, is certainly used by Toffler, although often in quotation marks, as if the term 'stress' has not quite finished its journey from specialist to everyday language. Since the 1980s, however, many theories of trauma have used similar studies to formulate the neuroendocrinological basis of post-traumatic stress (see Young). What people remember about Toffler is the snappy phrase 'future shock' that grasps the headlong forward tilt of advanced capitalist modernity in its accelerated cycles of novelty and obsolescence, tripping on the heels of its own futurity. But one of the blindnesses of Toffler's *Future Shock* was its failure to predict how the psychological language of 'adaptational breakdown' or 'environmental overstimulation' would be almost entirely replaced by the pervasive discourse of trauma.

Toffler was writing before the advent of post-traumatic stress in 1980, yet he might still have noted that it had long been established that notions of psychological trauma had been inextricably bound up with the emergence of modern technologies. Notions of disruptive psychological sequelae following a shock event were first formulated by medical specialists in relation to train accidents in the 1860s. 'Railway spine', as it was called, was 'the first attempt to explain industrial traumata' (Schivelbusch 168), a theory that rested controversially on the cusp of physiological and psychological explanations. Soon enough, Victorian medics spoke about the mental and physical depredations of modern urban life, prompting the emergence of terms like neurasthenia (sometimes called 'Londonism') in the writings and treatments of mid-century doctors like Silas Weir Mitchell. Moral and physical degeneration, a catastrophic slide down the evolutionary scale within one or two generations, was often explicitly associated with the nervous overstimulation of urban life. 'Even the little shocks of railway travelling … the perpetual noises, the various sights in the streets of a large town, or suspense pending the sequel of progressing events, the constant expectation of the newspaper, of the postman, of visitors, cost our brains wear and tear', the conservative commentator Max Nordau wrote in 1895 (39). Walter Benjamin explicitly borrowed the language of 'traumatic shock' from Freud to portray the modern city as a series of 'shocks and collisions' (155, 171). If the railway was the first 'machine ensemble' into which men were passively inserted and subject to the traumatic consequences of systems failure, the technologies of 'total war' after 1914 engineered a whole new set of trauma subjects, the shell shocked or NYDNs (not yet diagnosed – nervous). The inclusion of post-traumatic stress disorder (PTSD) in the official diagnostic manual of the American Psychiatric Association in 1980 was partly the result of psychiatric advocacy on behalf of Vietnam war veterans. The increasing use of technological prostheses through which contemporary warfare is executed has not diminished the amount of casualties from PTSD. Indeed, it has fostered new areas of cusp controversy between competing physical or psychic origins, such as Gulf War syndrome. And as the wired-in, webbed and networked computerized present of the third industrial revolution transforms subjectivity, narratives of the potential traumatic impact of these technologies on the meanings of the 'human' multiply, often simply repeating terms that Toffler had himself borrowed (see, for instance, Carr).

Trauma studies – this vast set of inter-related fields that emerged in the 1990s – has not been much concerned with the future. It inevitably begins with what it is that returns from the past or which remains so insistently in the present, such that unprocessed trauma might be figured as that which puts pressure on the very possibility of a future. As an emergent scholarly formation, though, trauma studies has reached a point where it is beginning to reflect on its future directions. In the recent collection *The Future of Memory*, however, there is a suspicion about both technological prosthetics of memory and neuroscientific explanations if they threaten to 'assume a master status' above psychodynamic and cultural conceptions (Crownshaw et al. xi). The future here seems very much like a refinement of the arguments of the past in the discourse of cultural memory, even retrenching somewhat against the perceived growing authority of neurological science.

Meanwhile there is, of course, a whole cultural genre that deals in the futures that technological and scientific advance might bring, and which has had fascinating things to say about subjects under the stress of 'future shock.' Science fiction (SF) is the written and visual culture of technologically saturated societies, often reflecting on nothing less than the collision of technology and subjectivity (Luckhurst 2005). Yet SF has barely featured in the literary wing of trauma studies, probably because, as I've argued elsewhere (Luckhurst 2008), there have been prescriptive tendencies around what is considered to be an appropriate aesthetics for the representation of trauma. In short, trauma aesthetics has tended to favour Modernist tactics of foregrounded difficult and disrupted representation and form to convey trauma, and therefore been suspicious of the investment in narrative pleasure often equated with mass cultural forms like SF.

This essay is the briefest of sketches about how we might bring into conjuncture trauma studies and SF. This will move from merely incorporating SF into the purview of trauma studies to suggest that the most challenging contemporary science fictions, precisely because they dismantle any recognizable human subject in challenging ways, intimate that we might need a rethinking of trauma itself even now, as imagined futures outgrow the psychodynamic frameworks that dominate conceptions of cultural trauma.

>NEW HARDWARE DETECTED

The relatively short history of academic criticism of SF has been dominated by Darko Suvin's crisp definition that it works through the principal device of 'cognitive estrangement' (61). SF offers an imaginative world different (estranged) in greater or lesser degree from the empirical world of the writer or reader/viewer, but it is different in a way that obeys rational causation or scientific law (it is estranged *cognitively*). An SF future is thus one that is meant to extrapolate consistently from tendencies within its current empirical environment. Whatever the limits of this definition (and they are manifold and much debated), Suvin at least established that SF could have serious ambitions because it was principally an allegorical form, made of fictions that could offer sustained social and political commentary on the cultures of their production in ways that more culturally sanctioned modes of representation perhaps sometimes could not.

One might argue that the emergence of generic scientific romances in the late nineteenth century (the term 'science fiction' was only coined in 1926) was the very consequence of a technological revolution in the electronic telecommunications that so often formed its subject. As Friedrich Kittler has observed of the era 1880–1920, 'in the founding age of technological media the terror of their novelty was so overwhelming that literature registered it more acutely' (xl). One of the pioneers of the scientific romance, H. G. Wells, undertook training in science education under T. H. Huxley at the Normal School of Science before beginning to write. His fictions of the 1890s registered the traumatic impacts of evolutionary thought and rapid technological advance, consistently toppling the imperious position of complacent Victorian man. In his early books, before his turn to technocratic utopias, enlightened science always slides inexorably towards Gothic horror, as in the cannibalistic Morlocks of *The Time Machine,* the animal–human splices of *The Island of Dr Moreau* or the efficient exterminations by our merciless biological superiors in *War of the Worlds.* Indeed, Wells contributed to a burgeoning popular genre of near future catastrophism, invasion and apocalyptic end that has surfaced and resurfaced at distinct historical junctures, as in the rash of contemporary ecological disasters and zombie apocalypses. Fictions of future shock on such a cataclysmic scale allegorize the felt traumas of dis-possession, the techno-cultural recasting of the boundaries of body and self under the relentless acceleration of neo-liberal economics (see Williams; Žižek). Contemporary horror in particular, as is often noted, is held together by the syntax of trauma (see, for instance, Lowenstein).

But it isn't always necessary to stretch this far for allegorical readings. As in so many areas of cultural life, the psychology of trauma can become a means to decrypt and translate recalcitrant forms of popular culture as displaced traumatic expressions. So, for instance, the difficult, avant-garde SF of J. G. Ballard was for a long time pushed to the margins of extreme fiction. His most provocative experimental work, *The Atrocity Exhibition,* made up of diverse textual interventions in the late 1960s that pushed at the limits of libel and obscenity, was set in a dystopian near future and concerned the dissolution of the self under relentless technological innovation and media bombardment. The protagonist is so effectively future shocked by intensifications of technological mediation that he is simply dispersed into global telecom networks, what Marshall McLuhan was already calling 'the extensions of man'. Similarly, Ballard's *Crash* explored a perverse rerouting of sexual desire into the matrix of motorway systems, cars, and violent collision, thus projecting an intensified alternate present marked by the techno-cultural inversion of traumatic pain for pleasure. The novel and later film of *Crash* were routinely condemned, but also, equally routinely, incorporated into burgeoning trauma theory (see Barker et al. for the former and Adams for the latter).

Yet Ballard's uncomfortable technological fantasies have been further retranslated as symptoms of a far more explicable traumatic experience with the appearance of Ballard's fictionalized autobiography, *Empire of the Sun,* written in a highly stylized but recognisably Realist mode. Knowledge that Ballard had witnessed, as a child, the fall of Shanghai to the Japanese in the Second World War and been interned in a civilian prisoner-of-war camp for a number of years began to 'explain' his extreme SF. His visions of entropic collapse, the death of affect and the ecstatic embrace of a post-human future published in SF magazines from the 1950s were retrospectively recast as compulsive reiterations of unprocessed wartime trauma, complete with obsessively repeated plots and tropes (see, for instance, Crosthwaite). The delayed decoding of this extremity – Ballard was thirty years into his career when *Empire of the Sun* appeared – only confirmed the logic of belatedness associated with the difficulty of narrating trauma. Another example of SF as translated trauma was the career of Kurt Vonnegut, typically held to hinge on *Slaughterhouse 5*, the author's fanciful time-travel novel that explodes the possibility of living in sequential time because the protagonist Billy Pilgrim, like Vonnegut himself, is a post-traumatic survivor of the fire-bombing of Dresden in February 1945 when tens of thousands of civilians were killed. So it goes. In another less convincing example, the compelling explanatory power of the trauma paradigm has even prompted one critic to propose, very controversially, that key aspects of the SF of Philip K. Dick, one of the most important post-war SF writers in America, could be largely explained through episodes of childhood sexual abuse that resulted in Dick's undiagnosed multiple personality disorder as an adult. Gregg Rickman's thesis appeared at the height of the 'recovered memory' movement in the early 1990s that claimed to retrieve buried and amnesiac traumatic memories (and just before multiple personality disorder was removed from the American Psychiatric Association's manual over problematic diagnostic inflation in 1994). In this contested reading, Dick's extraordinary *oeuvre* became an unlikely retrospective exemplification of America's trauma culture (see Rickman).

Whilst these accounts have a certain explanatory force, the more radical approach might be to recognize that if SF focuses on the technological transformation of subjectivity itself, this forces a reconsideration not only of how trauma might be represented and narrativized, but also, potentially, of the very notion of trauma itself. It becomes problematic to translate SF into pre-existent trauma models, because if future shock sets about reconfiguring selfhood and the boundaries of the human, would models of trauma also not have to change?

SF writing is sometimes rather artificially divided between 'hard' and 'soft' modes. Hard SF is supposed to be driven by the physical sciences, concerned with ideas rather than character, and very anxious to present extrapolated futures within a rhetoric of scientific rigour (see Slusser and Rabkin). Soft SF in contrast is more focused on the human sciences, on social and political impacts, and tracking the profound subjective responses to technological change. Ballard, Vonnegut and Dick are archetypal soft SF writers, more or less hostile to science where it is conducted within the framework of the military-industrial complex. Their familiarity with the language of psychological depredation might suggest that it is soft SF that is most likely to provide source material for these transformations of trauma. But as we sift through SF works, it seems to be hard SF that offers the most radical rethinking of trauma in the imagining of post-human futures. Let's start, however, with two classics of future shock.

>ALLOW CHANGES?

John Brunner's *The Shockwave Rider,* first published in 1975, was an explicit extrapolation of the cultural consequences of future shock outlined in Alvin Toffler's book. Characters refer to Toffler's Law, held to state that 'the future arrives too soon, and in the wrong order' (268). *The Shockwave Rider* is remembered principally for inventing the notion of the computer worm (those self-replicating programmes that eat up bandwidth and cause systems crashes) some years before hackers unleashed the real thing when computers became routinely networked together. Yet the novel is actually focused on exploring a culture that has undergone catastrophic collapse as a result of future shock. This disaster hits in 2010, when 'Beetling forward at full pelt split society. Some did their utmost to head the other way. A great many more decided to go sideways. And some simply dug their heels in and stayed put. The resultant cracks were unpredictable' (128). For those who cannot cope, there are anti-technology enclaves ('paid-avoidance areas'), or companies like Anti-Trauma Inc. that promise to reconstitute shattered selves. 'Hearing Aid' provides emergency telephonic therapy, a counterforce to a government that engages in total surveillance. The protagonist, Nicholas Haflinger, however, has been able to ride the shockwave and become a free and subversive agent, precisely because of a traumatic childhood in a secret government institution. He becomes a 'plug-in' personality, able to switch personae by faking computer records and erasing past histories of his selves with electronic tapeworms. He has experienced 'overload' in several personalities, an 'extremely traumatizing' experience (104), but has acquired extraordinary adaptive abilities to cycle through alternative selves. He relives these lives in full in 'fleshback' (a brilliant coinage), forced to confess once captured by intelligence operatives using coercive 'stimulus-response evaluation' techniques. After his escape, Haflinger engineers the release of all secret information, ending these dystopian controls, in another striking anticipation of the hacker imperative that 'all information wants to be free'.

As Fredric Jameson has argued, SF futures are limited by the horizon of their present: it is impossible to imagine the complete alterity of the future. Brunner's riposte to Tofflerian over-stimulation is strongly marked by narratives of authentic and unalienated enclaves, typical of the rhetoric of liberation in the 1970s. The psychological horizons of *The Shockwave Rider* are still Freudian rhythms of sublimation and desublimation. But what non-Realist possibilities of the SF genre allow Brunner to do is to embed in the radically disjunctive character of Haflinger, and in the shocking jumps and jolts of the narrative that force readers into their own readerly experience of discontinuity, a palpable sense of how technology might begin to change notions of subjectivity and therefore, necessarily, of trauma.

This sort of thing is also aimed at, with a little more aesthetic grace, in William Gibson's *Pattern Recognition*. Gibson's *Neuromancer* fleshed out the virtual worlds of his coinage 'cyberspace' in the 1980s and owed a fair bit to Brunner's trail-blazing fiction. Yet, nearly twenty years later, *Pattern Recognition* is barely science-fictional at all, not least because, as one character explains,

> we have no future. Not in the sense that our grandparents had a future, or thought they did. Fully imagined cultural futures were the luxury of another day, one in which 'now' was of some greater duration. For us, of course, things can change so abruptly, so violently, so profoundly, that futures like our grandparents' have insufficient 'now' to stand on. We have no future because our present is too volatile.
>
> *(57)*

This makes *Pattern Recognition* an 'ambivalent alternate present' (Easterbrook 499), an exercise in what Gibson calls 'speculative presentism', and Jameson reads this sense of time compression as futures now captured and traded on the markets of late capitalism. It means that the book over determines this heightened present with multiple traumatic layers. The protagonist Cayce consistently experiences disorienting soul lag as she jets across the globe from one abstract space to another. But modernity is also marked traumatically on her body: she is valued by marketeers and branding gurus because she is somatically allergic to offensive branding (accidental exposure to the Tommy Hilfiger logo causes instant vomiting in one memorable scene). This may or may not be linked to the obliquely introduced information that her father disappeared in New York on 11 September 2001, although she is initially unclear whether he was caught up in the attack on the World Trade Center. Belatedly, then, the book appears to emerge as a post-9/11 work (Gibson was halfway through the writing in September 2001, so it was literally a belated intrusion into the novel).

Yet the novel morphs again when Cayce is employed to hunt for the origin of an enigmatic, guerrilla filmic text known simply as 'the footage' that is being released in tiny fragments on the internet. Her employers want to know if it is a brilliant piece of stealth marketing or a work of art ambitiously seeking for a fugitive place outside commoditized cultural production. It transpires that the footage has been created by a young Russian woman left with major wounds after a terrorist attack has left her brain damaged, and is her only means of communication with the outside world. The way the film is encoded is shaped around the shrapnel fragment of the Claymore mine that killed her parents that has been left buried in her skull. The footage is nothing less than 'the wound, speaking wordlessly in the dark' (305). In a sense, it is impossible to think of a narrative that more literally conceives of trauma as the intrusive wounding of a consciousness. Gibson, as he often does, organizes his SF plot around the ambivalent prospect of the possibility of a surviving avant-garde practice, which in this case seems distinctly aligned to a modernist aesthetic of trauma. This attests to Gibson's own very ambiguous relation to SF history, whose crude optimistic futurism he rejected in his early short story, 'The Gernsback Continuum'. Even so, he is still far more interested than mainstream literary fiction in the ways in which technology and subjectivity are necessary in an ongoing dynamic of transformation.

What, though, if we were on the cusp of a technological transformation so profound that subjectivity, as conceived by psychodynamic models, were effectively to disappear? What would 'trauma' mean then? For that, we have to turn to contemporary hard SF.

>VIRUS SCAN RECOMMENDED

In Greg Egan's short story, 'Reasons to be Cheerful', the first-person narrator recalls a childhood of growing, ecstatic bliss. It soon becomes clear that this is a neurological side-effect of a brain tumour that causes him to over-produce endorphins. An experimental treatment involves inserting a genetically engineered virus into his cerebrospinal fluid designed to kill infected cells. Unfortunately, it interferes catastrophically with the uptake of endorphins, and he collapses into a profound and immovable depression, segments of his brain withering away from lack of use. Two decades later, another experimental treatment inserts a nanotech polymer foam into the dead regions of his brain, its neuronal connections composed from the imprinted matrix of thousands of other brains. It is meant to allow him to determine his own neuronal pathways and thus retain his sense of self; instead, he is supplied with so many options, so many routes and pathways to desire or happiness or pleasure that he ends up having arbitrarily to choose, leaving him in a permanent existential state of utter inauthenticity.

Egan's story is hard SF because it extrapolates from contemporary medical investigations in neurological brain science and portrays the psychodynamic sense of self as epiphenomenal rather than central. Importantly, though, the story is about unforeseen consequences of experimental methods. This is not a confident, deterministic fantasy that control of the body can master and control subjective states. Hardcore technological futurists like Ray Kurzweil often resort to metaphors of self as 'software' that can be uploaded or file-copied and thus be rescued from the feeble 'hardware' constraints of what is contemptuously dismissed as human 'meatspace'. This is a dream of immortality by the reduction of the human to informational bits, the vision of the human rendered as 'the inhuman' condemned by the philosopher Jean-Francois Lyotard. Egan's story resists that fantasy, but is perhaps best read in context with a more sophisticated set of cultural encounters with the neurocognitive sciences that resist reductionism. After Antonio Damasio's accessible introductions to these more dynamic accounts, critics have begun to explore more dynamic interactions between culture and neurology (see Salisbury and Shail).

Yet some of the strange corners of hard SF have fully embraced technological literalism and the idea of trauma as a programming glitch that can be de-bugged to restore machine efficiency. In 1950, one of the key magazines that published extrapolative, allegedly scientifically rigorous, hard SF, *Astounding Science Fiction,* published a non-fiction research article by one of their writers of space operas, L. Ron Hubbard, which was called 'Dianetics: A New Science of the Mind'. The article, endorsed by the legendary hard SF editor John W. Campbell, was premised on the view that 'the human mind was a problem in engineering' (47) but that it was a computer riddled with 'aberrative circuits' that produced irrational behaviour from neurotic compulsions to full-scale psychosis, suicide and even nuclear mass-death (54). Hubbard envisaged the mind as scored – literally 'like the wax indentations on a record' (78) – with what he called 'engrams', the traces of trauma that produced errant programmes. Dianetics was a science and also a discipline of mental hygiene intended to 'clear' the brain of engrams, and potentially unlock the infinite possibility of the human brain. 'Clears', in effect, realize the superpowers of the SF heroes of the pulp magazines. In the push-button optimism of the 1950s, Hubbard's resultant book, *Dianetics*, sold a million copies; within a few short years, for tax purposes, Dianetics became the considerably weirder Church of Scientology, which still controversially trains people in de-bugging their traumatic engrams and self-overcoming.

Elements of this hard SF dream are still alive: old-school Futurians have become modern-day Extropians and Transhumanists. The argument now is that we are on the threshold of a technological Singularity, a notion popularized by Vernor Vinge in 1993 as the moment when technological advance reaches a point of transformation that makes it 'an exponential runaway beyond the hope of control' (Vinge). This is usually seen as the point when machines reach a level of intelligence able to produce other machines, outside of human agency (the idea of the dystopian film *Terminator*). Vinge placed this somewhere between 2005 and 2030. Since the Singularity is always a proleptic prospect, vanishing ahead of us as we move forward, Kurzweil has since suggested 2040. For utopians, the Singularity transcends the trauma of being embodied; for the rest of us, the Singularity might be intrinsically traumatic because it dethrones human control. But since the Singularity must also reconfigure notions of subjectivity, can 'trauma' be relevant at all?

The novel that rigorously works out the genuine oddness of a post-Singularity world is Charles Stross's *Accelerando,* which came out in 2005. Set just a little into the future, it follows the experience of the 'constant burn of future shock' (8) until the Singularity actually occurs, after which the post-human future accelerates past any notion of traumatic subjectivity, or so it appears. In the first part, Manfred Macx is a techno-geek who 'lived on the bleeding edge of strangeness, fifteen minutes into everyone else's future' (5). He is moving faster than most in a 'world of the terminally future-shocked', humans who will shortly be left behind or traded by intelligent AI corporations (64). He is a post-national, post-capitalist, post-punk, postmodern but (just) pre-Singularity trader with a 'thalamic-limbic shunt interface' that plugs his brain directly into whatever it is that is morphing out of the internet. In a parody of memory studies, Manfred at one point loses his cool shades, a prosthetic device that contains much of his enhanced memory storage. He awakes with no idea who he is, feeling '*blunt.* And slow. Even *obsolete*' (103): '*Is this what consciousness used to be like?*' (93) he complains. Later, to avoid such risks, Manfred distributes his consciousness into a flock of enhanced seagulls for a few years.

Manfed's daughter, Amber, the next generation created out of DNA storage in a fit of neurotic pique by her ostensible mother, grows up 'with neural implants that feel as natural to her as lungs or fingers. Half her wetware is running outside her skull on an array of processor nodes hooked into her brain by quantum-entangled communication channels' (122). She lives through virtual avatars and becomes, in a proper sense, post-human. Her son, Sirhan, has inevitably accelerated well beyond any human conception. With Sirhan, Stross, in an information-dense, hi-tech prose that carries its own future shocks, pursues the logical outcomes of post-human subjectivity. He has such immense processing power available to him that he is able to model every lived human life, and every forking possibility in those lives. Growing up, he 'lives a dozen lives, discarding identities like old clothes' (310). He 'had lived through loads of alternate childhoods in simulation' (410). In this model, the fixations of traumatic childhood become meaningless. These pasts can be monetized (as Steve Shaviro observes, Stross's future is always and forever hyper-capitalist), and Sirhan seeks shareholders for raising enough memory to 'archive the combined sensory bandwidth and memories of the entire population of twentieth-century Earth' (311–12). This is the 'history futures market' (314) where trauma has all the fixity of traded informational bits.

Weirdly, however, by the fourth generation (which is so post-human it can't really be conceived of in biological generations), Manni, a sort of remixed Manfred, gets into retro stylings, embodying himself in human form again, and choosing to live in a perfect simulacrum of the 108th floor of New York's World Trade Center on 11 September 2001, moments before the impact of the planes. Rather oddly, in this utterly future-shocked post-Singularity conception, 'the fall of the Two Towers that shattered the myth of Western exceptionalism' remains the event that 'paved the way for the world he was born into' (411). Right at the end of this wild, overloaded imaginary trajectory, we circle back to a classical conception of the punctual traumatic event. This only goes to prove, perhaps, Jameson's insistence that the (traumatic) horizon of the present cannot escape into any genuine place of alterity.

Hard SF fictions about the neurology of trauma are, needless to say, future fictions bounded by the limits on the imagination of today. They explore a side of the multiform discourse of trauma that cultural and literary studies have been uncertain or even censorious about addressing. But since so much of the medicalization of trauma has pushed beyond the comfortable formulae of psychodynamic theories of trauma, these visions challenge us to address the rapid development of new scientific understandings that are likely to reconceptualize notions of trauma in the very near future.

Works cited

Adams, Parveen. 'Cars and Scars'. *New Formations* 35 (1999): 60–72.
Barker, Martin, Jane Arthurs and Ramaswami Harindranath. *The* Crash *Controversy*. London: Wallflower, 2001.
Benjamin, Walter. 'On Some Motifs in Baudelaire'. *Illuminations*. Trans H. Zohn. London: Fontana, 1973. 152–96.
Brunner, John. *The Shockwave Rider*. London: Orbit, 1977.
Carr, Nicholas. *The Shallows: What the Internet is Doing to Our Brains*. London: Atlantic, 2011.

Crosthwaite, Paul. '"A Secret Code of Pain and Memory": War Trauma and Narrative Organisation in the Fiction of J. G. Ballard.' Available online at www.jgballard.ca/jgb_secretcode.html (accessed 28 June 2011).

Crownshaw, Richard, Jane Kilby and Antony Rowland, eds. *The Future of Memory*. New York: Berghahn, 2010.

Easterbook, Neil. 'Alternate Presents: The Ambivalent Historicism of *Pattern Recognition*'. *Science Fiction Studies* 33.3 (2006): 483–504.

Egan, Greg. 'Reasons to be Cheerful'. *Luminous*. London: Orbit, 2008. 213–53.

Gibson, William. *Pattern Recognition*. London: Penguin, 2003.

Hubbard, L. Ron. 'Dianetics: The Evolution of a Science'. *Astounding Science Fiction* (May 1950): 43–87.

Jameson, Fredric. *Archaeologies of the Future: The Desire Called Utopia and other Science Fictions*. London: Verso, 2005.

Kittler, Friedrich. *Gramophone Film Typewriter*. Trans. G. Winthrop-Young and M. Wurz. Stanford: Stanford UP, 1999.

Kurzweil, Ray. *The Singularity is Near: When Humans Transcend Biology*. London: Duckworth, 2003.

Lowenstein, Adam. *Shocking Representation: Historical Trauma, National Cinema, and the Modern Horror Film*. New York: Columbia UP, 2005.

Luckhurst, Roger. *Science Fiction*. Cambridge: Polity, 2005.

Luckhurst, Roger. *The Trauma Question*. London: Routledge, 2008.

Lyotard, Jean-Francois. *The Inhuman: Reflections on Time*. Trans. G. Bennington and R. Bowlby. Cambridge: Polity, 1991.

Nordau, Max. *Degeneration*. London: Heinemann, 1895.

Rickman, Gregg. 'On Our Philip K. Dick Collection'. *Science Fiction Studies* 20 (1993): 139–41.

Salisbury, Laura and Andrew Shail, eds. *Neurology and Modernity: A Cultural History of Nervous Systems, 1800–1950*. Basingstoke: Palgrave, 2010.

Schivelbusch, Wolfgang. *The Railway Journey: Industrialization of Time and Space in the Nineteenth Century*. New York: Berg, 1986.

Selye, Hans. *The Stress of Life*. New York: McGraw-Hill, 1956.

Shaviro, Steve. 'The Singularity is Here.' In M. Bould and C. Mieville eds. *Red Planets: Marxism and Science Fiction*. London: Pluto, 2009. 103–17.

Slusser, George and Erik Rabkin, eds. *Hard Science Fiction*. Carbondale: Southern Illinois UP, 1986.

Stross, Charles. *Accelerando*. London: Orbit, 2006.

Suvin, Darko. 'On the Poetics of the Science Fiction Genre'. In M. Rose, ed. *Science Fiction: Twentieth Century Views*. New York: Prentice-Hall, 1976. 57–71.

Toffler, Alvin. *Future Shock*. London: Pan, 1978.

Vinge, Vernor. 'The Coming Technological Singularity' (1993). Available online at www.accelerating.org/articles/comingtechsingularity.html (accessed 28 June 2011).

Williams, Evan Calder. *Combined and Uneven Apocalypse*. Ropley: Zero Books, 2011.

Young, Allan. *The Harmony of Illusions: Inventing Post-Traumatic Stress Disorder*. Princeton: Princeton UP, 1995.

Žižek, Slavoj. *Living in the End Times*. London: Verso, 2010.

INDEX

Please note that page numbers relating to Notes will have the letter 'n' following the page number.

aborigines, 33
Abraham, Nicholas, 86
Abrams, Meyer, 30
Accelerando (Stross), 165–6
acknowledgement, 88
acute dissociative disorders, 84
Adams, Parveen, 160
adaptational breakdown, 158
Adorno, Theodor W., 14, 50, 94, 97, 98, 99–100, 102, 107n, 108n
aesthetic/aesthetics, xiii, 30, 40, 83; of Adorno, 97; aestheticization of violence, 24; feminist literature, 49, 58n; of fragmentation, 46; normative trauma aesthetics, 46; trauma aesthetics, beyond, 50–1
affect-worlds, xii, 71–2, 73
'afterwardsness,' 12, 14, 16–19
Agamben, Georgio, xiii, 7, 34–5, 37, 92, 113, 123n, 143–4, 153n; on biopolitics as sovereignty, 143–5; *Homo Sacer: Sovereign Power and Bare Life*, 143; *Remnants of Auschwitz*, 144; *The Signature*, 153n; on time and personhood, 127–8, 130–1, 133–4, 135, 137, 138; *The Time that Remains*, 127–8, 133
Aghaie, Kamran, 48, 58n
Alexander, Amy, 49
Alexander, Jane, 102
Algeria, 78

alienation, 98, 99
Alisch, Stephanie, 69, 70
allegory, 79, 82
Alphen, Ernst van, 80, 81, 82
Alter, Joseph, 72
Althusser, Louis, 29, 30
American Psychiatric Association, 2; Diagnostic Manual (DSM), 49, 153n, 158
amnesia, protective, 56
Ancestor Stones (Forna), 52
Anderson, Benedict, 105
Angelus Novus (Klee), 93
Anglo–Afghan War (1860), 71
Anglophone modernities, 66
Angola, xiii, 69–71
Anil's Ghost (Ondaatje), 73
Animals in the Third Reich (Sax), 33
animism, 102, 108n
animus, quasi-ritualistic, 37, 39
Anna Karenina (Tolstoy), 17–18
Anthropocene, xvi
anthropomorphism, 117–18, 120
anti-Semitism, 24, 28, 33, 35; redemptive, 39; *see also* Holocaust
anti-teleology, 63, 66
Antze, Paul, 64, 65
Arab world, 78
Arendt, Hannah, 6, 32, 34, 113–23; *Eichmann in Jerusalem*, 116; 'human being

general,' 114, 115, 120; *The Human Condition*, 113; Jew-Stranger, 118–23; 'new kind of human beings,' 116–17, 118, 121; *The Origins of Totalitarianism*, 114, 118, 122; 'We Refugees,' 115, 116, 117, 119, 122, 124n
Aristotle, 18
art, works of, 97, 100
al Assad, Mehmet, 115, 119; 'Asylum,' 113, 114, 117, 122, 123n
Astounding Science Fiction (magazine), 164
'Asylum' (al Assad), 113, 114, 117, 122, 123n
asylum seekers, 115
Athanasiou, Athena, 146
atrocities, 14
Atrocity Exhibition, The (Ballard), 160
Auschwitz death camp, 11, 15, 16, 17, 34; poetry following, 50
auto-immunity, 26, 41n

bad faith, 25
Baelo-Allué, Sonia, 58n
Bal, Mieke, 65
Ball, Karyn, 15
Ballard, J. G., 7, 160–1
Bangladeshi fires, xiv
barbarism, 2, 36, 40
bare life, 130–1, 136, 144, 153n
Barker, Martin, 160
Barth, Karl, 26
Bartov, Omer, 34
Bataille, Georges, 25, 30, 31, 38; *Trauma: Expectations in Memory*, 58n
Bauman, Zygmunt, 34
beauty, 29, 40
'Before the Law' (Kafka), 18
Beirut, 78; Sabra and Shatila massacres in (1982), 79; Tel al-Zaatar, siege and massacre of Palestinians (1976), 80
Belzec death camp, 34
Bengal, 66
Benhabib, Seyla, 67, 124n
Benjamin, Walter, 93, 96, 105, 119, 124n, 127, 133, 135, 158
Bennett, Jane, 29
Bennett, Jill, 50–1, 58n
Bergson, Henri, 24, 25
Beyond Feminist Aesthetics: Feminist Literature and Social Change (Felski), 58n
Beyond the Pleasure Principle (Freud), 91, 149
Bhabha, Homi, 68, 93
Bhakti cult, 66
binary oppositions, 26, 28
biological organisms, 91, 150

biopolitics, xiii, 7, 92, 93, 130, 141–55; vs. biopower, 152n; defined, 142–3; and governmentality, 143; as sovereignty, 143–5, 153n; thanato political tendency, 153–4n; and trauma post 9/11, 141–3
biopower, 32, 34; vs. biopolitics, 152n
Bíos: Biopolitics and Philosophy (Esposito), 145, 148, 153n
Birkenau death camp, 11, 15, 34
Bischoff, Lizelle, 70
Black Atlantic, xii, 71, 72
Black Skin, White Masks (Fanon), 58n
Blücher, Heinrich (husband of Hannah Arendt), 122
Blumenberg, Hans, 30
Bodhi tree, in Buddhism, 68
Bodies that Matter (Butler), 92
body, 72, 153n
'Bollywood,' 66
Bourdieu, Pierre, 28
Brazier, David, 68
Breithaupt, Fritz, 153n
Brod, Max, 119
Broderick, Mick, 58n
Brown, Jayne, 69, 71
Brown, Laura S., 7, 49, 106, 145
Brown, Wendy, 141, 152n
Browning, Christopher, 16, 34
Bruckner, Pascal, 14
Brunner, John, 7, 157, 162, 163
brutality, 36, 38, 39
Buck-Morss, Susan, 72
Buddhism, xii, 68, 69, 71, 72
Buelens, Gert, 58n, 145
Bultmann, Rudolf, 26
bureaucracy, 7, 119, 147, 148; and fascism/Nazism, 32, 34, 36
burial sites, 106
Burrows, Victoria, 58n
Butler, Judith, 6, 7, 92–3, 94, 96, 105, 141–2; on 9/11, 92, 94; *Bodies that Matter*, 92; vs. Esposito, 149, 150; *Frames of War: When is Life Grievable?* 2, 47, 142; vs. Freud, 92; *Precarious Life: The Powers of Mourning and Violence*, 2, 20, 91, 92, 141, 153n; *The Psychic Life of Power*, 92
Butler, Mark, 69
buzzing, in works of history, 16

Caillois, Roger, 25
Cambodia, Pol Pot regime, xii, 67, 68
Campbell, Timothy, 149
capitalism, xiv, 152n, 163
carnivalesque practices, 40

Carr, E. H., 16
Carr, Nicholas, 158
Caruth, Cathy, 2, 12, 13, 14, 17, 46, 47, 48, 65, 72, 81, 92, 142; *Trauma: Explorations in Memory*, xi, 3, 58n, 144–5; *Unclaimed Experience: Trauma, Narrative and History*, xv, 3, 45, 132
Castle, The (Kafka), 119, 120
Catholic Church, 30
Césaire, Aimé, 2
Chakrabarty, Dipesh, xvi, 64, 67
Cheah, Pheng, 145
Chelmno death camp, 34
chiasmus, 79, 82, 88
Christian theology, 27, 30
chronological/linear time, 6, 127, 128, 131, 133, 134
Church of Scientology, 165
Ciceronian tradition, 27
City Gates (novel by Khoury), 5–6, 78–88; collapse of narrative voice, 83–4, 85, 87; failure of novel as symbolic form to represent the event, 81–2; fragmentariness of, 79, 82; man and stranger in, 79–80, 82, 84, 88; narrative in, 78–9, 79, 80, 82, 83–4, 85, 87; paradox of, 80; plot, 79–80, 80; protagonist in, 79, 84, 86–7; PTSD in, 79; publication (1981), 78, 80; sadness of, 80–1; style, 80, 83; vulnerability, portrayal in, 79, 83–4, 85, 88
civil religion, fascism/Nazism as, 24, 32
Civilization and Its Discontents (Freud), 30
Claymore mine, 163
Clear Light of Day (Desai), 65
clerico-fascism, 30
climate change, xiv
closure, 55, 57, 65; emotional, 78, 79, 82; psychoaffective, 81
Coetzee, J. M., 69, 106
cognitive estrangement, 159
Cold War, 32, 63, 70, 72
collective memory, 2
collective trauma, shift from individual, 92
collectivist societies, 50, 65
colonialism, Angola, 70
Communitas: The Origin and Destiny of Community (Esposito), 145
community, 148, 149, 153n; corporeal, 104–5
Comparative Studies of South Asia, Africa and the Middle East (Saunders and Aghaie), 58n
Complex PTSD, 49
concentration camps, 34; *see also* death camps

consciousness, 86
conspiracy theory, 36–7
'contemporary narrative,' 14
Continuum: Journal of Media and Cultural Studies (Traverso and Broderick), 58n
Convention Relating to the Status of Refugees (UN), 1951, 115, 123n
coping mechanisms, 55
corporeality, common, 92, 94, 102
counter-narratives, 5, 78
Craps, Stef, xii, xv, 4, 5, 12, 13, 48, 145; *Postcolonial Witnessing: Trauma Out of Bounds*, 58n; *Studies in the Novel*, 58n
Crash (Ballard), 160
Crazy like Us: The Globalization of the American Psyche (Watters), 48–9
Critchley, Simon
critical historiography, 12
critical melancholia, 73
critical refugee studies, 113
Criticism: A Quarterly for Literature and the Arts (Craps and Rothberg), 58n
Croisy, Sophie, 58n
cross-cultural context, 46, 48, 50, 51
Crosthwaite, Paul, 161
Crownshaw, Richard, 159
Crutzen, Paul, xvi
cultural imperialism, 48
cultural transfer routes, 72
cultural trauma, 13
culture industry, 97
Currie, Mark, 17
cyberspace, 163

Daiya, Kavita, 65
Damasio, Antonio, 163
'Darkling Thrush, The' (elegy by Hardy), 101, 102
Dawidowicz, Lucy, 37
De Man, Paul, 12, 13, 14
death camps, 11, 15, 16, 34, 123n; disorientation, 17; *see also* Holocaust
death drive, 41, 150
decolonization, 67
deconstructive thought, 2, 12, 14, 45, 92
Deleuze, Gilles, 124n, 153n, 154n
depersonalization, 83
Derrida, Jacques, 2, 3, 13, 14, 24–5, 123n, 124n; 'Faith and Knowledge: the Two Sources of "Religion" at the Limits of Reason Alone,' 24, 26–7; 'Force of Law: The "Mystical" Foundation of Authority,' 41n; 'Structure, Sign, and Play in the Discourse of the Human Sciences,' 27

Desai, Anita, 65
destruction, machinery of, 32, 33–4, 36, 39
detachment, 72
detention camps, 113, 114, 117, 120
Devi, Mahasweta, 107n
Devji, Faisal, 71
Dialectic of Enlightenment (Adorno and Horkheimer), 40, 107n, 108n
Dianetics (Hubbard), 165
Dick, Philip K., 161
difference/*différance*, 26
disciplinary power, 142–3, 144
discipline-specific knowledge, 12
discourse, 19, 20, 81
discursive distance, 82
disenfranchisement, 26; legal, 47; National Socialist policy, 30
Disorders of Extreme Stress Not Otherwise Specified, 49
domination, 97, 100
Douglas, Kate, 58n
Douglas, Mary, 25
dreamworld, 72
Dresden bombing (1945), 161
Dube, Surabh, 67
Dufourmantelle, Anne, 124n
Duran, Edwardo, 49
Duras, Marguerite, 47
Durkheim, Emile/Durkheimian tradition, 25, 28
Durrant, Sam, 4, 6, 89n, 107n; *Postcolonial Narrative and the Work of Mourning*, 58n, 107n

Eaglestone, Robert, 4, 13
Early Modern Period, 19, 20
Easterbrook, Neil, 163
Edkins, Jenny, xii, xiii, 7, 92, 123n, 127, 130, 131, 134, 136; *Trauma and the Memory of Politics*, 6, 151
Egan, Greg, 164
Eichmann, Adolf, 39
Eichmann in Jerusalem (Arendt), 116
Einsatzgruppen (special task forces), 33
electrified fence, 15
Elinga Teatro, Angola, 69
embodiment/embeddedment, 72
emergency, state of, 135
empiphany, 87
empire, trauma of, 46–8
Empire of the Sun (Ballard), 160–1
empire of trauma, 48–50
empty time, 133
engrams, 165
Epic and Empire (Quint), 97

Erikson, Kai, 87
eschatology, 133
Esposito, Roberto, xiii, 142, 148–51, 152n; *Bíos: Biopolitics and Philosophy*, 145, 148, 153n; vs. Butler, 149, 150; *Communitas: The Origin and Destiny of Community*, 145; vs. Foucault, 148; *Immunitas: The Protection and the Negation of Life*, 145
Eternal Treblinka (Patterson), 33
ethics: ethical turn, 12, 45; and trauma, 18, 19
ethnocentrism, 31
Euro-American academy, xvii
Eurocentrism, 5, 33; bias of, 46, 47, 68; breaking with, 48; empire, trauma of, 46–8; empire of trauma, 48–50; excessive concentration on, in trauma theory, 12–13; trauma aesthetics, beyond, 50–1; trauma theory beyond, 45–61; *see also Memory of Love* (Forna)
event-based trauma model: limitations, 49, 50, 53, 54, 144; missing 'person,' 132–3; Partition of India (1947), as event, 64, 65, 66, 67; and repetition, 81; *see also* Holocaust
exceptionalism, European, 144, 166
exclusive inclusion, 153n
existential choices/questions, 11, 12, 14
expansionism, European, 72
experience, vs. representation, 81, 82
experimentation, avant-garde, 57
exploitation, xiv
extermination camps, 113; *see also* death camps
'external relations' of literature, 12
extreme violence, xiii, xiv, 78, 141, 144; *see also* violence
extremity, 25

factory fires (2012), xiv
faith, 25, 27, 28, 35
'Faith and Knowledge: the Two Sources of "Religion" at the Limits of Reason Alone (Derrida), 24, 26–7
'family camp,' Auschwitz, 15
Fanon, Frantz, 14, 58n, 93
fantasy, of mastery/storytelling, 84–5, 85–6
Farrier, David, 123n
fascism, xii, 4, 23–43; comparative, 23; and Nazism, 23, 31–2; prominent characteristics, 31; and religion, 24, 25, 30; sacred in, 23, 24; salute, 26; as secular religion, 24
Felman, Shoshana, 2, 12, 14, 45, 46, 92; *Testimony*, 3

Felski, Rita, 58n, 88
feminist literature, 49, 58n
fence, electrified, 15
films, 65, 66
'final solution' *see* Holocaust
Finchelstein, Federico, 30
First World War, 19, 29, 93
Flatley, Jonathan, 89n
Flores, Paulo, 71
'folk psychology' language concept, 13
'Force of Law: The "Mystical" Foundation of Authority' (Derrida), 41n
foreclosure, 77, 79, 85
formlessness, 79; of *City Gates*, 83
Forna, Aminatta: *Ancestor Stones*, 52; *The Hired Man* (Forna), 51; *Memory of Love*, 5, 46, 51–7, 59n
Foucault, Michel, xiii, 19, 20, 93, 130, 144, 153n; on disciplinary power, 142–3, 144; vs. Esposito, 148; on governmentality, 145–8, 152n; *Security, Territory, Population*, 146
fragmentariness, of *City Gates*, 79, 82
Frames of War: When is Life Grievable? (Butler), 2, 47, 142
framing, 141–2
Frank, Arthur, 2
Freetown, Sierra Leone, 51, 52
Freud, Sigmund, 12, 29, 32, 64, 72, 73, 104, 150, 158; *Beyond the Pleasure Principle*, 91, 149; vs. Butler, 92; *Civilization and Its Discontents*, 30; melancholia vs. mourning, 65, 68, 69; *Moses and Monotheism*, 47, 48; protective shield of, 91, 93, 94, 97, 106, 149
Frey, Hans-Jost, 80–1
Friedlander, Saul, 11, 14, 16, 33; *Nazi Germany and the Jews*, 39
Frye, Northrop, 30
fugue, 56
future shock, 7, 157–67
Future Shock (Toffler), 7, 157, 158

Gana, Nouri, xiii, 4, 5–6, 107n
gas chambers *see* death camps
Gaus, Gunter, 117, 123n
Genel, Katia, 153n
genocide, 14, 20, 32–3, 35, 39, 40, 46; *see also* Holocaust; Nazism; violence
Genocide Museum, 67, 68
genre, 65
Genter, Robert, 72
Gentile, Emilio, 32
geological agency, xvi
ghettos, 32, 36

Gibson, William, 162–3
Gift of Death (Derrida), 25
Gilroy, Paul, 71, 89n
Girard, René, 25
globalization, xiii, xiv, 4, 46, 151
'god's eye view point,' 17
Goebbels, Josef, 39
Goldberg, Greg, 147, 153n
Goldhagen, Daniel, 35
good faith, 25
'The Good Old Days': The Holocaust as Seen by its Perpetuators and Bystanders (Trevor-Roper), 37–8
Göring, Hermann, 35
Gottlieb, Susannah Young-ah, 124n
governmentality, 145–8, 152n; and biopolitics, 143
'Great Death' (gas chambers), 15, 16; *see also* death camps
Greenhouse, Steven, xiv
Griffin, Roger, 32, 40–1n
Gross, Jan T., 33
Guattari, Felix, 124n
guilt, 14
Gulf War Syndrome, 158
Gurs detention camp, South West France, 114, 119

habitus, 28
Hacking, Ian, 2
Haidu, Peter, 64
hailing, 25, 26, 30
Halbwachs, Maurice, 2
Hamacher, Werner, 124n
hands-on killing, 34
happiness, 18
Haraway, Donna, 153n
Hardt, Michael, 77, 152n, 153n
Hardy, Thomas, 101, 102, 106
Harmony of Illusions: Inventing Post-Traumatic Stress Disorder (Young), 48
Hartman, Geoffrey, 45, 46
healing, traditional, 54
Hegel, Georg Wilhelm Friedrich, 28
Heidegger, Martin, 25, 34, 88
Herman, Judith, 2, 12, 49
hermeneutic tools, 64
Herrero, Dolores, 58n
Hess, Rudolf, 35
Hilberg, Raul, 14, 34
Himmler, Heinrich Luitpold, 24, 35, 39; Posen speech (1943), 36, 37, 38
hiphop, 71
Hired Man, The (Forna), 51
Hiroshima, bombing of, 47

174 Index

Hiroshima mon amour (film), 5, 47–8
Hirsch, Marianne, 65, 72
historical precision, 13
historical trauma, 13, 92; *see also* event-based trauma model
history: buzzing, in works of, 16; and narrative, 14; trauma as, 14–16, 45
History and Its Limits: Human, Animal, Violence (LaCapra), 23, 41n
Hitler, Adolf, 28, 35, 38, 39; charisma of, 31, 36; *Mein Kampf,* 29–30
Hitler's Willing Executioners (Goldhagen), 35
holiness, 25, 26, 29
Holocaust, xi, 4, 18, 20, 23, 37, 46, 119; whether excessive concentration on, in trauma theory, 12–13, 58n, 64, 144; as 'limit-event,' 64; as population control, 32; survivor testimonies, 11–12, 14, 16; *see also* Second World War
Holy Spirit, 25
homeland, concept of, 98
homeland security, breach of, 92
homelessness, 115, 124n; *see also* refugees
homo sacer, 130, 131, 136, 145, 152
Homo Sacer: Sovereign Power and Bare Life (Agamben), 143
hope, need for, 54
Horkheimer, Max, 94, 107n, 108n
Hubbard, L. Ron, 164–5
Hulme, T. E., 30
Human Condition, The (Arendt), 113
human rights violations, 100, 114
humanitarianism, 121, 130
Huxley, T. H., 160
Huyssen, Andreas, 67
Hyder, Syed Akbar, 71
hyperbolic suggestion, 19–20

identification, 47
identity, pure, 26
ideology, 24, 25, 29, 30, 32, 38; Nazi, 34
immanent sacred, 28
Immunitas: The Protection and the Negation of Life (Esposito), 145
immunity, 148, 149, 150, 152, 153n
immunization, 149–50
inaccessibility of trauma, 45
inanimate, objectification or instrumentalization of, 128
incarnation, 'scandal' of, 27
inclusive exclusion, 153n
Indian Ocean trade routes, 72
Indian Partition (1947), 64, 65, 66, 67
individualistic approaches to trauma, limitations, 49–50

injury, insistently unredeemable, 141
insidious trauma, 49, 106, 145
'internal laws' of literature, 12
interpellation, 30, 67
interwar period, 29, 30
Iraq, 71, 78
Irish Famine, 94, 95, 100
Irish Folklore Commission, 107n
Islam, 63, 71, 72
Islamo-fascism, 25
isolation of traumatized individuals, 46
Israel, 16–17, 136, 137

Jain, Kajri, 66
Jalal, Ayesha, 66
Jameson, Fredric, 162, 163, 166
Janoff-Bulman, Ronnie, 49
Japan, 67
Jay, Martin, 77
jazz, 71
Jedwabne pogrom (1941), 33
Jewish people, 24, 30, 32; conspiracy theory, 36–7; hatred of *see* anti-Semitism; history, biblical account, 105; middle-class European (eighteenth and nineteenth centuries), 116; as refugees, 115; ritual murder charges, 33, 36; 'sheep to slaughter' metaphor, 36; *see also* Holocaust
Jew-Stranger, 118–21; and Arab-Stranger, 121–3
Joffé, Roland, 67
Johnson, Barbara, 117, 118, 120
Judaism, 26; *see also* anti-Semitism; Holocaust; Jewish people
Jünger, Ernst, 29
juridical framework, 68–9

Kabir, Ananya Jahanara, xii, xiii, 4, 5, 63, 64, 65, 66, 71
Kafka, Franz, xii, 6, 18, 118–21, 124n; *The Castle,* 119, 120; Zionism of, 122
Kansteiner, Wulf, 13, 17
Kant, Immanuel, 24, 28, 38
Kaplan, E., xii, 58n
Kaunas, Lithuania (murder of Jews at), 37–8
Kelly, David, 130
Kelly, Erica, 101
Kennedy, Rosanne, 51, 58n
Khanna, Ranjana, 73, 89n
Khmer Rouge regime, Cambodia, 67, 68
Khoury, Elias, xiii, 77; *City Gates,* 5–6, 78–88; 'Sociology and the Novelist,' 89n

Khulumani Support Group, 101, 108n
Kielce pogrom (1946), 33
Kierkegaard, Søren, 12, 27
Kilby, Jane, 12, 46
killing, direct, 34
Kindly Ones, The (Littell), 34
King, Stephen, 51
Kittler, Friedrich, 160
Klebes, Martin, 124n
Klee, Ernst, 37–8
Klee, Paul, 93
Klein, Kerwin Lee
Kligerman, Eric, 38
knowledge, 12, 88
Kok, Ingrid de, 6, 94, 105, 106; 'Parts of Speech,' 101, 102, 104; 'A Room Full of Questions,' 101, 102; 'Some there Be,' 105; *Terrestrial Things*, 101
Kolk, Bessel van der, 81, 83
Kovner, Abba, 36
Kristeva, Julia, 25
kuduristas, dance of (Angola), xiii, 69–71
kuduro (Angolan electronic music–dance complex), xiii, 69, 70, 71
Kuehn, Alex and Felix, 63
Kulka, Otto Dov, 12, 14, 18–19; as historian, 15, 16; *Landscapes of the Metropolis of Death*, 4, 11, 15–16, 17; Temple Mount visit (in 60s), 16, 17
Kumar, Priya, 65
Kurzweil, Ray, 164

Lacan, Jacques, 2, 26, 36, 87, 93, 129–30, 131, 134, 136, 137
LaCapra, Dominick, xii, xiii, 3, 4, 35, 38, 45, 46, 64; *History and Its Limits: Human, Animal, Violence*, 23, 41n
Lacoue-Labarthe, Philippe, 34
Laila and Majnu myth, 63, 64, 66, 71
Lambek, Michael, 64, 65
Landscapes of the Metropolis of Death (Kulka), 4, 11–12, 15–16, 17
Langah, Nukhbah Taj, 66
language, 13, 14, 19–20, 99; and Arendt, 115, 116, 117
Latour, Bruno, xi
Laub, Dori, 14, 45, 46; *Testimony*, 3
Lazare, Bernard, 116
leadership, and fascism/Nazism, 31
Lebanese civil war literature, xii, 77–90; *City Gates* (Khoury), 78–88
Lebanon, 78
Lebensraum, 32
Lemke, Thomas, 146, 152n
Lerner, Paul, 48

Levi, Neil, 33
Levi, Primo, 144
Levinas, Emmanuel, 25, 26, 92
Leys, Ruth, xv, 153n
licensed displacements, 78
linear/chronological time, 6, 127, 128, 131, 133, 134
'linguistic turn,' 13, 17
lip-sewing, refugees, 113, 123n, 136
Lischoten, Trick van, 63
Liska, Vivian, 122, 124n
listening, 85
literary realism, 57
literature, internal laws and external relations of, 12
Littell, Jonathan, 34
Lloyd, David, 94, 95, 96, 97, 98, 99, 100, 101, 107n
'Londonism,' 158
losses, traumatic, 92
love, unrequited, 63, 66
Lowenstein, Adam, 160
Luanda, Angola, 69, 70, 71
Luckhurst, Roger, xi, 1, 6, 7, 12, 51, 93, 145, 147, 149, 150, 153n, 159
Lyotard, Jean-François, 164
lyric and law, 117
lyric iterations, 64–6, 69
lyric poetry, 101, 102
lyric voice, 118

machinery of destruction, 32, 33–4, 36, 39
Magona, Sindiwe, 100–1
Majdanek death camp, 34
Malkki, Liisa H., 115
Mallett, Robert, 40–1n
Mamdani, Mahmood, 107n
Man, Paul de, 2, 3, 118
martyrdom, Holocaust victims, 37
Marx, Karl/Marxism, 28, 32
mass public, 31
Massimo, Donà, 153n
master signifier, 129–30
mastery, fantasy of, 84–5, 85–6
materialism, 92, 94
materialistic capitalism, 32
Maus (Hirsch and Spiegelman), 65
Mauss, Marcel, 25
Mbembe, Achille, 92, 144
McFarlane, Alexander C., 81
McLuhan, Marshall, 160
meaning, 25, 27; personhood, 135–7; search for, 79
medieval medicine, 20
meditation, bodily, 72

176 Index

Mein Kampf (Hitler), 29–30
melancholia, 65, 68, 69, 105
memorialization, 94, 95, 97
memoro-politics, 2
memory, 2, 12, 64, 78; collective, 2; 'dominant and dominated' sites of, 67; European, 122; multidirectional, 72; postmemory, 65; practices of, 128; unforgettable, the, 127, 133
Memory of Love (Forna), 5, 46, 54, 59n; PTSD discussed in, 52, 54, 56; Sierra Leone war as depicted in, 51–7, 52, 58n
mental health and illness, 49
Merleau-Ponty, Maurice, 154n
messianic time, 6, 128, 133, 134, 136
messianism, 27, 133
meta-history, traumatic, 15, 16
meta-narrative, 83
meta-texts, 15
meta-trauma, 67
metonymy, 79
Micale, Mark S., 48
Michlic, Joanna B., 33
Michman, Dan, 32
'midst of life,' 136
militarism, 31
Miller, J. Hillis, 119
mimesis, 100, 101
mimicry, 68
minority groups, trauma of *see* non-Western cultures, trauma of
Mir, Farina, 66
miracle, 136, 137
mirror stage, 131
misleading symbolic equivalency, 13
misrecognition, 87
missing 'person,' 7, 128, 137–8; biopolitically missing, 130, 131; in contemporary politics, 129–30; vs. the dead, 129; ontically missing, 129, 131; ontologically missing, 129, 131; politically missing, 130, 131; when missing, 131–5; *see also* personhood; time
Mitchell, Silas Weir, 158
modernism, 46, 50, 51, 99
modernity, 30, 36, 40, 72, 145, 149; Anglophone, 66; meta-trauma, 67; semantemes of, 77; therapeutic, 94, 101, 103; traumatic onset of, 93
Moglen, Seth, 89n, 144
Moorman, Marissa J., 70, 71
moral specificity, 13
Morrison, Toni, 107
Moses and Monotheism (Freud), 47, 48
moth and flame attraction, 63

Mother to Mother (Magona), 100–1
mourning, 65, 68, 69, 78, 80, 92, 95; critical or material, 100, 101; postcolonial, 94–7, 98; temporality, 105
movement/the movement, 31, 35
Mufti, Aamir, 66
multidirectional memory, 72
Multidirectional Memory: Remembering the Holocaust in the Age of Decolonization (Rothberg), xv, 58n
Multiple Personality Disorder, 161
Muselmann, 130, 145, 152
Mussolini, Benito, 31, 32

Nachträglichkeit (afterwardsness), Freud on, 12, 17; *see also* 'afterwardsness'
Naficy, Hamid, 72
Nagasaki, bombing of, 47
Nair, Supriya, 63
Nancy, Jean-Luc, 77
Naqvi, Akbar, 66
narrative, 14, 15, 17, 65, 66; in *City Gates* (Khoury), 78–9, 79, 80, 82, 83–4, 85, 87; collapse of narrative voice in *City Gates*, 83–4, 85, 87; first and third person, 84
narratocentric framework, 68–9
nationalism, 31
Natural Supernaturalism (Abrams), 30
Nazi Germany and the Jews (Friedländer), 39
Nazism, xii, 2, 11, 15, 33–4, 36, 46; and fascism, 23, 31–2; sacred in, 24; *see also* Holocaust
Nealon, Jeffrey, 144, 152n
Negri, Antonio, 77, 152n, 153n
neighbour, 136, 138
neo-liberal economics, xiv, 160
nervous shock, 147
neurasthenia, 158
Nevers, French city, 47
New Historicist analysis, 97
Nicholsen, Shierry Weber, 100
Night of the Long Knives, 38
Nijhawan, Michael, 65
9/11 terrorist attacks, 46, 92, 93, 163; trauma following, 141–3
Nixon, Rob, xv, xvi
non-national lives, 105
non-Western cultures, trauma of, 48, 50, 64; "other," non-Western people categorised as, 46–7; as shown in *Memory of Love* (Forna), 52–3
Nora, Pierre, 2, 67
Nordau, Max, 158
Norridge, Zoe, 55, 56

nostaliga, 98
nostos (homecoming), psychopathology, 106–7
Novak, Amy, xv
novel, 65, 66
NYDNs (Not Yet Diagnosed - Nervous), 158

'Ode to Joy' (song), 11
Odyssey, The, 94, 97–9, 104
Ofrat, Gideon
Ojakangas, Mika, 145, 153n
Omeros (Walcott), 72
Ondaatje, Michael, 73
ontic trauma, xiii, 131, 132, 135
ontological trauma, xiii, 132, 135
Operation Barbarosa, 33–4
operational time, 128, 133, 134
oppresson-based trauma, 49
Order of Things, The (Foucault), 19
Origins of Totalitarianism, The (Arendt), 114, 118, 122
Orsini, Francesca, 66
"other," non-Western people categorised as, 46–7
Other Cultures of Trauma: Meta-Metropolitan Narratives and Identities (Croisy), 58n
Otto, Rudolf, 25
Owens, Patricia, 123n

paintings, social-realist, 68
Pakistan, Siraiki poetry of, 66
Palestine, 78
Palimpsestic Memory: The Holocaust and Colonialism in French and Francophone Fiction and Film (Silverman), 58n
Pandey, Gyanendra, 66
'paradoxical duality,' 15
Partition of India (1947), 64, 65, 66, 67
Partition's Post-Amnesias (Kabir), 64
parvenu, 116, 119
pathos, 115, 118
Pattern Recognition (Gibson), 162, 163
Patterson, Charles, 33
Paxton, Robert, 32, 33
Payne, Stanley, 32
performativity, 29
'personality,' vs. 'self', 136
personhood: commodification/instrumentalization of, 128, 138; 'human being general,' 114, 115, 120; meaning, 135–7; 'new kind of human beings,' 116–17, 118, 121; question of What is a person? 117–18; and time, 128; *see also* missing 'person'; time

Peters, Benoit, 2
phantasms, 24, 29
pilgrimage, 67, 68
Pin-Fat, Véronique, 123n, 130, 136
poetics of occlusion, 79
poetry, 65; following Auschwitz, 50; on Truth and Reconciliation Commission, 94
Pol Pot (Saloth Sar, Cambodian leader), 67
Poland, Jews of, 33
political religion, fascism/Nazism as, 24
Polonsky, Anthony, 33
polyphony, 79
Popkin, Jeremy D., 11
possibility/impossibility, 26, 51
post-apartheid literature, and critique of reconciliation, 100–7
postcolonial commitment, 96
postcolonial mourning, 98; critique, 94–7
Postcolonial Narrative and the Work of Mourning (Durrant), 58n, 107n
postcolonial stress disorder, 49
postcolonial syndrome, 49
Postcolonial Witnessing: Trauma Out of Bounds (Craps), 58n
postcolonial world, 67
postcolonialism, 4
post-deconstructive thought, 12, 14, 20
postmemory, 65
postmonolingual tensions, 124n
postsecular, notion of, 24, 29, 36, 40
post-traumatic slavery syndrome, 49
post-traumatic stress disorder *see* PTSD (post-traumatic stress disorder)
Poteat, V. Paul, 49
Poussaint, Alvin F., 49
practice/Practice Theory, 28
Practicing History: New Directions in the Writing of History after the Linguistic Turn (Spiegel), 28
Precarious Life: The Powers of Mourning and Violence (Butler), 2, 20, 91, 92, 141, 153n
print cultures, South Asia, 66
Protestantism, 26
psychiatric universalism, 48
psychic experience of trauma, 50
Psychic Life of Power, The (Butler), 92
psychoaffective closure, 81
psychoanalysis, xiii, 30, 45, 64, 135, 137, 144, 147; psychoanalytical determinism, 72
psychotherapy, 53, 147
PTSD (post-traumatic stress disorder), 49, 50, 79, 153n; neuroendrocrinological

basis, 158; as shown in *City Gates* (Khoury), 84; as shown in *Memory of Love* (Forna), 51, 54, 56
Pupavec, Vanessa, 115
purity, notion of, 26, 28
pyrotechnics, 57

quasi-sacrificialism, Nazi, 36
Quint, David, 97

Rabkin, Erik, 161
racism/racial prejudice, 24, 28, 39, 50
Radstone, Susannah, 12, 46
Rae, Patricia, 89n
railway spine, 158
Rajaram, Prem Kumar, 123n
Ramazani, Jahan, 72, 89n
Rancière, Jacques, 124n
Reader, The (Schlink), 34
reading practice, 45–6
'Reasons to be Cheerful' (Egan), 164
recognition, 87–8
reconciliation, 96–7; critique of, 100–7
Red Cross, 15
redemptive anti-Semitism, 39
Redfield, Marc, 105
Reformation, 27, 28
Refractions of Violence (Jay), 77
refugee writing, 117, 118, 122
refugees, 6, 113, 114, 119, 121, 136
refusniks, Israel, 136, 137
religion, 23, 29; Derrida on, 24–5; and fascism/Nazism, 24, 25, 30; ideological links to fascism/Nazism, 24, 25; multiplicity of meanings, 25; and sacred, 25; sources, 25, 27; split, Romanticism as, 30; wars of, 27
Remak, Joachim, 35
Remnants of Auschwitz (Agamben), 144
repetition, 68, 79, 81, 150
representation, 14, 17, 45, 100; vs. experience, 81, 82; failure of *City Gates* novel as symbolic form to represent the event, 81–2; unrepresentability, 64
Resnais, Alain, 47
responsibility, 101
Ricciardi, Alessia, 89n
Richman, Michèle, 38
Rickman, Gregg, 161
Ricoeur, Paul, 87
Riefenstahl, Leni, 31, 35
ritual, 24, 25, 28
Rogbonko Project, 59n
Romanticism, 30
Ronell, Avital, 117

Root, Maria, 49
Rothberg, Michael, 12, 58n, 67, 72, 144; *Multidirectional Memory: Remembering the Holocaust in the Age of Decolonization*, xv
rule of law, 31
Rushdie, Salman, 93
Russell, Paul, 86

Sabra and Shatila massacres, Beirut (1982), 79
sacralization, 23, 29, 32, 40
sacraments, 28
sacred, the, 23, 24, 25, 29, 30; immanent sacred, 28
The Sacred in Twentieth-Century Politics: Essays in Honour of Professor Stanley G. Payne (Griffin, Mallett and Tortorice), 40–1n
sacrifice, 24, 25, 26, 28, 36, 37, 132, 135
safe-world violations, 49
Salisbury, Laura, 164
Sanders, Mark, 101, 108n
Sangari, Kumkum, 66
Santner, Eric, 29, 129, 130, 133, 135, 136, 137
Sapnierman, Lisa B., 49
Sarkar, Bhaskar, 66, 67
Satanic Verses, The (Rushdie), 93
Saunders, Rebecca, 48, 58n
Sax, Boria, 33
scapegoat, sacrificial, 26, 28, 36, 40
Schivelbusch, Wolfgang, 158
Schlink, Bernhard, 34
Schmitt, Carl, 144
science fiction (SF), 7, 157–67; 'hard' and 'soft' modes, 161–2, 166; origins of term, 160
Sebald, W. G., 15
Second World War, 47, 65, 161; *see also* Holocaust; Nazism
secularity, 24, 25, 30
Security, Territory, Population (Foucault), 146
sedimented content, 94, 97
'self,' vs. 'personality', 136
self-help books, 147
self-observation, 153n
Seltzer, Mark, 147
Selye, Hans, 157–8
sensemaking, 78
Shabad, Paul, 86
Shail, Andrew, 164
Shaviro, Steve, 166
Shell and the Kernel, The (Torok), 86
shell-shock, 54, 158
Shia Islam, 71

Shoah *see* Holocaust
shock, future, 7, 157–67
Shockwave Rider, The (Brunner), 7, 157, 162
Siddhartha Gautama (Buddha), 68
Siegert, Nadine, 69, 70
Sierra Leone, war as depicted in *Memory of Love* (Forna), 51–7, 58n
Signature, The (Agamben), 153n
signifying stress, 133
silence, 55, 56, 57
Silverman, Max, 58n
Simon, David, 16
Singer, Isaac Bashevis, 33
Singularity, 165
Slaughterhouse 5 (Vonnegut), 161
Slusser, George, 161
'Small Death' (electrified fence), 15
Sobibor death camp, 34
social-realist art, 68
solidarity, 77, 85
song, 65, 66
South Africa, post-apartheid, 95
sovereign power, 128, 130, 131, 135, 137
sovereignty, biopolitics as, 143–5, 153n
Soviet Union, former (USSR), 32
Spargo, R. Clifton, 89n
Spector, Scott, 36
speculative presentism, 163
Spiegel, Gabrielle, 28
Spiegelman, Art, 65
Spinoza, Baruch, 154n
Spivak, Gayatri, 96, 107n
The Splintered Glass: Facets of Trauma in the Post-Colony and Beyond (Herrero and Baelo-Allué), 58n
Sri Lanka, post-tsunami of 2004, 49
SS (*Schutzstaffel*), 34, 35, 37, 38
state of nature, 107n
statelessness, 115, 120, 121
Sternhell, Zeev, 32
stimuli, overexposure to, 91–2, 150, 158
Stonebridge, Lyndsey, xii, xiii, 6, 123n
storytelling, 84, 85
stress, 157–8
Stross, Charles, 165–6
structural trauma, xiii, 92, 98, 107n, 145
'Structure, Sign, and Play in the Discourse of the Human Sciences' (Derrida), 27
'structure of experience,' and trauma theory, 14
Studies in the Novel (Craps and Buelens), 58n
subjectivity, 77, 79, 83, 85, 87; post-traumatic, 88

sublimation, 23, 29, 32, 38
suffering, poetic qualities, 119–20
Sufism, 63, 66, 71
suicide, 130
Summerfield, Derek, 48, 49, 50
surfascisme, 30
survival strategies, 55
Surya, Michel, 38
Suvin, Darko, 159–60
symbolic order, 127, 129–30, 131–2, 135, 137
symbolic torsion, 133
symptomatology, 86
Szörényi, Anna, 116

Taliban, 63, 71
talking cure, 54, 55, 65; *see also* Freud, Sigmund; psychoanalysis
Tancred and Clorinda, story of, xv, 47, 48
Tatum, James, 78
Tegal, Megara, 59
Tel al-Zaatar, siege and massacre of Palestinians at (1976), 80
telos, 97, 99
Temple Mount, Jerusalem, 16, 17
temporality *see* time
Terr, Lenore C., 49
Terrestrial Things (de Kok), 101
terrorism, 32, 134–5; *see also* 9/11 terrorist attacks
testimony, 66, 102, 103, 105, 108n, 120; Holocaust, 11–12, 14, 16
Testimony (Felman and Laub), 3
textualist approach, limitations, 45–6, 50, 51
Thailand, 67
therapeutic modernity, 94, 101, 103
therapy, 54
time, 12, 127–39; chronological/linear, 6, 127, 128, 131, 133, 134; empty/homogenous, 133; messianic, 6, 128, 133, 134, 136; operational, 128, 133, 134; and personhood, 128; taking, 138; trauma, 127, 128, 132, 133, 134, 137; *see also* personhood
'Time is Coming, A' (poem by Taliban), 63, 71
Time that Remains, The (Agamben), 127–8, 133
time-travel, 161
Toffler, Alvin, 7, 157, 158, 162
Tolstoy, Leo, 17–18
Tommy Hilfiger logo, 163
Torok, Maria, 86
Tortorice, John, 40–1n

Index

totalitarianism, 32
'totally other' (Derrida), 25, 28
train accidents, 158
trans-Atlantic Silk Route, 72
transcendence/immanence aporia/paradox, 27, 28
transcendent sacred, 28
transgenerational memorialization of trauma, 65, 72
trauma: concept, 1, 12, 145; cultural, 13; of empire, 46–8; empire of, 48–50; and ethics, 18, 19; failed experience of, 81, 83; historical, 13, 92; as history, 14–16, 45; impact of, 14, 15, 20; inaccessibility, 45; incessantly quotidian, 145; individualistic approaches to, limitations, 49–50; insidious, 49, 106, 145; as medico-legal problem, 147; old and new problems, 23; ontic, xiii, 131, 132, 135; ontological, xiii, 132, 135; as origin and disruption of knowledge, 12; post-9/11, 141–3; psychic experience, 50, 91; structural, xiii, 92, 98, 107n, 145; and violence, 141–2
Trauma and Recovery (Herman), 2
Trauma and the Memory of Politics (Edkins), 6, 151
trauma counselors, 49
Trauma: Explorations in Memory (Caruth), xi, 3, 58n, 144–5
trauma knot, xi
Trauma Question, The (Luckhurst), 51
trauma studies, xii, xiii, xiv, xv, xvii, 1, 4, 5, 7, 17, 23, 64, 68, 70, 72, 88, 122; biopolitics, 92–3, 141, 142, 143, 144, 149, 150, 151, 152; collective trauma, shift from individual, 92–3; and end of trauma theory, 92–3; ethico-political agenda, 142; future of, 88, 159; as immunitary technology, 151–2; structural, 92
Trauma Texts (Whitlock and Douglas), 58n
trauma theory: 'afterwardsness' in, 12, 14, 16–19; critique of studies, 46, 49–50; end of, 91–109; Eurocentrism, beyond, 45–61; event-based model, limitations, 49, 50, 53, 54; future of, 63–4, 66–7; and Holocaust, 2; origins, 12, 45; and 'structure of experience,' 14; textualist approach, limitations, 45–6, 50, 51; Western model, 13, 48, 52, 54, 57; *see also* Holocaust
trauma time, 127, 128, 132, 133, 134, 137
traumatropisms, 29
Traverso, Antonio, 58n

Treblinka death camp, 34
Trevor-Roper, Hugh, 37–8
Trezise, Thomas
Triumph of the Will (Riefenstahl), 31, 35
Truth and Reconciliation Commission (TRC), 6, 94, 100–1, 102, 103, 104, 105, 106, 107n, 108n
tsunami, 2004, 49
Tuol Sleng, Phnom Penh, 67–9, 71
Turia, Tariana, 49
Type II traumas, 49

uncanny, the, 29
Unclaimed Experience: Trauma, Narrative and History (Caruth), xv, 3, 45, 132
unconscious, the, 72
uncontamination, notion of, 26
unforgettable, the, 127, 133
unification, 18
United States (US), trauma culture, 161
unreadability, 45
unrepresentability, 64
unscathed, notion of, 26, 27, 28, 41n
Urdu, 66
Ustorf, Werner, 28
utopia, racial, 28, 36

Van der Peer, Stephanie, 70
Vermeulen, Pieter, xii, xiii, 6, 7
vernacular lyric, 65, 66
vesicle, 91, 93, 107n
Vichy France, 33
victimization, 24, 39, 40
Vietnam War, 16, 158
Vinge, Vernor, 166
violence, 33, 39, 78; aestheticization of, 24; biopolitical, 144; everyday, 77, 83; extreme, xiii, xiv, 78, 141, 144; and fascism/Nazism, 31, 32; historical, 79; slow, xv; structural, 79; transgressive, 37–8; and trauma, 141–2; *see also* genocide; Holocaust
'viraha' (longing caused by separation), 66
Voegelin, Eric, 28
Volksgemeinschaft, 28, 36, 39
Vondung, Klaus, 28
Vonnegut, Kurt, 7, 161
vulnerability, 7; bodily, 149; in *City Gates* (Khoury), 79, 83–4, 85, 88; common corporeal, 92, 94, 102; of organism, 91–2; theory, 142

Walcott, Derek, 72
Walsh, Declan, xiv
war on terror, 32, 93

warfare, 77, 78, 132
wars, 27
Watters, Ethan, 48–9
'We Refugees' (Arendt), 115, 116, 117, 119, 122, 124n
Wells, H. G., 160
Wessells, Michael G., 50
Western trauma model, limitations, 13, 48, 52, 54, 57; *see also* Eurocentrism
When Memory Comes (Friedlander), 11
White, Hayden, 16
Whitlock, Gillian, 58n
Wiese, Christian, 30
Williams, Evan Calder, 160
Williams, Paul, 67
Willse, Craig, 147, 153n
witnessing, 27, 46, 66, 85, 86, 101
Wittgenstein, Ludwig, 20
Wolin, Richard, 38
Wood, David, 17
Woomera detention camp, South Western Australia, xiii, 113, 123n

working through, 150
works of art, mimesis, 100
World Memory: Personal Trajectories in Global Time (Bennett and Kennedy), 50–1, 58n
wound culture, 147
Wounded Storyteller, The (Frank), 2
Wretched of the Earth, The (Fanon), 58n

Yale deconstruction school, 12
Yale French Studies (Rothberg), 58n
Yale School, 92, 97
Yerushalmi, Yosef, 2
Yildiz, Yasemin, 123n, 124n
Young, Allan, 48, 54, 158
Young-Bruehl, Elisabeth, 119

Zabuli, Sadullah Sa'eed, 63, 64
Zakhor: Jewish History and Jewish Memory (Yerushalmi), 2
Zeleza, Paul, 71
Zionism, 122, 124n
Žižek, Slavoj, 2, 92, 93, 131, 136, 160

Printed in Great Britain
by Amazon